VOYAGE
TO
THE ISLE OF FRANCE
THE
ISLE OF BOURBON
AND THE
CAPE OF GOOD HOPE

1768-1771

WITH OBSERVATIONS AND REFLECTIONS UPON

NATURE AND MANKIND

VOYAGE
TO
THE ISLE OF FRANCE
THE
ISLE OF BOURBON
AND THE
CAPE OF GOOD HOPE

1768-1771

WITH OBSERVATIONS AND REFLECTIONS UPON

NATURE AND MANKIND

J. H. B. DE SAINT PIERRE

GYAN

Published by

Gyan Publishing House
5, Ansari Road
Daryaganj, New Delhi-110002
Phone: 011-47034999, 9811692060
E-mail: books@gyanbooks.com

Distribution Network
gyanbooks.com
India, USA, Canada, UK, Australia, France

ISBN : 978-81-212-4205-9 (PB)
First Published, London, 1800

2nd Impression 2020

Printed at: Gyan Press, Delhi.

Voyage to the Isle of France
Author: J. H. B. De Saint Pierre

VOYAGE

TO

THE ISLE OF FRANCE.

THE

ISLE OF BOURBON,

AND THE

CAPE OF GOOD HOPE;

WITH OBSERVATIONS AND REFLECTIONS

UPON

NATURE AND MANKIND.

BY

J. H. B. DE SAINT PIERRE,

AUTHOR OF STUDIES OF NATURE.

Homo sum; humani nihil a me alienum puto.

TER.

TRANSLATED FROM THE FRENCH.

To which is added

SOME ACCOUNT OF THE AUTHOR

LONDON:

Printed by J Cundee, Ivy Lane,

FOR VERNOR AND HOOD, IN THE POULTRY; J. CUTHELL MIDDLE-ROW, HOLBORN; AND J. WALKER, PATERNOSTER-ROW

1800

OF THE AUTHOR,

J. H. B. DE SAINT PIERRE.

THE very flattering reception given to the *Studies of Nature* by every description of readers in this country, renders whatever has fallen from the pen of *James Henry Bernardin de Saint Pierre* of high request. His *Voyage to the Isle of France*, which he frequently mentions in this great work, is here republished, in compliance with public solicitude. And it will be found, by such as peruse it with discernment, to indicate the same worthy intentions, the same indefatigable investigation of the various laws which regulate the universe, the same aversion to dogmatism and hypothesis, the same extended benevolence, the same rational and exalted piety, the same brilliant imagery, and the same majesty of genius which distinguish that masterly performance.

The author is no otherwise known among us than by his writings, and from the celebrity of *these* to whom is not *some account of him* now become desirable. All means of communication between the two countries have been long shut up by the sanguinary mandates of war. Even the innocent and useful intercourse of letters is still subjected to this cruel interdiction. Ah! happy for society and human nature, were this horrid conflict attended with evils of no greater magnitude. But even this trenches to a very considerable degree on one of the richest funds of our purest enjoyments.

Impressed with this sentiment, and eager to get some further intelligence of a favourite writer than is yet before the public, the editor embraced an opportunity that fortunately offered, of requesting a French gentleman resident at Vienna, whose high literary character, and extensive acquaintance in the learned world, rendered him perfectly competent to tell all he knew of *James Henry Bernardin de Saint Pierre.*

And

And he very complaisantly writes to this effect.—" That he is a sweet, simple, modest " man, of great sensibility, and true worth; " that *J. H. B. de St. Pierre* had been a long " time the intimate friend of *John Jacque* " *Rousseau*, and like that illustrious author, " shewed himself late in life among men of " letters: that the French Jacobins spared " him from respect to the great esteem in " which he is held by all parties, though " his opinions are essentially different from " theirs, and though he is well known to " favour the cause they would crush: that " his gentle temper and love of ease, pre- " vented his putting himself among the " ranks of such as have opposed the revo- " lutionary frenzy with courage and per- " severance; that it is principally towards " moral sentiment, and the improvement " of the heart, his *studies* are directed: " that he was appointed professor of this " species of philosophy at a *new school*, " which they wished to establish at Paris " three years ago: that his instructions in " that capacity procured him the most uni- " versal applause, but his lectures were not " published: that he was much solicited to " undertake a moral catechism, and work- " ed on the subject a long time, but neither " did this performance appear: that the " deplorable irreligion and corruption

" France still labours under, would now " render the true principles of Morals un- " acceptable: that these tenets, which " so long prevailed, engaged *Mr. de la* " *Cretelle*, who had likewise expended much " time and consideration on a similar " topic, but who was also impelled for the " same reason to renounce it: That the " silence of these two celebrated and va- " luable writers emboldened at last *Mr. de* " *St. Lambert*, an old encyclopediel writer, " and the public beheld from the pen of " this pretended philosopher, a *Moral* " *Catechism*, in three volumes, polluted " with gross impiety, and basely accom- " modated to the dissoluteness in fashion: " that morals are here represented altogether " independent of religion: that *J. H. B.* " *de St. Pierre* is he whose stile has most " of that kind of warmth and unction, " which characterize the works of *J. Jacque* " *Rousseau*, but he is less eloquent than " his master, though sometimes as brilliant " as Buffon, who is always more noble and " manly: that as to the purity of language, " and all the nicety of composition, he is " not considered on the continent as the " most unexceptionable model: that his " most esteemed production is a novel, en- " titled *Paul and Virginia*: that his *Studies* " *of Nature*, in France at least, had original- ly

" ly no great success, and are calculated to
" excite a taste for natural history without
" teaching it: that his account of the new
" system* of botany is more amusing
" than instructive: that all he advances
" on general physics is still worse: that the
" theories by which he would solve the
" phenomina of the tides, are palpably
" erroneous: that many other things in
" this voluminous work, merit reprehen-
" sion, and youth ought not to dip into it
" till their studies are finished, and their
" faculties matured: that the author is,
" however, a man of honour and strict
" probity, whose labours have all the most
" virtuous tendency, and inspire not only
" admiration of the varied excellencies they
" disclose, but love for the mind that
" conceived them: that his stile, though
" not a standard of correctness, is every
" where elegant and beautiful: that he
" often wants precision, and seems to
" hold in contempt both logic and meta-
" physicks, has many false ideas and opi-
" nions, more paradoxical than just; but
" the ardent philosophy he breathes, and
" the sentiments of refined humanity he
" uniformly inculcates, more than atone
" for all his imperfections."

* That some of our most eminent naturalists have notwithstanding adopted his ideas, may be seen *sufficiently* exemplified by consulting *Dr. Darwin's Phytologia.*

That our readers may be still further acquainted with the elegant and laudable pursuits of this amiable man, we make no apology for inserting the following paper, which has but lately appeared in one of the French journals* It shews his ardour for science, and the improvement of the species to be still unabated, as well as what may yet be expected from his labours, should his life and faculties be preserved to any length of time. He sanctions the fragment with his name, but though he had not, every one in the least acquainted with his genius and turn of thinking, must perceive it sufficiently stamped by marks of internal unequivocal authenticity.

" I, some time ago, accompanied two of " my friends to the house of *Citizen de Non*, " an able artist, who had but a short time " before returned from Egypt. He shewed " us with the most obliging complaisance a " number of designs, which he had copied " from hieroglyphical inscriptions. He " shewed us likewise several hieroglyphics " engraved, and others done in relief, on " splinters of stone which he had broken " off the monuments: they were as distinct " as when they received the last touch of

* February, 1800

" the

" the chisel. He told us that he ha l seen " large squares entirely covered with these " characters, inscribed on statues, columns, " obelisks, towers, and gates of cities and " temples. These ancient temples are so " spacious, that the modern villages built " upon their ruins appear like fortresses.

" Among other Egyptian curiosities, " which *Citizen de Non* has brought home " with him, I remarked the foot of a " young female mummy. It is as hard and " as black as ebony, and of as exquisite a " form as the feet of the most charming " Grecian statues. It has a slight bend, " the toes are separated from each other, " are full, round, and in their natural pro- " portion; they were not compressed by " narrow and sharp-pointed shoes. But " what appeared to me no less curious, was " a small roll of paphyrus, found under " one of the mummy's arms. By a small " opening at one end, we observed that it " was filled with hieroglyphical writing, " containing without doubt the principal " events of her life. Thus has the history " of a young female been preserved on the " rind of a rush, as long as that of Egypt " on its monuments of granite. But it is " a subject of regret, that there now exists " none capable of decyphering the one or "the other. The characters of the an-"cients have descended through a period "of 4000 years, but their language is for "ever extinct.

"These objects of antiquity suggested "several original reflections to my mind. "I have a thousand times heard, that the "art of printing will transmit our dis-"coveries to the latest posterity; but, at "the sight of those unintelligible hierogly-"phics which, though engraved on gra-"nites, have not been capable of trans-"mitting to us those of Egypt. I ex-"claimed—What will become of the fu-"ture glory of our arts and sciences, when "printed only on paper made of rags?

"I then reflected on the arrow-shaped "letters, disposed like musical notes on "the friezes of the temple of Chelminar, "in Persia; the small parallel lines of the "ancient Chineselanguage; the knots of the "quipos of Mexico; and the types of se-"veral other ancient languages, of which "the signification is totally lost;—and I "said to myself, in vain does the man of "letters console himself for the persecu-"tion he suffers from his cotemporaries, "by the hope of having justice done to his "character by posterity, since the know-"ledge

"ledge of the very language in which he
"writes will not reach them.

"Yet the sentiment of our immortality "is felt even by those who formally deny "it. They refer it, not to their souls, but "to their writings, which they imagine to "be already stamped with the seal of im-"mortality, by means of printing, and a "little lamp black. What a strange con-"tradiction! Certainly all our productions "must perish, because they are the work "of perishable man; but our souls are "immortal, because they are the work of "God.

"Our arts and sciences are but transitory "emblems of a permanent nature. The "language of ancient Egypt is irrecover-"ably lost. The past ages, which have "obliterated the meaning of its hierogly-"phics, have already exfoliated its pyra-"mids, which surpass mountains in height, "and marble in hardness; succeeding ages "will crumble them to dust, and mingle "their materials with the surrounding "sands. But while they destroy the mo-"numents of art, they there incessantly "develope those of nature. The feet of "young females in that country still retain "their charming proportions. The rushes, "on the rind of which they wrote their histories

" histories, are, like them, still reproduced " on the banks of the Nile; and whoever " should be able to read their ancient ad- " ventures in the writings of the Pharaohs, " would at least trace in those of our own " time the same sentiments.

" All that we know of the greater part " of these hieroglyphical characters, of " which we are acquainted with nearly " 225 different kinds, is, that the *barking* " *Anubes*, the *meagre Ibes*, the *winding* " *serpents*, the *large pitchers*, termed *ca-* " *nopes*, were emblems alike of political " and natural laws. They were so nu- " merous, that I do not wonder the people " forgot them. The term law comes ori- " ginally from *ligare* to bind; that of re- " ligion from *religare*, to bind again. When " these laws or bands are too much multipli- " ed, the people cannot support them, and " they, at least, disburden their memory of " them. All the monuments of the Egyptians " were real tables of law: their jurisprudence " was sculptured on their walls, as ours are " recorded in our books; but, as they were " not engraved on their hearts, nothing " of them has remained in their remem- " brance.

" It is well known, that among those " laws, those of nature predominated much

" beyond

" beyond those of civil government. The " Spynx, the obelisks, the figures of Isis, " Orus, and Typhon, the twelve signs of " the zodiac, completely similar to those " now in use, represented the phases of " the moon and sun. From these natural " laws were derived the comparatively " small number of their social laws.

" With us every thing is in a contrary " order. We strive to reduce to the single " principles of attraction all the laws of " nature, whose productions are so varied; " while we have already extended to 34,000 " those of political government, of which " the productions have been so few. The " legal, has with us extinguished the na-" tural order, in the proportion of 34000 " to 1.

" Now, though I possess only a very " ordinary sagacity, having long studied " nature, I can assert, that I have discover-" ed at least a dozen primitive laws, the " existence of which is no less certain than " that of attraction. They spring all from " one first principle, and uniting with each " other, comprehend at once in their har-" monies the physical and moral order. I " hope speedily to point them out in a " course of lectures, if time permit me to " prepare it.

" The

"The Egyptian laws were originally but "few, for they had but one legislator— "namely, Osiris. The largest building "requires only one Architect. Osiris en- "acted only a very small number of laws, "but they were well digested: and he left "the application to the conscience of the "rulers, who in their transmission from "Father to Son, by means of extensions "and comments, converted them into a "very discordant science. Ah! what an "Osiris of equal talents with that of Egypt, "will bring back ours to their ancient "simplicity.

"I cannot observe, without regret, our "34000 social laws, overturning all the "laws of nature, which they have reduced "to one only. Being the production of a "great number of Legislators, they are "vague, destitute of order, incoherent, and "sometimes contradictory; the conse- "quence is, that they present a thousand "caverns to shelter the serpents of chicane. "They lay snares for unexperienced pro- "bity, and those which are intended to "punish villainy remain unexecuted. Owing "to them, the most simple processes "have become endless. The man who "wishes to know all their abuses, which "are already of considerable standing,

"need

"need only read the two chapters of "Michael Montaign, entitled on Custom "and Experience. This father of our "philosophy says, that even in his time the "laws amounted to about 100,000. With "the exception of a few which have been "repealed, we may, therefore, state our "present laws at 134,000. Sooner or "later, their fate will be consigned to "oblivion like those of Egypt. At present "it is indispensibly necessary to oppose a "barrier to their alarming overflow."

"Our wisest sages have felt the necessity "of balancing the powers of government. "This is, in fact, one of the first harmonic "laws of nature. I should, therefore, wish "that the tribunals of justice, and even of "appeal, were balanced by a tribunal of "equity. A court of justice is attentive "only to forms; a court of equity con- "siders principles alone. The members of "a court of justice proceed only according "to their legal knowledge: those of a "court of equity decide according to their "conscience. The latter would in some "measure resemble, on a large scale, the "court of a justice of the peace, or an "arbiter; but it would differ from it in "this, that it would have power to oblige "the litigants to submit their claims and

"reasons

"reasons to arbiters appointed from its "members, and would pronounce judgment, without advocate, without procurator, and without appeal.

"Be pleased, Citizens, to insert these "ideas of an individual in your Journal. "The voice of the people will join yours, "in demanding that they should be carried into execution. A tribunal of "equity would be the most durable monument a people could erect. They see "with astonishment, but without interest, "the monuments of our Sciences and our "Arts, and they will one day view with the "same indifference, those of our sanguinary "victories, but they will always bestow "benedictions on those of humanity. Thus "to the wandering Arab, the trophies of "learned and victorious Egypt present "only unintelligible hieroglyphics. They "know not even the names of those who "raised them. He regards them with "terror, as the work of demons, and he "destroys them when he can, or when he "dare. But he still recollects with gratitude those who have made wells in the "midst of the sand. Of them he takes the "greatest care, and still gives them their "ancient and affecting names of *Baba "Joseph, Baba Abou, Babà Ibrahim*— "Father Joseph, Father Abou, Father "Abraham."

"Do

" Do good then to the unfortunate, you " who would transmit your glory to " posterity. Imprint it not on granite " with the chisel of the sculptor, not on " paper by the press, but on grateful hearts, " by the benefits you bestow. Recollect " that the proud pyramids, erected near " populous cities, have lost the names of " their founders, while the humble wells " have preserved those of such as are dry " in the midst of the deserts."

Such is the Writer so celebrated among all the learned circles of Europe, and so variously employed to this moment in developing new sources of intellectual worth, and extending the sphere of human felicity whose first production is here presented in an English version. The Voyage was made full twenty five years ago, when the author's sensibilities were vigourous and perfectly alive to all he could either hear or see. He seems to have been so deeply impressed by the picturesque scenes which then presented themselves to his imagination, that he never after lost the recollection of them. And his reflections and delineations concerning every subject which fell in his way, are so natural, so full of vivacity, and so very interesting to every person of a well formed

formed taste, and a susceptible heart, that it is not surprising to find him as is still very well known to have been the case, a peculiar favourite of the late *Dr. Goldsmith*, who possessed in an eminent degree a congenial mind, and an happy predilection for all that is most tender and sublime in the *Studies* to which *St. Pierre* appears exclusively attached.

This Voyage is a striking instance in what an enchanting light the various aspects of nature are contemplated by original minds; and certainly no man could make a better use of the curious materials thus laid before him by her diversified operations than our Author.

His speculations on the vegetable world, contained in the three last letters, appear in the original in the form of a dialogue. But without adhering to this mechanism, we have compressed the whole in as few words as possible. A long table of sea terms, and various other matters, but little interesting to an English reader, are also omitted. The Editor has endeavoured to present his countrymen with the spirit and essence of this elegant work, stript of its native *verbiage*, and he doubts not but it may contribute in this form both to amuse the imagination and better the heart.

THE

THE

AUTHOR'S PREFACE.

THE following Letters were all regularly written to my friends, during my voyage. I put them in the best order I could on my return, and published them, as a public testimony of my acknowledgments of the good offices I had received.

Having given an account of the plants and animals natural to each country; and of the soil, both in its unimproved, and improveable, state; I then speak of the characters and manners of the inhabitants.

Many things suggested in the course of this correspondence, may, perhaps, be deemed a satire;

satire; but, I can say with truth, that in speaking of men, I have spoken of their good actions with satisfaction and alacrity, and of their faults with perfect candor, and even some reluctance.

Having spoke of the Colonists, I next enter upon a detail of the vegetables and animals with which they have replenished the country. The industry, the arts, and the commerce, of these countries, are all included in agriculture, It should seem, that this art, so simple, would be productive of the most amiable manners; but the life led by the people of the Isle of France, is far from a primitive one.

Monsieur de Tolbach, Governor of the Cape, who had been very obliging to me, is alas! no more. If the place allotted him in these memoirs cannot now serve as acknowledgments, it may, at least, exhibit an useful example of conduct to those Frenchmen who may be appointed governors in India. If from my account, they are induced to imitate his virtues, I shall then, indeed, do honour to them.

What apology can I make for having ventured to treat on subjects with which I am not scientifically

tifically acquainted? I have written upon plants and animals, but am no naturalist. Natural history, however, is not shut up in libraries; it has rather seemed to me, a volume to be read by the whole world. I have consulted, and traced throughout, the most evident proofs of a Providence, which I am always happy to consider, not as a system that is pleasing to my fancy, but as a sentiment with which my heart is filled.

a

At least, I do trust I shall have been of use to mankind, if the faint sketch here given of the miserable lot of the Negro slaves, should save them from one stroke of the whip; and if the Europeans who so loudly exclaim against tyranny, and among whom are composed such beautiful treatises of morality; may be induced by my means, to cease being in India the most barbarous of all tyrants.

I have doubtless done some service to my country, if I prevent but one single man of worth from quitting it, and if I have determined him to cultivate one additional acre in some heath which has never yet felt the plough.

A man to be truly penetrated by the love of his country must first quit it. I am attached to

mine,

mine, though neither by my fortune, nor the rank I hold in it: but the place where I first saw the light, is dear to me: There, I have felt, have loved, have spoken.

This delightful country, so agreeable and attractive to strangers, facinates me. Here all that can be desirable, is in abundance; and France, by the temperature of its climate, the excellence of its vegetables, its delicious fruit, its transcendent wines, and the industry of its inhabitants, is to be preferred to either India.

In fine, my whole heart, is in my country, where my connections are numerous, where esteem is the most refined, friendship most intimate, and virtue most amiable.

A

VOYAGE, &c.

LETTER I.

L'Orient, Jan. 4, 1768.

AT L'Orient we are just arrived, after having felt the most severe cold. The road was frozen from Paris to within ten leagues of Rennes. This city, which was burnt in 1720, has now a grandeur which it owes to its misfortune. There are several new buildings, two handsome squares, a statue of Lewis XV. and also one of Lewis XIV The inside of the Parliament-House is handsomely decorated, but with rather too much uniformity. The pannels of the wainscot are painted white, and have gilt moldings. Most of the churches and public buildings are in this taste. In other respects, Rennes is but a dismal town. It is situated at the confluence of the *Villaine* and the *Isle*; two small rivers. Its suburbs are formed of some dirty houses; the streets are ill paved. The common people dress in a coarse brown stuff, which gives them very much an air of poverty.

A vast deal of waste land is still to be seen in Britany. Nothing grows upon it but broom, and a shrub a shrub with yellow flowers, which appeared to me a composition of thorns. The country people call it furze. They bruise it to feed their cattle The broom serves only to heat their ovens; it might be turned to better account, and especially in a maritime country. The Romans made a cordage of it, which they preferred to hemp, for their shipping. I owe this observation to Pliny, who is known to have commanded the fleets of the Empire.

These lands might surely be sown to good purpose with potatoes, a certain subsistence, which can neither suffer by inclement seasons, nor the storehouses of monopolizers.

Industry seems checked equally by an Aristocratic government, or in a *pays d'etats**. The peasant, who is without a representative in the assembly, is likewise without protection. In Britany he is ill clad, drinks nothing but water, and lives upon black bread.

Human misery always increases in the same degree as men are dependant. I have seen the peasant rich in Holland; at his ease in Prussia; in a tolerable comfortable state in Russia, and labouring under the greatest penury in Poland: I shall then certainly see the Negro, who is the peasant of our colonies, in a deplorable state. I account thus for what I have said; in a republic there is no sovereign, in a monarchy, but one; but in an

* As the text was composed under the old government of France, many allusions are made to the forms then in use, and this refers to their provincial parliaments. EDITOR.

aristocracy,

aristocracy, every peasant is subject to his particular tyrant.

The parent of industry is Liberty. The Swiss peasant is ingenious, the *villain* of Poland is without imagination. This stupor of the soul, which enables a man, even more than philosophy, to bear up against misfortune, seems to me to be a peculiar blessing. *When Jupiter,* says Homer, *reduces a man to the state of a slave, he takes from him one half of his understanding.*

Pray excuse my occasional reflections. When I see mankind struggling with great miseries, I cannot help enquiring, what will remedy them, or from whence they arise.

Nature seems every where, in Lower Britany, stinted in growth. The hills, vallies, trees, men and animals are all of diminutive size.

In several places we meet with quarries of slate, and of black and red marble, and mines of lead, mixed with silver, which is very ductile. But the real riches of this country are its linens, its threads, and cattle. Industry revives with liberty, from the vicinity of the sea-ports. This is, perhaps, the only good consequence of a maritime commerce, which is little else than an avarice, pointed out by law. Strange lot of man, that he should frequently deduce greater benefits from the indulgence of his passions, than from the exercise of his reason.

Here the peasant is much at his ease; he looks upon himself at liberty, from the neighbourhood of an element, all the roads to which are open.

Oppression cannot extend itself to any thing beyond his fortune: Is he hard pressed, he embarks himself, and on shipboard finds the oak of his own inclosures; the linens woven by his own family, and grain, the growth of his own fields · Houshold Gods by whom he has been abandoned! In the commander of the vessel, he frequently recognizes the Lord of his own village, and in their common misery sees him a man, whose fortune is more to be complained of than his own. At liberty to judge of his own situation, he becomes master of it; and seated on the yard-arm, decides in the fury of a storm upon that, which on shore, he durst not make an object of enquiry.

Port L'Orient I have not yet seen. Half a league before our arrival, we crossed a small arm of the sea in a ferry-boat: I could scarcely distinguish the town. A thick fog covered the horizon: This is occasioned by the vicinity of the sea; but the winter is the less severe on this account.

Such is generally the case as well in the neighbourhood of pools and lakes, as of the sea. May not this be to favour the propagation of a multitude of insects, and water vermin that inhabit the sands of the shore? Whether this conjecture is right or not, the facility of living there, and the mild temperature, draw from the North an infinite number of sea and water-fowls.

Who knows not that nature may well reserve for them some portion of the coast, and of mild air, when she has allotted to the fishes alone, above half the world.

I am, &c.

LET-

LETTER II.

L'Orient, Jan. 18, 1768.

THIS is a small town in Britany, which the commerce of the East Indies renders daily more flourishing. It is, like all other new towns, regular, the streets in strait lines, but unfinished. It is but indifferently fortified. There are some fine warehouses, the Hotel del Ventes, and a tower, whence one may see, wharfs which are only just begun, and ground plats whereon buildings are marked out.—It is situated at the bottom of a bay which receives the rivers *Blavet* and *Ponscorf;* they are navigable, and a vast many ships come down by them to L'Orient. The entrance to this bay is narrow, and defended by a work they call Port Louis, or Blavet. The citadel of which is too much raised, and must occasion the shot fired from it, to be, but of little effect. Its flanks, too narrow in themselves, have also Orillons, which are never of use, but for defending the ditch ; and there is none here but the sea, which washes the foot of the ramparts.

What an old, and deserted city, is Port Louis! 'Tis a gentleman of an ancient family in the neighbourhood of an East India nabob. The people of fashion live at Port Louis ; but the merchants, the muslin, and silk warehouses, the money, and the pretty women, are all at L'Orient. Their manners are the same here as in other commercial ports

ports. Every man's purse is open: but he lends money in the gross only; the interest of a sum for the Indies is twenty-five or thirty *per cent. per ann.* The borrower is much worse off than he that lends; his profits are uncertain, his bonds are not so. The law authorises this lending of money by contracts, and they give the creditors a sort of claim upon the whole ship's cargo. A power which extends over the entire fortune of most of the seafaring people.

Here are three ships ready to sail for the Isle of France, the *Digue*, the *Condè*, and the *Marquis de Castries*. Others are fitting out, and some more on the stocks. The noise of the carpenters and caulkers, the concourse of strangers, and the perpetual moving about of vessels in the road, excite in the people a thirst after every thing that is maritime: the idea of fortune, constantly accompanying that of the Indies, adds to the illusion. You would think yourself a thousand leagues from Paris. The people of the country no longer speak French; those in town, know no other mafter, than the East India Company. The better sort of people talk of the Isle of France and Pondicherry, as if they were just by. You will suppose that counting-house disputes come here in the bales from India, for interest rather tends to separate men from each other, than to bring them together.

I am, &c

LET-

LETTER III.

Port L'Orient, Feb. 20, 1771.

A FAIR wind to set sail only keeps us here. My passage is taken on board the *Marquis de Castries*, a ship of eight hundred tons, and one hundred and forty-six men, loaden with naval stores for Bengal. My birth is a little recess from the great cabin. There are fifteen passengers, most of whom are lodged in the gun-room, the place where they put the cartouches, and ordnance stores. The master gunner has the care of this part, and lodges here, as do also the secretary, chaplain, and surgeon. Over this is the great cabin, where the passengers dine with the captain. Over this again is the * council chamber, and the captains cabin; it is decorated on the outside with a gallery, and is the finest room in the ship. The officers cabins are before you come to these abovementioned, that they may with the more ease look to what is going forward upon deck.

The forecastle is the birth allotted for the crew, and between decks, a dismal hole, where one can see nothing. The † galliards are the length of the whole ship, which is level with the great cabin, and has a gangway before it, as the cabin has. The kitchen, or cook-room, is under the

* Called in English, the coach. *E.*

† Galliards; the ship must, from this description, have had a spare deck. *E.*

forecastle. The provisions and merchandizes in the hold; and the powder-room is under the gun-room.

This is a general sketch of the disposition of our ship; but to describe the disorder of it, is impossible. There is no getting along for the casks of Champagne, wine, trunks, chests, and boxes, every where about. Sailors swearing, cattle lowing, birds and poultry screaming upon the poop, and, as it blows hard, we have the additional noise of the whistling of the ropes, and the cracking of the timbers and rigging as the ship rolls about at anchor. Several other ships lay near us, and we are deafened by the hallowing of their officers to us, through their speaking trumpets.

Distracted by this uproar, I got into a boat and went ashore at Port Louis.

We walked through the streets, but met nobody. The wind blew fresh. From the walls of the citadel, I saw the horizon very black, and the island of *Groi* covered with a thick fog; upon the shore crouds of women chilled with cold and fear, and a centinel at the point of the bastion, in astonishment at the hardiness of the poor wretches, who were fishing in the midst of the tempest.

Close buttoned up, wet through, and holding on our hats with our hands, we made shift to return. As we went along, the streets were covered with fish; white and purple skait, thornbacks, dog-fish, conger eels of a monstrous size, large baskets full of crabs and lobsters, heaps of oysters, muscles and cockles, codlings, soles, and turbots;

turbots; in short, as miraculous a draught as that of the apostles.

When they fish for pilchards, a priest goes in the first boat, and gives his benediction to the water. One might see among them the conjugal affection of old times; for as they came dropping in, their wives and children hung about their necks: it is among these hard working people, that some remains of virtue is to be found, as if man retained his morals no longer than while he was in a state between hope and fear.

No part of the coast abounds more in fish than this: each species of which is, in general, larger than they are elsewhere; but their taste is inferior. I was assured, that the pilchard fishery brought in four millions of livres, annually, to the revenue of the province. It is rather singular, that there are no craw-fish in the rivers of Britany; occasioned, perhaps, by the stillness of the water.

Once more are we got to our inn; the noise of the wind and sea still buzzing in our ears. Two Parisians, the Sieurs B***, father and son, who were to have gone in our ship, without saying a word to us, ordered a chaise, and are gone to Paris.

LETTER IV.

On board the Marquis de Castries, March 3,
Eleven in the Morning.

TIME is only just allowed me to say—adieu; we are setting sail. Pray take care of the letters inclosed; three are for Russia, Prussia, and Poland. Wherever I have travelled, I left somebody whom I regret.

Our anchor is a-peak. I hear the noise of the boatswain's whistle, the capstern, and the sailors heaving anchor. The last gun is just fired. We are under sail, and the shore, the ramparts, and roofs of Port Louis begin to disappear. Adieu, ye friends, who are dearer to me than the treasures of India. Adieu! Adieu!

JOURNAL.

JOURNAL.

MARCH, 1768.

WE were under way on the third at a quarter past eleven in the morning, the wind at N. E. the tide not being high enough, we were very near touching upon a rock, to the right of the Channel. When we were abreast of the island of *Groi,* we lay to for some of the passengers and officers.

The weather was fine on the 4; but the wind began to rise, and the sea to run high in the evening.

A violent storm arose on the 5; the ship was on her way under her courses. I was terribly sea-sick. At half past ten in the morning, being in bed, I felt a great shock; somebody cried out, that the ship had struck. I went upon deck, where I found all the people in consternation. A wave struck us on the starboard-side and carried away the yawl, with the mate and three men One of them only remained, entangled in the shrouds of the main-mast, from whence he was taken, with his shoulder and hand shattered to pieces. It was impossible to save the others; they were seen no more.

The disaster was occasioned by the vessel not answering the helm. Her poop was too low in the water, to suffer the rudder to act properly upon her. The bad weather lasted all day, and the

the motion of the ship killed most of the poultry. I had a dog on board, that panted incessantly with uneasiness. The only animals that seemed insensible, were some sparrows and canary birds, accustomed to a perpetual motion. These birds are carried to India as curiosities.

All the other passengers, and myself amongst the rest, were exceedingly sick. There is no remedy for this evil, which occasions the most dreadful reachings. It is good, however, to take some dry food, and above all acid fruits.

The weather being fine on the 6, we offered up our prayers for the souls of the poor sailors we lost in the late storm. The sea, in breaking upon the vessel, had split the beam that goes round the hatchway, though it was ten inches thick.

We reckoned ourselves to be in the latitude of Cape Finistere the 7, where gusts of wind, and a great sea, as at all other capes, are very common.

We had a beautiful sea and fair wind on the 8. We saw flying about, some white birds with black borders round their wings; they call them Manches de Velours *Velvet Sleeves*.

The air grew sensibly hotter, and the sky more pleasing on the 9 and 10. We approached the *Fortunate* island the Azores if it be true, that heaven has placed good fortune in any particular island.

We had a calm the 11, the sea was covered with bonnets de feu *bonnets of fire* a kind of

 mucilage,

mucilage, formed into the shape of a cap, with a progressive motion. In the morning we saw a ship.

Some good regulations were made the 12 and 13. It was agreed that each passenger should have but one bottle of water a day. Breakfast was to be at ten every morning, and was to consist of salted meats and dry vegetables. Our afternoon meal, at four o'clock, was a rather better repast. All fires were to be put out at eight o'clock.

We expected to see the island of Madeira on the 14, but were too much westward; it was calm all day. We saw two birds, brown, and of the size of a pigeon, flying to the westward, as high as the masts. We took them for land birds, and judged, from their appearing, that some island was to our left hand.

We continued calm the 15; but the wind rose a little towards night: an English brig passed us in the afternoon, and saluted us with her flag.

About sun-rise, we saw the island of Palma before us the 16; on the left is the island of Teneriffe with its Pike, which is in the shape of a dome, with a pyramid on the top. These islands were enveloped in a fog all day, and at night in storms of lightning: an appearance which terrified the mariners who first discovered them. It is known, that the Romans had heard of them; because Sertorius was desirous of retiring to them. The Carthaginians, who traded on the coast of Africa,

Africa, knew them well. *Juba*, the historian, says, there are five of them; and describes them at large: he calls one of them the Isle of Snow, because it is covered with it all the year. The Pike, is, in fact, covered with snow, though the air is so hot. These islands are the ruins of that large island of Atlantis, of which Plato speaks. By the depth of the cavities, out of which their mountains are raised, one would think they were the ruins of this original world, when overturned by an event, the tradition of which remains among all nations. According to *Juba*, the island of Canary took its name from the large dogs bred there. The Spaniards, to whom they belong, got excellent *Malmsey* from thence.

We passed through the midst of these islands, having Teneriffe on our left, and Palma on our right, the 17, 18, and 19. Gomera was to the eastward. I took a draught of these islands, which are cut in with very deep ravines or furrows.

Here a flying fish was distinctly seen. A lapwing came and perched on our ship, and took its flight to the west; it was of an orange-colour, its wings and aigrette mottled with black and white, its beak is black as ebony, and a little bent.

We left the island of Ferro the 20, to the west, and lost sight of all the Canaries. The sight of those islands, situated in so fine a climate, excited in us many fruitless wishes. We compared the repose and abundance, the union and pleasures of these islands, to our own unquiet life

life of agitation. Perhaps, at seeing us pass by, some unhappy Canarian was upon a burning rock, wishing himself on board a ship, that steered under full sail for the East Indies.

We saw a land-swallow, and afterwards a shark, the 21. While we were in the latitude of these islands, we were becalmed all day, the wind rising in the evening only.

The weather became so hot by the 22, as to occasion several bottles of Champagne to break, though they were cased in salt; this is a store, that most of the officers going to India take with them; it is sold there at a pistole a bottle. This inundation, which penetrated every thing, destroyed some lettices and cresses, that I had sown in wet moss, where these plants grow surprizingly. This salted liquor was so very corrosive, as to entirely spoil all my papers that got wetted with it.

We had a very fresh wind the 23; the sea appeared to be grey and greenish, as upon banks, or in soundings; they pretend to find soundings above eighty leagues from the coast of Africa, which is but little raised in these latitudes. We saw a ship bearing away foı Senegal.

The trade-wind prevailed from the N. W on the 24. The ship rolled very much.

With fine weather and fair wind, the 25 and 26, we passed the latitude of the Cape de Verd islands, but did not see them; they belong to Portugal; fresh provisions are to be had there; but water, the chief article, is very scarce. We

saw

saw some flying fishes and a land swallow. The French wheat, in the bread-room, heated to such a degree, that there was no bearing one's hand in it. It has happened sometimes, that ships have been set on fire by this means. In 1760, an English ship, loaden with hemp, was burnt in the Baltic. The hemp took fire of itself. I saw the wreck of her on the coast off the isle of Bornholm.

From head to stern an awning was spread the 27, to shelter the people from the heat. We saw some *galeres*, a species of living mucilage.

We saw flying-fish, and a great number of tunny-fish, the 28 and 29.

Our men got ready for fishing the 30, and took ten tunny-fish, the least of which weighed sixty pounds; we saw a shark. The heat increased, and the crew bore their thirst with great impatience.

We took a bonnito the 31; some thirty sailors in the night opened the water jars of several passengers, who by that means found themselves, as the crew were, reduced to a pint of water a day.

SEAFARING PEOPLE.

IT may not be improper here to say a few words of the influence the sea has upon these men, in order that those faults, which are the consequences of their way of life, may meet with suitable indulgence.

Dispatch

Dispatch in every thing so absolutely necessary in operations on board a ship, renders them coarse in their expressions. Living at a distance from land, they think themselves independent; hence it is that they frequently speak of princes, laws or religion, with a freedom equal to their ignorance. Not but they are, in some circumstances, devout and superstitious. I have known more than one, who would not so much as touch a rope on a Sunday or Friday. But, in general, their religion depends upon the weather.

Their lounging and gossiping habits make them fond of scandal and stories. The quarter-deck is the place where the officers deal out fables and wonders.

New acquaintance which they make continually renders them inconstant in their society and taste. At sea they wish for land, on shore they murmur that they are not at sea.

It is best to give way, especially in long voyages, a little, and never to dispute. The sea naturally sours the temper; and the slightest contradiction will breed a quarrel. I have seen one arise on a question in philosophy. It is true these questions have sometimes caused no small mischief on shore.

These men are, for the most part, rather silent and thoughtful. Ah! who can be gay, when surrounded with dangers, and deprived of the prin cipal necessaries of life?

We must not, however, forget their many good qualities. They are open, generous, brave, and above all, good husbands. A seaman looks upon himself as a stranger when ashore, and mostly so in his own house. Unaccustomed to the manner of living, he leaves to his wife the management of a world, of which he is ignorant.

This odd mixture of good and bad qualities derives a peculiar cast from the vices of their education. They are given to drunkenness. Every day a ration of wine or brandy is issued. There are seven men in a mess, and I have seen them agree among themselves to drink alternately the allowance of the whole seven. Some of them are given to thieving; and there are of these, men so dextrous as to strip their comrades while sleeping; others again, are of an extraordinary probity The master and gunner are commonly the men entrusted, upon whom devolves the government of the crew. One may add to these, the chief pilot, who, I don't know why, does not hold among us that rank which his merit deserves; he is but the first *officier marinier**. Upon these three men depends the good behaviour of the crew, and very often the success of the navigation.

* In British men of war, the captain and lieutenants, are considered as gentlemen by their office, and generally are so by their behaviour and birth. They all have commissions. The master, his mates, and the carpenter, gunner, &c. are only warrant officers, and in general are low born uneducated people, who by their good behaviour, and application in their respective branches in seamanship, have qualified themselves for their particular commands. These are what the author probably means by *officieres mariniers*. F.

The

The cook is the last, but not the least important in the ship. The cabbin boys are often used very barbarously. There is scarce an officer or sailor, that does not make them sensible when he is in an ill humour. They even amuse themselves on board some ships, with flogging them in calm weather, to procure a wind. Thus man, who is so often complaining of his weakness, seldom has power, but he abuses it.

From all this you will readily conceive that a ship is a place of dissention; that a convent and an island, which is a kind of ship, must be filled with discord; and that the intention of Nature, which is in other respects so plainly pointed out, is, that the earth should be peopled with families, and not with societies and fraternities.

APRIL, 1768.

Some sharks were perceived, and we took one, as also a bonito, on the 1. I intend to continue my observations on fishes at the end of my journal for this month.

We had calm weather the 2, and now and then squalls.—We are upon the borders of the southern trade winds. In the afternoon we had a squall that made us reef all our sails. We draw near to the line; and have now very little twilight.

A few bonitos were taken the 3, and a shark. We were constantly surrounded by the same shoal of tunny fish.

A stormy sky, and a violent squall, with thunder at a distance, marked the 4. A sailor died of the scurvy. Many others are ill of it. This disorder shewing itself so early, spreads an alarm through the whole crew. We took several bonitos and sharks.

The 5 and 6, yesterday morning at three o'clock, it blew a most terrible storm, and obliged us to reef all our sails except the mizen. I have always remarked, that the rising of the moon dispels the clouds very perceptibly. Two hours after it is above the horizon, the sky is perfectly clear

clear. We had a calm these two days, and some drops of rain.

We took some bonitos on the 7. I saw some glass cut with scissars under water; the cause of which I am ignorant of.

One shark was caught the 8 and 9, some sucking-fish, or remoras, and two tunny fish. Although near the line, the heat was not very troublesome to me; the air is cooled by the storms.

The ducking at the line, was announced, the 10, we were within one degree. A sailor disguised in a mask, came to the Captain, and desire l him to cause the old custom to be observed. This is a frolic designed to divert the melancholy of the crew. The sailors are very dispirited; the scurvy gets a-head among them, and we have not gone one third of the voyage.

The ceremony of dipping was performed the 11. The principal passengers were ranged along a cord, to which their thumbs were tied with a ribband. Some drops of water were poured on their heads, and they then gave some money to the pilots.

Now the sky and the sea were very fine, but the wind was contrary.

We could not get past the line the 12. The currents ran northward. We now see the polar-star no more We saw a ship to the East.

On the 13, however, we crossed the line. The fea appeared at night, as if covered with phosphorus. The lower deck is cleaned every Sunday; the chests and hammocks of the crew are brought upon deck, and then pitch is burnt between decks; the third part of the water-casks were found to he empty, though we had not gone near a third of our voyage.

Our winds varied the 14, 15, and 16. It was very hot. We were continually surrounded with bonitos, tunny-fish, porpoises, and flemish-caps. We saw a shark of an enormous size. The weather calm in general, but sometimes stormy.

Our calms and heats continued the 17, 18, and 19. The pitch melted from the rigging. Spleen and impatience increased aboard the ship. 'Tis not unusual to lay becalmed a whole month under the line. I saw a whale going to the westward.

This distressing calm, and our uneasiness lasted the 20, 21, and 22. The ship was surrounded with sharks. We saw one tied to a *paillaison*, in a large ridge of surf running from East to West. It was alive; some ship had certainly passed by just before.

Some tunny-fishes, bonitos, five or six sharks, and a porpoise, with a very sharp pointed head were all catched. The sailors say that the porpoise forebodes wind; in effect, at midnight it began.

We

We entered at last into the South-West trade-winds the 23, which were to carry us beyond the other tropic. Here we took some bonitos and tunny-fish. As we were drawing one of these out of the water, a shark catched it by the tail, and broke the line. We saw a frigate-bird; it is black and grey, and nearly of the same form as a stork. Its flight is very lofty.

Some squalls occurred the 24 and 25, which occasioned the wind to change. Towards evening the moon was encompassed with a large halo, or red circle. We catched bonitos, and tunny fish.

Frigate-birds, flying-fish, tunny-fish, bonitos, and a white bird, which the crew said was a booby, appeared the 26. In the evening, all the sails being set, we were attacked by a violent squall, which laid us on one side for some minutes. Our ship is a bad sailer, and when the wind is quite fair, makes but about two leagues an hour.

The sea ran high the 27, the wind was fresh, and had some squalls of rain. We saw the same fishes, and a halcyon, which the English call the Bird of Storms*. I shall reserve an article of my journal for sea-fowl.

We had fresh winds the 28, and squalls with rain. Six guns were carried forward, from the aft-

* Petrels, alluding it is said, to St. Peter, when our Saviour walked on the sea. They seem to walk in a ship's wake, particularly in storms. The common sailors call them *Mother Carey's Chickens.*

part of the ship——that being deeper in the water forward, she might steer the better. We had very stormy weather, which is rare in these latitudes. Saw the same tunnies.

Fine weather, but sometimes squally, prevailed on the 29. We saw some frigate-birds, and a white bird, with wings marked with grey. At sun-set, we saw a ship to windward, steering the same course as we.

We enjoyed a fine fresh wind and beautiful sea the 30. The air cooler. We saw the ship we had seen last night, a little to windward. She had crouded sail; we did the like; she hoisted English colours; we ours. We catched tunnies, and saw flying-fish.

THE SEA AND FISHES.

A MORE dismal sight than the main sea is scarcely to be seen. A man becomes presently impatient of being in the centre of a circle, the circumference of which he never attains. It however presents some very interesting scenes. I do not speak of it when tempestuous only. During a calm, and especially at night in hot climates, it is surprizing to see the sparkling of it. I have taken in a glass some of those luminous points of which it is full; and have seen them move about with great vivacity. They are said to be the fry of fish; and are sometimes seen in a heap together, appearing like moons. At night,

night, when the ship is under way, and is surrounded by fish that accompany it, the sea appears like a vast fire-work, all sparkling with serpents and silver spangles.

You may consider at your leisure of what a prodigious quantity of living beings this element must be the native region. I confine myself to some observations upon different species of fishes found in the main sea.

I believe the ancients called the bonnet-flamand *pulmo-marinus*. It is a species of animal, formed of a very glaring substance. It is not unlike a champignon, or mushroom. Its upper part has a power of contraction and dilatation, by the which it moves very slowly. I know no other property of it; 'tis so common, that we found the sea covered with it for many days. It can change its shape and colour; but the shape naturally is always the same. They are found very large upon the coast of Normandy.

Of the same substance is the *galere;* but it seems endued with more intelligence and malignity. Its body is a kind of oval bladder, covered lengthways with a tuft or sail, which is always out of the water, in the same direction as the wind. When overturned by a wave, it rises again quickly, and always presents the convex side of its body to the wind. I have seen many of them together, ranged like a fleet of ships. There might, perhaps, be some kind of sail contrived upon this principle, by means of which a bark might get on, though the wind were contrary.

From

From the lower part of the *galere*, hang several long blue filaments, with which it seizes whatever attempts to take it. These filaments burn immediately, like the most violent caustic. I one day saw a young sailor who swam after, and attempted to catch one of them, burnt on the arm so terribly, that the fright nearly occasioned his being drowned. The *galere*, while alive, is of the most beautiful colours; some of them are of a sky-blue, and some of a rose-colour. The bonnet-flamand *, is found in our seas, and the *galere* in those near the tropics.

I saw, in the latitude of the Azores, a kind of shell-fish, floating and living on the surface of the sea, shaped like the beard of an arrow, or beak of a bird. It is small, transparent, and very easy to break. This is, perhaps, the same that is found in ambergrease.

Here also we found some snails, that were blue, and floated on the surface of the water, like bladders filled with air. Their shell was very thin and brittle, and filled with a liquor of a beautiful purplish blue colour. This is not, however, the purple-fish of the ancients.

A shell-fish much more common, is that which sticks itself to the sides of the ship, by means of a ligament, which it shortens or contracts, in bad weather. It is white, shaped like an almond, and composed of four pieces. It puts out a number of filaments, that have a regular motion. They

* Or Flemish bonnet.

multiply

multiply so very fast, that the course of the ship is sensibly retarded by them.

Between the tropics the flying-fish is very common. It is of the size of a herring. It flies in a troop, and at one single spring, the usual flight of a partridge. In the sea, 'tis hunted by the fishes, and in the air by the birds. Its destiny seems a very unfortunate one, that in the air the same danger should await it, which it fled from in the water. But it has a compensation for the misfortune, for as a fish, it often escapes from the birds, and as a bird from the fishes. 'Tis in storms chiefly, that it is seen flying from the *frigattes* and tunnies, which make prodigious leaps in pursuit of it.

The same manœuvre is nearly made by the *encornet*, as the flying-fish. It has the faculty of blackening the water, by throwing into it a very black ink, and it does not swim altogether so well; it is of a conoid form. These two kind of fish frequently fall on board of ships, and are very fine eating.

Of these seas, the tunny-fish differs in taste from that of the Mediterranean. It is very dry, and has no fat but in the eye. It has very little entrails. Its flesh appears pinched, or compressed together by the skin. Eight muscles, four large, and four small, form its body, the transverse section of which resembles that of a tree. They fish for it at sun-rise, and sun-set, because then the shade of the waves disguises the bait, which is made to represent a flying-fish. This shoal of tunnies

tunnies followed us these six weeks past. They are easily known; among them there is one, which has a red wound on the back, from being struck with a harpoon a fortnight ago: but his course was not retarded by it.

It has sometimes occurred to me, can a fish exist without sleep, and is sea-water of a healing quality to wounds? I have somewhere read that Monsieur de Chirac, cured the Duke of Orleans of a wound in the wrist, by ordering it to be steeped in the waters of Balaru

When eaten fresh, the tunny is wholesome, though it occasions thirst,—it is dangerous in these latitudes to eat it salted—for one of our sailors having done so, his skin turned as red as scarlet, and he had a fever for twenty-four hours after.

We took a number of bonitos among laminæ. They are a sort of mackarel, some of which are as large as tunnies. In the flesh of many were found living worms, as big as a grain of barley, which did not seem at all troublesome to the fish.

Near the line sharks abound. As soon as it is calm the ship is surrounded with them. This fish swims along slowly, and without noise. It is preceded by many small fishes, called pilot-fish, speckled with black and yellow. If any thing falls into the sea, they instantly reconnoitre, and return to the shark, who approaching his prey, turns himself, and devours it. If it is a bird, he does not touch it; but when pressed by hunger,

hunger, he swallows every thing, even iron nails.

He is the tyger of the sea. I have seen some more than ten feet long. By Nature it is very short-sighted. It swims very slowly, from the round form of its head, which joined to the position of its mouth, that obliges it to turn upon its side, in order to swallow, preserves a number of fishes from its voracity. It has no bones, but cartilages, like other fishes of prey, as the sea-dog, the thornback, the polypus. These like the shark, see but badly, are slow swimmers, and have their mouths placed quite beneath, and are also viviparous.

The chops, or jaws of this monster, are armed with five or six rows of teeth above and below. They are flat, and sharp at the sides, which are serrated. They have but two rows perpendicular, the others are hidden, and disposed in such a manner, that they replace by an admirable mechanism, those that frequently are liable to be broken.

He is baited for with a piece of flesh, fastened upon an iron crook. Before they draw him out of the water, they fix round the sail a sliding knot, and as soon as he is upon the deck, and attempts to strike or wound the sailors, they cut him with a hatchet. His tail has but one fin, shaped like a sickle. The Chinese esteem this as an aphrodisiaque. In other respects, this fish is of no utility. Its flesh has a taste of the thornback, and a smell of urine, and is reckoned feverish.

feverish. The sailors fish for this creature, merely to destroy it. They put out the eyes, gut them, tie two or three together by the tails, and throw them into the sea; a spectacle worthy of a sailor. The shark is so vivacious, as to move, long after the head is cut off; yet I have seen them drowned very fast, by being plunged several times in the sea, after being struck by a hook, which keeps their mouth open.

Upon the shark is almost always found a fish called a sucking-fish, or *Remora*, about as big as a herring. It has upon the head an oval surface, a little concave, with which it fixes itself upon any body, by forming a vacuum, between the oval surface and the body, to which it adheres in the manner of a leathern sucker. I have put some of them alive upon an even smooth glass, from which I could not afterwards take them. This fish has this singularity, that it swims with the head and gills out of water, its skin is coarse and rough, and its mouth armed with several rows of small teeth. We often have eaten the sucking-fish, and have found the taste like fried artichokes.

The shark nourishes under its skin, not only the pelot and sucking-fish, but also an insect shaped like the half of a pea, with a beak that projects a long way. It is a kind of louse.

The fish we call a porpoise, is a fish well known. I have seen of one sort, that has the snout very pointed. The sailors, on account of its swiftness, call it the sea-arrow. I have seen them go go quite round about the ship, while she made two leagues an hour. They throw a dart at this animal, which pants when taken, and seems to complain; it is a bad fish; its flesh is black, hard, gross and oily.

A *Dorado*, which they say is the lightest of all fish, I have also seen. This, it is said, is the dolphin of the ancients, so fully described by Pliny. Be as it may, we did not experience much of its friendship to mankind; but saw, at a great depth, the shining of its golden fins, and its back of a beautiful azure.

We frequently observed, at half a league's distance, whales, snorting and spouting water, as their custom is, with great velocity. They are smaller here than in the north, and appeared to me, afar off, like a boat, bottom upwards.

These are most of the fish I have yet seen. Sharks are seen in a calm, and are commonly followed by the *dorados;* the porpoises appear when the wind freshens. The tunnies have followed us constantly for six weeks past.

Consider if this detail has been tiresome to you, what my pleasures must have been. There are none for a man, upon an element, with the inhabitants of which he cannot connect himself.

MAY, 1768.

AT sun rise the 1, the vessel we had seen some days before, was in our wake, and gaining upon us insensibly; at ten in the morning she was along-side of us. We remarked, that all her sails were very old, that the chests and beds of the crew were upon deck. They asked us in English, *What cheer? What's your ship called? Where do you come from? Where are you bound?* We answered in English, and asked them the same questions. She came from London, sixty-four days before, and was bound for China. She was pierced for twenty-four guns, and was of about five hundred tons burthen. She wished us a good voyage, and continued her way. Saw some frigate birds, tunnies, and bonitos.

We again saw the English ship, which the tunnies followed, after having borne us company so long. The 2 and 3 we had violent squalls from the west. These variations, in my opinion, arise from the neighbourhood of *All Saints* Bay; and, I believe, the currents and leeway she made by not answering her helm, have carried her nearer to America* than we were aware of.

Our wind was violent and changeable the 4 and 5. We saw a fouquet, a bird that is black and

* The Abbè de la Caille says, that in his voyage to the Cape of Good Hope, the ship was constantly and considerably to the westward of the reckonings. *E.*

and grey; some frigate-birds and boobies, that were diving to catch fish.

A good breeze and fine sea continued the 6 and 7; last night we had violent squalls. We saw some frigate-birds taking their course to the N. E.

Yesterday, the 8 and 9, the wind was very violent, and the sea very high. The ship lay on her side, and the water came in at the ports. Towards the evening the wind fell calm, which it commonly does when the sun gets in the opposite quarter. We saw a great number of land birds and some gulls, signs that we were near land, whence these squalls arose.

The sea was quite calm the 14. At nine in the evening, as I stood talking in the gallery with the captain, I saw all the horizon enlightened by a very luminous fire, running from the east to the north, and shooting forth red sparks. In the daytime the clouds stopped and appeared like land to the southward.

Violent squalls soon followed, with some thunder. Here the S. E. winds commonly end, but sometimes they reach to twenty-eight degrees of latitude. We now looked for the westerly winds, with which they double the Cape of Good Hope.

Fine weather the 17, 18, 19, though foggy; we perceived a surge coming from the west, which always precedes a wind from that quarter. Last night we saw a second luminous

 appearance,

appearance, and in the afternoon a whale to the S. W. a league and a half from us. They imagined in the morning, that they saw a sea fowl, called the Mouton de Cap, or Cape Sheep * This bird is found in the latitudes of the Cape of Good Hope.

THE SKY, WINDS, BIRDS.

EASTWARD, the stars seem more luminous than those to the west. One may distinguish, besides the cross of the south, the magellanic constellation, which are two white clouds, formed by multitudes of little stars. One side of which are seen two spaces more dark than the other parts of the sky.

As we verge on the line, the twilight decreases so much, that the day is almost entirely distinct from the night. It is easily explained, why the twilight increases with the refraction of the rays toward the poles. In these regions, scarcely inhabited, light is mingled with the darkness, especially in the Aurora Borealis, which in all places, is the greater, the less the sun is elevated above the horizon. How very inconvenient would it have been, had the night between the tropics partaken of day-light. The night seems made for the blacks of Africa, who wait the close of day

* We call them Albatrosse. Their wings, when extended, will measure ten feet, sometimes more, and have one more joint than the wings of other birds; for this reason, if they are put on their feet upon deck, they cannot fly away, being unable to rise; but from the water. *E.*

that

that they may dance and revel. 'Tis at this time that the wild beasts of these parts come to refresh themselves in the rivers, and that the turtles go on shore to lay their eggs. Is there not then a sensible heat in the rays of the sun, though refracted? The torrid zone would have been uninhabitable, had there been long twilights. In other respects, the night in these climates is finer than the day. The rising moon dispels the vapours with which the air is impregnated. I have so often made this remark, that I am of the sailors opinion, who say, that the moon swallows up the clouds. On the other hand, can the influence of the moon upon our atmosphere be denied, when we allow it to have so great a one upon the ocean *.

The winds, on this side the line, in general are N. E. and on the other side S. E. These winds appear to arise from the air being dilated by the sun, and reflected by the poles. The S. E. winds extend farther than the N. E. as may be seen by the journal of winds. They are commonly met with in three or four degrees of N. latitude. The S. pole is moreover colder than the N. perhaps because the sun is longer on the northern side. Navigators, who have attempted to discover the

* On these matters we believe very little is known, but the conjectures indulged by old women and astronomers, shew at least that the influence of the moon is not wholly confined, either to the sea or the weather. We readily except from this remark the very ingenious and sublime *System of the World, of M. Lambert,* of which our language has been lately enriched by a masterly version from *James Jacque, Esq.* No work we have hitherto seen on a subject so transcending common observation, seems, in our opinion, so likely to render it popular, or is better calculated to compensate the reader's perusal. *E.*

southern continent, have found ice in forty-five degrees †.

The vapours raised by the sun from the Atlantic, are continually wafted to America by these winds. Those of the South Sea, serve to fertilize a part of Asia and Africa. The wind in general blows harder by day than by night.

There would be no rivers but for clouds; and they do not contribute less to the beauty of the heavens, than to the fruitfulness of the earth.

Who can but admire the rising and setting of the sun. This is a spectacle not less difficult to describe than to paint! Figure to yourself the horizon of a beautiful orange colour, tinged with green, which as it approaches to the zenith, loses itself in a lilac hue, while the rest of the sky is of a most glorious blue. The clouds floating to and fro of a clear pearl-coloured grey, sometimes disposed in long streaks of crimson or scarlet; all the tints lively, distinct, and bordered with a fringe of gold!

The clouds to the westward one evening appeared in the shape of a vast net, like black silk. As soon as the sun began to pass behind it, each mesh of the net looked as if it rose in a thread of gold. The gold then changed into flame colour and scarlet, and the deeper part of the sky was coloured with light tints of purple, green, and sky blue!

† Some have sailed as far as 56 deg. before they met with ice. *T.*

Great

Great variety of landscapes are frequently formed in the sky, and the most uncouth figures present themselves to imagination. We see in them, promontories, steep and rugged rocks, towers, and villages, over which the light diffuses all the colours of the prism. 'Tis to the brilliancy of their colours we must attribute the beauty of the birds of India, and the shell-fish of these seas; but why are not the birds of the sea of these countries so handsome as ours? I will reserve the examination of this problem to another article, and now describe to you those I saw flying about our ship, with the names given them by seafaring people. You may imagine that this description cannot be a very accurate one.

In all latitudes the most common bird is a species of swallow, or halcyon, called by the English, the *foul-weather bird*, or *petrel*. It is of a blackish brown, skims on the surface of the water, and in bad weather follows the wake of the ship. It probably follows ships at that time, to find a shelter from the wind; for the same reason that it flies between the two surges in skimming the water's edge.

Even as high as Cape Finisterre, we saw some sea-mews, the wings of which are bordered with black. They are about the size of a duck, and fly, fluttering their wings, on the surface of the sea. They do not fly far from land, whither they retire every evening.

In two and an half deg. of N. latitude, we saw first the frigate-birds. They were thought to come from the Island of Ascension, which is in 8 deg. S. latitude. In form and size, they are like a stork, are black and white, have wings that extend a great way, and they have a long neck. The males have under their bills, a puff of skin, round as a ball, and red as scarlet. This is the lightest of all sea-birds. It never rests upon the water, yet is seen three hundred leagues from land, whither, 'tis affirmed, that it returns every evening to roost.

Something larger, but more compact, is the booby. It is white, mingled with grey, and dives when pursuing its prey, which is fish. The point of its beak hooks downwards, and the sides of it are full of little sharp points, which assist it in seizing its prey. The frigate-bird is at war with the booby, which is better furnished with arms, though the former has more swiftness and cunning. When the booby has filled its craw with fish, the frigate attacks it, and makes it give up its spoils, which it receives in the air.

When *goelettes* are found in great flocks, it denotes shallow water, and that the land is near. They are white, and by their flight and shape, may be taken for pigeons.

Something bigger, of the height of a large duck, is the *envergure*. It is white under the belly, and of a greyish brown on the wings and back. It takes its name from the great extent of its wings

Near the Cape of Good Hope only, are *damiers* found. They are as big as pigeons, have a black head

head and tail, a white belly, the back and wings marked regularly with black and white, like the checks of a draught-board.

We next saw the *mouton-de-cap;* 'tis a bird something larger than a goose, has a flesh-coloured beak, very extensive wings, mixed with grey and white. They are seldom found but in the latitude of the Cape of Good Hope. I have seen all these birds at rest upon the water, except the frigate-bird and the *envergure.* The sight of them is an indication of the latitude, when we have been many days without taking an observation, or when the currents have made us lose way in our longitude. It is to be wished that able seamen would give the world their observations on this. Some species do not go far from the land, and roost there every night. *Goelettes* seen out at sea, are signs of some land, or broken rocks being near; but the manches-de-velours, or sea-mews, are a certain token of its neighbourhood.

A certain species of bladed grass, or floating algæ, deserve also very particular attention. These several notices may be of use, instead of a method which is not yet discovered, of determining the longitude. They make an observation of the variation morning and evening; but this is not to be depended on. One cannot every day see the sun rise and set; moreover the variation, which is the declination of the needle, varies from one year to another, under the same meridian.

JUNE, 1768.

WESTERLY winds having announced themselves on the 1, we now hoped we should soon double the Cape.

Necessary precautions for this purpose were taken the 2. New cordage was put to the wheel of the rudder, and some additional ones to the shrouds, for securing the masts. We bent four new sails. The boats, and all things that were moveable on board, were strongly lashed. The wind was very fresh. We saw some birds, but the frigates no longer appeared.

Each day to the 7 the wind was very fresh, except yesterday, when it subsided a little. We saw every day a prodigious number of goelettes, moutons, and damiers, and the Cape reed *, which resembles the long trumpet used by shepherds. The sailors make a kind of trumpets of these hollow stalks. The sea was covered with surf, another sign of our being near the Cape. Fifteen men are rendered unfit for service by the scurvy.

At noon the 7, a bird of the size of a goose, with short wings, tawny coloured and brown, a head like a hen, a short tail, shaped like a leaf of trefoil, has fixed upon our masts for some time.

* English sailors call it trunk weed. *T.*

By

By all the bearings, we ought to find the Cape hereabouts. Saw the same birds.

Disorders and dejection increase in the ship the 9. One of the mates has just died of the scurvy.

As the sea appeared greenish, we sounded the 12, but found no bottom. The wind very fresh and a great sea.

Next day we at length came into soundings of ninety-five fathoms, a muddy and greenish bottom. This rejoiced us exceedingly. The great depth convinced us that we had lost way to the westward. We saw two ships, one a-astern, the other over our starboard Cat-head. The soundings ascertain where we are, but inform us, that we have misreckoned above two hundred leagues in our journal.

It blew fresh on the 15. The vessel a-stern hoisted English colours, and soon passed by us at about a league and a half to leeward. The other hoisted French colours, and as she was before the wind, she lowered her sails in order to join us, bearing up as near as she could. Our captain did not think proper to come to, she proved to be the *Digue* man of war, that sailed a month before us. Towards evening she hoisted all her sails, and steered in our course.

It proved calm the 17. We saw some whales and dorados.

The

The morning following we had a gale of wind, that obliged us to remain till eleven at night under our mizen. There arose at the extremity of each wave a white powder, like the dust blown by the wind along a road. At seven o'clock we shipped a sea at the great cabbin windows. At eight o'clock it hailed, and at midnight the weather grew fine.

We had a very fresh wind and a rolling sea the 22. The opinion of the ancients that the weather was calm during the solstice, was erroneous. I have this afternoon read an observation in Dampier's voyages, that the sun's disappearing at about three in the afternoon, behind a range of high and thick clouds, is a sign of a violent storm. When I went upon deck, the sky discovered all these signs described by Dampier.

About half past twelve in the night of the 23, a great sea beat in four of the five great cabbin-windows, though the dead-lights were barred like a St. Andrew's cross. The vessel pitched, as if she would have stood an end in the water. Hearing the noise, I opened the door of my chamber, which was instantly filled with water, and the furniture floated about. The water ran out of the door of the great cabbin, like the sluice of a mill; above thirty hogsheads of water came in by this accident. The carpenters were called, lights were brought, and new boards nailed against the windows as quickly as possible. We now ran under a mizen, and the wind and sea were truly frightful.

Hardly

Hardly was this error rectified, before a large chest, that served for a table, full of salt and bottles of Champagne, broke its lashings. The rolling of the ship threw it to and fro like a die. This enormous box weighed many tons, and threatened us with being crushed to pieces in our rooms. At last it burst open, and the bottles rolling about and breaking, caused a confusion that is inexpressible. The carpenters returned, and with the greatest difficulty replaced and fastened it.

This uproar and tumult not suffering me to sleep, I lay down upon the bed in my boots and morning-gown: my dog seemed in the greatest fright, and while I amused myself with soothing him, I saw a flash of lightening through the crevice of the port-hole, and heard it thunder. 'Twas about half past three in the morning. In a moment, a second clap of thunder broke, and the dog began to fly about and howl. The lightning flashed again in an instant. Thunder immediately following, I heard them cry out upon deck, that some ship was in danger; in fact, the noise was like the report of a cannon fired near us, as it did not roll at all. Perceiving a strong smell of sulphur, I went upon deck, and immediately felt it excessively cold. Every thing was silent, and the night so dark, I could distinguish nothing. I presently perceived somebody near me, and asked, what was the matter? The man answered, "They are carrying the quarter-master to his birth; he has fainted away, and so has the pilot. The thunder has fallen upon the ship, and shivered the main-mast." Indeed, I found the main-

main-top-sail yard was fallen upon the main-top. Neither mast nor rigging appeared, the crew were all retired to the council-chamber*

A ring was instantly formed on the fore-castle. The thunder had descended so far along the mast. A woman who had just lain in, had seen a globe of fire at the foot of her bed; yet nobody could discover any trace of the fire. Day light was looked for with impatience.

I again went upon deck about day break. Some very black clouds appeared, and others of a copper colour. The wind was westerly, where the horizon appeared of a flaming red, as if the sun was going to rise in that quarter. The East was totally black. The sea formed monstrous waves, that rose like pointed mountains, composed of a number of smaller hills; on their summits were raised spouts of foam, coloured like so many rainbows. They were thrown so high, as to appear from the quarter-deck, to be higher than the tops. The wind made so much noise in the rigging, that we could scarcely hear each other speak. We ran before the wind under a mizen only. A piece of the top-mast hung from the end of the main-mast, which was split in eight places to a level with the deck. Five of the iron rings with which it was bound, were melted. The gangways were covered with the broken pieces of the top, and main top-mast.

* There is no council-chamber in our English ships, nor do I know what part is so called by the French in theirs. *E.*

At

At the rising of the sun, the wind also rose with a redoubled and inexpressible fury. The ship no longer to be guided by the helm, went which way soever the wind or the waves drove her. The mizen-sail having gibed its braces, broke soon after; the force with which it was continually striking against the mast, we feared would have broken the latter by the board. In an instant, the forecastle was under water. The waves broke over the larboard cat-head, in so much, that the bowsprit was not to be seen. Clouds of surf inundated even as high as the poop. The ship, by not steering, presented her side to the waves, and at every roll took in water even to the foot of the main-mast, and rose again with the utmost difficulty.

In this moment of danger the captain called out to the Pilots to put before the wind; but the vessel could not be in the leaſt affected by the helm. He ordered the sailors to reef the mizen, which the wind was carrying away piece-meal; the poor fellows were sheltering themselves under the quarter-deck, some crying, others fallen on their knees, and praying. I crept along the larboard gangway, griping fast by the tackling, and was followed by a Dominican, who was chaplain of the ship, a passenger, and by several of the seamen, and we at length did reef the sail, though above half of it was carried away. They wanted to have bent a stay-sail, in order to put before the wind, but it was torn like a sheet of paper.

In this disastrous condition we remained then like a log, rolling about in a most frightful manner; having one time let go the tackle I held by, I slid as far as the foot of the main-mast, where the water was up to my knees. In short; next to God, we were indebted for our safety, to the strength of the ship, and to her having three decks, without which she must have filled. Thus we were tossed about till the evening, when the storm abated. The moveable furniture was almost entirely topsy-turvy, or broken to pieces: and I more than once found myself upright on my feet upon the wainscot of my cabbin.

To such a state were we reduced, and so costly the tribute we paid in the streights of Mosambique*. The passage through which is more dreaded by seamen, than doubling the Cape of Good Hope. The officers declared, they never saw so great a sea. All the upper works of the ship were so shaken by it, that into the joints of the pilasters of the great cabin, I put mutton bones, which were crushed to pieces by the play of the timbers.

At four in the morning of the 24 it fell calm, the sea was still very high. The people worked hard all day, in bringing the main-yard to its right place, and in fitting two fishes to strengthen the main-mast. The effects of the lightning are not

* In this strait the Aurora frigate, with the East-India Supervisors on board, is supposed to have been lost. The Portuguese have a large settlement at Mozambique, which is situated on an island in 15 deg. S The town is populous and well fortified; and the harbour safe and commodious. *E.*

to

to be described. The main-mast is split in a zig-zag, five feet of the mast immediately under the top, is splintered, forward, or towards the head of the ship; then five feet on the afterside, or towards the stern, is splintered; and so five feet alternately, the whole length of the mast to the deck; so that the sound on the one side, answers to the shattered on the other. In these cracks I could not perceive any smell or blackness, the wood being of its usual colour.

It was now we saw some Moutons de Cap. The weather killed the remains of our live stock, and doubled the number of men sick of the scurvy.

We spent the 25 in belaying and fastening the two fishes round the mast; they were two pieces of timber, forty-five feet long, hollowed out in grooves, to fit the circumference of the mast. Every man put his hand to this work, on account of the sickly state of the crew. A whale passed us, within pistol shot, it was scarcely the length of the long boat.

The weather became tolerable the 26; *Te Deum* was sung according to custom, to thank God for having passed the Cape, and the Straits of Mosambique.

We completed the mast so far the 27, that it would carry the main sail. One man died of the scurvy; and twenty-one men were rendered unfit for service by sickness.

An

An infant of only eight days old died the 29, of the scurvy. There are now twenty-eight sailors in the Lazarette. To make out the watch, we have been forced to take the domestic servants that are on board, and also the passengers, that are not of the great cabbin.

Our apprehensions were encreased, by the melancholy condition of the crew. Here the westerly winds are at an end. We keep in a high latitude, that we may have the S. W. winds which blow constantly hereabouts, and endeavour to keep to windward of the island of Rodorigue, to make the Isle of France with the greater certainty.

OBSERVATIONS THAT MIGHT BE OF USE FOR BETTER MANAGEMENT OF SEAMEN.

TO me there did not seem to be a proper subordination among the officers; the superiors are afraid of the interest of their inferiors. The chief part of these appointments being obtained by favour, I do not think that an authority can be established among them as it ought to be; and the evil being dependant upon the manners of the persons concerned, is, in my opinion, without remedy.

More than three months at sea no ship should stay without going into port. The sailors have not water enough for a longer trip, in these hot climates; being frequently reduced to half-a-pint a day.

a day. Could not that part of the ship, where the ballast is put, be divided into leaden cisterns and filled with fresh water; or could not some kind of wax or mastic be found out, with which the casks might be done over to prevent the water from corrupting. It is sometimes so much tainted, and so full of worms, as to be really intolerable.

Salt water rendered fresh by a machine, is not thought wholesome: besides, a great deal of sea-coal must be taken on board, which occupies too much room, and is subject to take fire; and the additional dangerous inconvenience of keeping a furnice burning night and day.

For the most part sailors prefer their biscuit, which is full of worms; the salt beef, in a short time, becomes both a disagreeable and unwholesome food. Could not provisions be dressed and preserved in fat. The great cabin was served with meat so prepared, which kept as well as the salted beef.

Seamen ashore generally spend as much money in a week, as they have been a year in earning. I should think each man might be provided with proper cloathing, which they should be obliged to take care of, by the frequent reviews of its condition by proper officers. Such a precaution would certainly, in some degree, prevent their extravagance. Several other regulations might be thought of, which properly attended to by the officers, would tend much to their cleanliness and decent appearance. The major part of these poor fellows need always be under a tutor.

JULY, 1768.

THIS evening, the 3, one of the carpenters died of the scurvy; forty people are now ill of it, and it makes a sensible progress, owing to the exhalations from the hold filled with masts, that have for a long time been laying in mud.

One of the sailors upon the watch died suddenly on the 9. We have all been very faint and weak to day; some have had vertigoes and sickness at their stomachs. We are, notwithstanding, more than one hundred leagues to windward of any known land.

We had a fair wind the 11, sixty-six of the men are now sick in their beds; if we should remain eight days longer at sea, we must infallibly perish.

Both fine weather and a fine sea favoured us the 12; there are no more than three foremast men to each watch; the officers and passengers help to work the ship.

On the morning of the 13, at half past eight, land appeared. We are so cast down, that the news rejoices no body. Eighty men are now ill with the distemper.

Approaching the land the 14, many of the people found themselves sick. I felt uneasiness

 all

all over me, and sweated abundantly. We hoisted the colours and fired guns for assistance; but a pilot alone came on board. He told us of the differences among the chief people of the island, about which, I suppose, he thought us very anxious: on the other hand, many of the people on board were of opinion that the complaints and miseries we had laboured under, would be a matter of great concern to the inhabitants on shore.

We now left to our right, two small inhabited islands, called Round Island, and the Isle of Serpents: we next passed within gun-shot of *Coin de Mire,* another island on the left. We kept at a good distance from the shore, on account of the shoal, at *Point aux Cannoniers.*

It was afternoon, about half past one we entered the harbour: two hours after, I landed, thanking God for having delivered me from the dangers and fatigues of so dreadful a voyage.

Four months and twelve days had we been at sea, without touching at any port. According to my journal, we have sailed about three thousand eight hundred marine, or four thousand seven hundred common leagues: and have lost eleven persons, including the three men carried away by the sea, and one who died as he was going ashore.

ON

ON THE SCURVY.

THE bad quality of the air and of the provisions occasions the scurvy. The officers, who are better fed and better lodged than the sailors, are the last attacked by this disorder, which affects even the animals on board: my dog was very much troubled with it. There is no absolute cure for it, but the air of the land and the use of fresh vegetables, though there are some palliatives which may moderate its effects; as the use of rice, acid liquors, coffee, and abstinence from all salted provisions. Great virtues are attributed to the use of turtle, but like other prejudices, this is adopted by seamen upon flight grounds only. At the Cape of Good Hope, where there are no turtles, the scurvy is cured as quickly as in the hospital at the Isle of France, where the patient is fed with broths of this animal. On our arrival, almost every body used this remedy; but not being fond of turtle, I did not eat of it, but of fresh vegetables; I was well before any of them.

The primary symptom of this grievous disease is a general lassitude; the sick person wishes for rest, is uneasy in his mind, and disgusted with every thing; all day long he is in disquiet, and is only relieved from it by the night: its next, are red spots on his breast and legs, and bleeding ulcers in the gums. There are frequently no external symptoms; but, if a man gets the slightest wound imaginable, it is incurable, while at sea;

 and

and makes the most rapid progress. I myself had a very slight wound at the end of my finger; in three weeks the sore had taken off the ſkin entirely; and notwithstanding all the remedies that were applied, extended itself to my hand. A few days after my landing, it healed of itself. Before the sick were landed, they took care to expose them for a whole day to the air from the shore. Notwithstanding these precautions, it cost one man his life, who was not able to bear the change.

The miserable situation we were in at our arrival is not to be described. Figure to yourself a ship, with its main-mast shattered to pieces by lightning, with a waft upon its ensign, and firing minute-guns as signals of distress; sailors more like spectres than men, sitting upon deck, the scuttles all open and emitting a vapour that infected the air; the forecastle and poop covered with sick men, exposed there for the benefit of the sun, and who died even while speaking to us, I shall never forget a lad of eighteen years old, to whom I had promised some lemonade the evening before. I was seeking for him among the rest, when they shewed him to me, lying dead in the cook-room.

LETTER V.

NAUTICAL OBSERVATIONS.

IT may be of use to add to my journal the observations of the most able seamen upon the voyage we have made, before I give you an account of the Isle of France.

The trade winds though in general regular and uniform in the main sea, are, notwithstanding, variable along the coast, and in the neighbourhood of islands.

There is a breeze off the land almost every night, along the shores of the great continent. This wind blowing in a different direction from the sea breeze, brings the clouds together into one long motionless range, which vessels rarely fail seeing as they approach the land.

It is in general, stormy near the coast, especially in the neighbourhood of islands. The winds in these parts vary much. At the Canaries, the S. and S. E. winds blow sometimes for eight days successively.

About twenty-eight degrees North latitude we first meet with the trade winds, but they seldom continue so far as the Line. An experienced seaman has given me the following account of the ceasing of the trade winds, which he has with much labour collected from more than two hundred and fifty journals of this voyage:

In January, between the 6 and 4 degrees of North latitude.
In February, between the 5 and 3 degrees.
In March and April, between the 5 and 2 degrees.
In May, between the 6 and 4 degrees.
In June, in the 10 degree.
In July, in the 12 degree.
In August and September, between the 14 and 13 degrees.
And during the months of October, November, and December, they blow as far as the Line.*

† There is a difference between the trade and general winds; the trade winds, particularly

* The southern trade wind has been known to blow farther North than the Line; and the northern, at other times, to be extended to the southward of the Line: but this rarely happens. *E.*

† B. Varenius, in his *Geographia Generalis,* gives a particular account of the winds, (*cap.* 20 *and* 21.) and of the variation of the needle, (*cap.* 38.)—and in the appendix prefixed by Sir Isaac Newton and Dr. Jurin, to the edition they published in 1712, (*page* 31 *and* 49) are collected Dr. Hailey's observations upon the same subjects.. *F.*

South

South of the line, where we commonly find the winds variable and stormy. What are called general winds extend much farther than the trade; even as far as twenty-eight degrees South. Beyond which latitude the winds vary more than in the seas of Europe; and the higher the latitude the more violent they are; blowing generally from the N. to N. W.; and from the N. W. to the S. S. W.—when they get round to the S. a calm succeeds.

Near the Cape of Good Hope, S. E. and E. S. E. winds are frequently met with. It is a general maxim to keep to the windward of the place intended to be made; yet not too much as the ship would then make too much leeway. It is best to cross the Line as much to the eastward as possible.

Vessels in want of provisions may be better supplied at the Cape de Verd Islands than at Brasil, where all necessaries are very dear; besides, the air of the place is very unwholsome. Turtle is caught in great plenty at the island of Tristan d'Aconia, but water is hard to be got, on account of the trees, which grow in the sea.

To put in at the Cape of Good Hope is dangerous from April to September; but the anchorage is perfectly safe at False-bay, which is very little distant. If a vessel misses the Isle of France, it may put in at Madagascar, at Port Dauphin, or Bay of Antongil; but there are

are dangerous epidemical distempers, and hurricanes on that coast, which last from October till May.

There is St. Helena, an English settlement, on our return; and the island of Ascension, where, however, nothing can be got but turtle. In time of war, the two islands are commonly cruizing stations, all ships from the other side of the Cape endeavour to make them, in order to ascertain their route.

Monsieur Dapre's charts are most in use, as esteemed the best. Sailors are also much indebted to the learned and modest Abbé de Caille. But the geography of these parts is yet very imperfect. The longitude of the Canaries, and of the Cape de Verd islands, is not well laid down. Between Cape Blanco and Cape Verd, the chart says, there are thirty-nine leagues difference, though there really are not twenty.

At about twenty minutes South of the Line, and about twenty-three degrees ten minutes longitude a shoal is suspected. In 1764, two French ships touched the bottom.

Pilots may be led into great errors by the currents. I am of opinion, that nothing certain relative to them can be determined upon, 'till a method is discovered, of ascertaining the quantity of a ship's leeway: even the angle she forms with her wake, will not lead to a decision of this matter; because the ship and her trace have one cause, the ship's motion.

Their

Their enterpriſe and hardihood who first made these voyages, without experience and without charts, cannot be sufficiently admired. Those of the present day have much more information, and less resolution. Navigation is become a mere routine. Ships sail at a particular season, make the same places, and steer the same courses. It were to be wished, that some vessels might be risked in making discoveries, that might assure the safety of others.

LETTER VI.

A PORTUGUEZE navigator, of the family of Mascarenhas, discovered the Isle of France, and called it Isle de Cerné. It was afterwards possessed by the Dutch, who gave it the name of Mauritius. They abandoned it in 1712, and soon after the French, inhabitants of the Isle of Bourbon, which is only forty leagues distant, came and settled themselves there.

In this island are two ports; that on the S. E. where the Dutch settlement was, and where remains of their buildings are still seen, is the principal port. It may be entered before the wind; but it is difficult to get out of it: the winds being almost ever at S. E.

Port Lewis, which is the smallest, is to the N. W. a ship may go in or out of it, large, before the wind. Its latitude is twenty degrees ten minutes S. and its longitude, from the meridian of Paris, fifty-five degrees E. This is the capital of the island, though situated in the most disagreeable part of it. The town called also the Camp, and which has scarcely the appearance of a market town, is built at the bottom of the port, and at the opening of a valley, which is about three

three quarters of a league long, and eight hundred or a thousand yards wide. This valley is formed by a chain of high mountains, covered with rocks; but without trees or bushes. The sides of these mountains are covered six months in the year, with a burning herb, which makes the country appear black, like a colliery. The edge of the rocks, which form this dismal vale, is broken and craggy. The highest part is at the extremity, and terminates in a rock, standing by itself, which they call the Pouce. This part, however, has a few trees; and there issues from it a rivulet, which runs through the town; but the water is not good to drink.

The town or Camp, consists of wooden houses of one story high; each house stands by itself, and is inclosed in pallisades. The streets are regular enough, but are neither paved nor planted with trees. The ground is every where so covered, and as it were staked with rocks, that there is no stirring without danger of breaking one's neck. The town is neither walled nor fortified in the least, except that on the left, when looking to the sea, there is a sort of intrenchment of stone, reaching from the mountain to the harbour; on this same side is Fort-Blanc, that defends its entrance; on the other side is a battery upon the Isle of Tonnelliers.

By the measurement of the Abbé de Caille, the Isle of France is ninety thousand, six hundred and sixty-eight fathoms in circumference; its greatest diameter is thirty-one thousand, eight hundred and ninety fathoms from N. to S.; and twenty-

twenty-two thousand, one hundred and twenty-four from E. to W.; its superficial content is four hundred thirty-two thousand, six hundred and eighty acres, of one hundred perches the acre; and twenty feet the perch.

The island is apparently level in the N. W. part, and the S. W is covered with ridges of mountains, from three hundred to three hundred and fifty fathom high. The highest of all is four hundred and twenty-four fathom, and stands at the mouth of the river Noire. The most remarkable, called Pieterboth, is four hundred and twenty toises high; it is terminated by an obelisk, which is again covered with a cubical rock, upon which no person has ever yet been. At a distance, this pyramid and its capital, resemble the statue of a woman.

More than sixty rivulets, water this island, some of which have no water in the dry season, especially since so much timber has been cut down. The interior part of the island is full of ponds, and in this part it rains nearly all the year round, the clouds being stopped by the mountains, and the woods at the top of them.

A more perfect account of a place, in which I am but just arrived, you can hardly expect. I may probably pass a few days in the country, and will endeavour to describe to you what relates to the soil of this island, before I speak of its inhabitants.

Port Louis, Aug. 6, 1768.

LET-

LETTER VII.

NATURAL PRODUCTIONS.

THE very herbage, and every thing here differs from what is seen in Europe. To begin with the soil: It is almost every where of a reddish colour, and mixed with veins of iron, which are frequently found near the surface, in the form of grains, the size of a pea. In the drier parts, especially near the town, the ground is very hard. It resembles pipe-clay, and to make trenches in it, I have seen them cut it with axes, as they do lead. As soon as it rains, it becomes soft and tenacious; notwithstanding they have not yet been able to make it into bricks.

In the soil there is no real sand. That which is found on the shore, is composed of fragments of madrepores and shells, which will calcine in the fire.

Almost every where the ground is covered with rocks, from the size of one's fist to a ton weight. They are full of holes, the bottom of which is in the form of a lentil.

These, for the most part, are formed of concentrical laminæ, like an onion. Some of them are in large masses, that adhere together. Others seem

seem as if they had been broken, and were again joined together. The island is in a manner paved with these rocks; and the mountains are formed entirely of these strata, which are oblique to the horizon, though parallel to each other. They are of an iron grey colour, vitrify in the fire, and contain a great deal of iron ore. I saw at the foundry, some grains of beautiful copper and lead, that were taken from some of the fissures in the rocks, but in a very small quantity. Experiments of this nature afford no encouragement here. The mineral appears to be too much dispersed. In the broken pieces of these stones, there are little cavities crystalized, some of which contain a down, that is white and very fine.

Three species of herbs, or gramen only, seem natural to the soil.

A sort of turf is found along the shore, that grows in beds, very thick and elastic. Its leaf is very small, and so sharp pointed, as to prick through one's clothes. The cattle will not touch it.

Pastures, in the hotest parts, produce a kind of dog's grass, which spreads much upon the ground, and puts out little branches from the joints. This herb is very hard. The oxen like it very well, if not too dry.

The airy and windward side of the island are distinguished by the best herbs. 'Tis a gramen, with large leaves, and is green and tender all the year.

Most

Most of the other species of herbs and shrubs that are known, are, a plant that yields for fruit, a husk filled with a kind of silk, of which an advantageous use might be made.

A prickly kind of asparagus grows here, above twelve feet high, round the trees, as the bramble, or briar. It is not yet known whether this is good to eat.

Here is also a species of mallow shrub, with small leaves, that grows in the paths, and sides of the roads. There is likewise a kind of thistle with yellow flowers, the seeds of which kill the birds that eat them; and a plant that is like the lilly, bearing long leaves. It grows in marshy ground, and has a flower of a grateful smell.

I found upon walls, and by the sides of the roads, some tufts of a plant, whose flowers resembles the plain red July-flower; it has a bad smell, and this singular property, that only one flower flourishes upon each branch at one time.

There grows, at the foot of the neighbouring mountains, a sweet basil, the smell of it is like that of a July-flower. Its stalk is ligneous. It is of a healing quality.

Here they make very dangerous hedges of the roquettes, bear a yellow flower, marbled with red. This plant is stuck full of very sharp prickles, that grow upon the leaves; and also upon the fruit. The leaves are very thick. The fruit is never used, and is of a sour taste.

On the sand by the sea-shore grows the veloutier. Its branches have a down upon them, like that of velvet. The leaves are entirely covered with glittering filaments. It bears flowers in clusters. This shrub exhales an odour, that at a distance is agreeable, less so when you draw near, and when quite close is perfectly loathsome.

Here, a plant, half bramble, half shrub, produces in pods, bristled with prickles, a sort of nut, very smooth and hard, of a pearl-colour grey, and the size of a musquet-ball. Its kernel is very bitter. These nuts are said to be good for the venereal disease.

There grows a great number of a kind of shrub that has large leaves, in the shape of a heart, in such parts of the island as are cleared. Its smell is sweet enough, and like that of balm, whose name it bears. I know of no use made of it, except in baths.

Another plant equally useless, is the false potatoe, which grows twining along the sea-side. It spreads on the ground like the liseron. Its flowers are red, and like a bell. It thrives in the sand.

A ligneous herb called, pannier grass, is found on the borders of the woods. They have attempted to make thread and cloth of it, which is not bad. Its leaves are small. Taken in barley-water, they are good for complaints in the breast.

A great

A great variety of shrubs, all comprized under the general name of * *liannes*, some of which are as thick as a man's leg, and grow round the trees, making the trunks look like a mast furnished with rigging. They, however, support the trees against the hurricanes, of whose violence I have seen frequent proofs. When they fell timber in the woods, they cut about two hundred trees near the root, which remain upright till the *liannes*, which hold them, are cut down also. When this is done, one whole part of the forest seems to fall at once, making a most horrid crash. Cords are made of their bark, stronger than of hemp.

Many shrubs, natives of the place, bear a flower like that of the box-tree.

Here too we find a shrub prickly and spongy, with a red flower, in a hoop, and scolloped. Its leaf is large and round. The fishermen use the stalk of it (which is very light) instead of cork.

A very pretty one also, is called, † Bois-de-demoiselle. Its leaf is scolloped at the edge, like that of the ash, and its branches ornamented with small red seeds.

Please to notice all along, that I know nothing of botany. I describe things as I see them; but if you will rely upon my opinion, I declare to you, that I think every thing inferior to the productions of Europe.

* A rattan, or supple jack. *E.*

† Lady's wood. *E.*

Not a single flower adorns our meadows, which are entirely covered with small stones, and overgrown with an herb as hard, and as tough as hemp. No plant bears flowers of a pleasant smell, nor is any shrub in the island to be compared to our white thorn. The *liannes* have not the fragrancy of the honey-suckle or ivy. Not one violet in all the woods. As to the trees, they have large whitish trunks, that are bare, except a little kind of nosegay of leaves of a dull green. I will describe them in my next letter.

Port-Louis, Sept. 15*th*, 1768.

LET-

LETTER VIII.

I PERCEIVED a few large trees in the middle of some rocks, and being desirous of cutting a piece with my knife, was surprized at the whole blade entering without my using the least force. It was of a substance like a turnip, and of a very disagreeable taste; for some hours after, though I did not swallow any part of it, my throat was much inflamed, and felt as if pricked by pins. This tree is called *mapou*, and is looked upon as poisonous.

All trees here take their names, in general, from the fancy or caprice of the inhabitants.

The *bois-de-canelle*, which is not like the real cinnamon-tree, is one of the largest in the island. It is peculiarly appropriate for joiner's work, and resembles walnut-tree, both in colour and veins. When it is worked green, it smells like human excrement, and like the blossoms of the real cinnamon. This is the only resemblance I could perceive between them. The seed of it is inveloped in a red skin, which has an acid, yet not a disagreeable taste.

We have a stinking wood, properly so called, from its horrid smell, which is very good for carpenter's use.

The trunk of what goes by the name of iron-wood, seems blended with the roots, and shoots up in a kind of ribs or spars, like so many boards. It turns the edge of the axe that fells it.

The leaves of the ebony are large, the lower side white, the upper of a dingy green. The center only of this tree is black, the sap and the bark being white. In a trunk, from which may be cut a timber six inches square, there is frequently no more of real ebony, than two inches square. This wood, if worked while green, smells like human excrement, and its flowers like the July-flower; the very reverse of the cinnamon, whose flowers are stinking, and the wood and bark of a pleasant smell. The ebony bears a fruit like a medlar, full of viscous juice, that is sweet and pleasant tasted.

A different sort of ebony we find in these parts is beautifully veined with black.

In cool and damp places only, the citron bears. The fruit is small, but full of juice.

In similar soils also, the orange-tree thrives; its fruit is bitter and sharp-tasted. Many of them grow in the neighbourhood of the Great-Port; yet I doubt if these two species are natural to the island. The sweet orange is very rare, even in gardens.

A species

A species of the sandal-wood is sometimes seen here, but seldom. Somebody gave me a piece of it, which was of a greyish white. It had a faint smell.

A kind of small palm-tree, named *vacoa*, whose leaves grow spirally round the trunk, has also been met with; they make mats and bags of them.

A large kind of palm-tree is the *latanier*, it bears at the top, one leaf only, in the shape of a fan, with which they cover their houses.

Above all the trees in the forest may be seen the palm-tree, rising perpendicular to the skies. It bears at the head a cluster of palms, whence there issues a shoot, which is all this tree affords fit to be eaten; and to get at this, the tree must be cut down. This shoot, which they call the cabbage, is formed of young leaves, rolled one over the other, very tender, and of a very pleasant taste.

In the sea only the manglier, or mangrove *, is to be found. Its root and branches creep along, and interweave themselves in the sand, so that it is impossible to pull them up. Its wood is red, and stains of an ugly colour.

* The mangrove is also called *paletuvier*; its wood is very proper for building, and of its bark, the people in some part of the East-Indies make clothes. The elephants are extremely fond of the young leaves of this tree, and eat them with avidity. *E.*

That the greater part of these trees have but a very thin bark, has been noticed; some of them even have nothing but a sort of skin over them, differing widely from the trees in the North, which Nature has furnished with a variety of coats, to protect them from the cold. Most of them have their roots upon the surface of the earth, and twist round the rocks as they shoot up. They are but short; their heads little, furnished with leaves, and are very heavy; which with the *liannes* that grow round them, is their only support against the hurricanes, which would else presently tear up the firs and chesnuts.

None of these trees can compare for durability and solidity to the oak, to the elm for pliancy, to the fir for the lightness and length of its timber, or to the chesnut for its usefulness in general. Their foliage has the same disagreeable quality as is common to every tree, whose leaves last the year round, being hard, and of an ugly dark green. Their wood is heavy, brittle, and easily rots. Those that in other respects are fit for cabinet-work, soon turn black, when exposed to the air, which gives their furniture a very disagreeable look.

The rivulets which flow through the woods, afford the most pleasing retreats imaginable. The waters run through the midst of the rocks; in one part gliding along in silence—in another, falling precipitately from a height, with a confused and murmuring noise. The borders of these ravines are covered with trees, from which

hang

hang large bunches of * *Scolopendria* and *Liannes*, which falling down, are suspended by their own twigs. The ground about them is rugged, with great pieces of black rock, overgrown with moss and maiden-hair. Large trunks, overthrown by the hand of time, lay, covered with fungus, waved with various colours.

An infinite variety of fern appears every where. Some, like leaves separated from the stem, meander among the stones, and draw their substance from the rock itself. Others spring up like a tree of moss, and resemble a plume of silken feathers. The common sort is of twice the size here, that it is in Europe. In lieu of the groves, and reeds, which so beautifully variegate the borders of our rivers, along the sides of these torrents, grow a kind of water-lillies, in great abundance, with very large leaves, in the form of a heart. They are called *Songes*. It will float upon the water without being wet, and the drops of rain amass together upon it, like globules of shining silver. Its root is an onion, of a malignant quality. 'Tis distinguished into the black and the white.

Alas! these savage desarts have been seldom enlivened by the songs of birds, nor have they ever seen reluctant maid with downcast eye, and listening ear attend to the fond lover's tale. The

* Spleenwort, or hartstongue, a medicinal herb. Pliny says, it was called in his time *Scolopendria*, *lingua cervina*, or *Asplenos*. There is a fish, and also an insect, called *Scolopendria*, both of which were called by the ancients *millipeda*, and the Italians now call them *Centogambo*. *E*.

ear

ear is sometimes grated by the croaking of the perroquets, or pierced by the shrill cry of some malicious monkey.

But with all this sterility of soil, even these rocks might have been made habitable, if the Europeans had not brought hither more and greater evils, than Nature herself, has heaped upon it.

The Port, October 8, 1768.

LET-

LETTER IX.

ANIMALS, NATIVES OF THE ISLE OF FRANCE.

THERE is not the most distant resemblance between the monkey of Madagascar, called *Maki*, and those of this island, or the baboons of the Cape.

Those most common here, are of a middling size, of a reddish grey cast, and have a long tail. This animal is fond of society. I have seen them in troops of sixty at a time. They frequently come in droves, and pillage the houses. Scouts are placed on the tops of trees, and the points of the rocks, who as soon as they see any dogs or hunters approach, cry out, to alarm the others, who immediately decamp. They will climb up the steepest mountain, and rest upon the slightest edge of a precipice, where no other quadruped of its size dare venture.

Thus Nature, which has covered even the holes of the rocks with herbage, and does nothing in vain, has also created beings to enjoy the benefit of it.

By

By right of possession, rats seem to inherit the island. There are prodigious swarms of them in every part; and it is said, that the place was abandoned by the Dutch, on account of their number. In some houses they are so numerous, that 30,000* are killed in a year. They make large hoards under ground, both of corn and of fruit, and climb up to the tops of trees to devour the young birds. They pierce the very thickest rafters. One may see them at sun-set, running about in all parts, and in one night they will destroy an entire crop. I have seen a field of maize, in which they have not left one single ear. They are exactly like the rats of Europe, and have, very possibly, come from thence in ships.

Here also are immense multitudes of mice, the havock they make is incredible.

Formerly, it is believed, a great many flamingos were also found about the isle; this is a large and beautiful sea-fowl, of a rose-colour; they say also, that three of them yet remain, but I never saw one.

Variety of *Corbigeaux* are also to be seen every

* This number may appear improbable, and I should have been inclined to think the author misinformed, had I not been told by a gentleman, upon whose veracity I can depend, that upon his return from the Havanna in the year 1766, in the Valiant man of war, the rats increased to such a degree, as to destroy a hundred weight of biscuit a day. The ship was at length smoked between decks, in order to suffocate them. This had the desired effect, and six hampers were filled daily for some time, with the rats killed by this means. *E.*

where

where on wing, and are reckoned the best game the island produces; but are difficult to shoot.

Our *Paillencus* are of two sorts, one of white, like silver, the other have the beak, claws, and tail red. Though this is a sea-bird, it builds its nest in the woods. Its name is not at all suited to its extraordinary beauty. The English more properly call it the *Tropic Bird*. It keeps near the sea, and is not intimidated at the sight of man.

The shores formerly abounded with turtles, which are now but rarely found. Their flesh is like beef; the fat green, and well tasted.

We have many sorts of parrots, but none very handsome. There is a species of green perroquets, with a grey head. They are as large as sparrows. It is impossible to tame them. These also are enemies to the harvest, but they are very good to eat.

Black-birds are seen in our woods, which when called to by a sportsman, will come to the end of his gun. This is a kind of game much in request.

Here is what they call the Dutch pigeon, of a most magnificent plumage; and another sort, which, though of a very pleasant taste, are so dangerous, that those who cat them are thrown into convulsions.

Bats

Bats, here, are of two kinds, one like ours, the other as big as a small cat, very fat; and is eaten by the inhabitants as a rarity.

Our sparrow-hawk, a beautiful bold bird, is in these parts called the chicken-eater; it is also said to eat grasshoppers.

Our shores are all full of holes, in which lodge a great number of *Toulouroux*, they are a kind of amphibious crab, and make burroughs under ground like moles. They run very fast; and if you attempt to catch them, they snap their claws, and present their points, by way of menace.

A very extraordinary amphibious animal is the *Bernard L'Hermite*, a kind of lobster, whose hinder part is not provided with a shell; but it instinctively lodges itself in empty shells, which it finds upon the shore. One may see them run along in great numbers, each with its house after it, which it abandons for a larger, when its growth makes it necessary.

No insects are here more baneful and mischievous, than grasshoppers. I have seen them light upon a field, like a fall of snow, and lay upon the ground several inches deep. They will eat up the verdure in the course of one night. This is the most dreadful enemy of agriculture.

We have many sorts of snails, and a large butterfly, which has upon its body the figure of a death's head. It is called *Hai* *, and flies about

* Odious, or hateful; so called, the author says, from the fear it excites. *E.*

chiefly

chiefly in rooms. It is said that the down of its wings will blind those whose eyes it touches.

Every building and habitable place are infested with ants, which destroy provisions of every kind. The pantries are not safe from their ravages, except they stand in water. Numbers of them are killed by an insect called a *Formicaleo.*

Centpied, or *Centipedes,* are frequently found in marshes and damp places. This insect seems destined to drive mankind from the unwholesome air they breed in. Its sting is very painful. My dog was bit by one of them, which was more than six inches long; the wound turned to a kind of ulcer, and was three weeks in healing. I was highly pleased with seeing one of them carried off by a vast number of ants; they had seized it by all its legs, and bore it along as workmen do a arge piece of timber.

A most desperate wasp, yellow with black rings upon the body, is not less formidable for its stings, than the scorpion, which is very common here. It builds in trees, and even in houses, its hive is of a substance like paper. There was one of them in my chamber; but I soon grew weary of so dangerous a guest.

That which is known by the name of *Maçonnel,* or the *Mason,* builds itself a nest of earth, which one would think, was the work of a swallow, were any in the island. It lodges in rooms that are not frequented, and chiefly in the locks, the wards of which are filled with its labours.

In

In gardens we frequently find leaves of the size of a six-pence; this is the work of the wasps, who shape with their teeth these circular pieces, with a nicety and readiness truly admirable. They carry them into their nests, and having rolled them into the shape of a horn, deposit their eggs in them.

An insect like an ant, is not less industrious with regard to their habitations. They make great havock among the trees and timber, the wood of which they reduce to a powder; with this dust they construct little caverns of about an inch broad, under which they live; these caverns or pipes, are black, and will sometimes run over the timber of a whole house. They will penetrate through trunks, or furniture, in one night. I found no remedy so effectual as to rub the places they frequented very often with garlick. They call these insects *Carias*. Many houses are quite ruined by them.

Here reside three species of *Cancrelas*, the dirtiest of all the *Scaraboea*. One of them is flat and gray; the most common one is of the size of a cock-chafer, of a reddish brown. It attacks furniture, especially books and papers, and harbours constantly in the offices and kitchens. The houses are very much pestered with them; especially in wet weather.

Its greatest enemy is a species of *Scaraboea*, or green fly, very gawdy and very nimble. When the *Cancrelas* is met with, and touched by this fly, it becomes motionless. The fly then seeks fcr for some crack or chink, to which it draws the *Cancrelas*, and thrusts it in, deposits an egg in its body, and then leaves it. This touch, which some look upon as a charm, is the stroke of the sting, the effect of which is instantaneous, the insect being otherwise hard to kill.

Here a large worm nestles in the trunks of trees, and has a sort of paws with which it picks and hollows them; they call it *Montac*. The blacks, and even the white people eat them greedily. Pliny observes, that they were served up at the most capital tables in Rome, and were fattened with meal for that purpose. That found in the oak-tree was in the highest estimation, and was called *cossus*. Thus have abundance and scarcity combined in the same taste; and like all other extremes, approached very near to each other.

The sides of the rivulets abound with lady-birds, of a fine violet colour, with a head like a ruby. This insect is carnivorous. I have seen it carrying a beautiful butterfly through the air.

All our chambers are, at certain seasons, filled with moths, or small butterflies, that come and singe themselves in the candle. They are so numerous, that the candles are frequently obliged to be put into cylinders of glass. They draw into the houses a very handsome small lizard, about a finger's length. Its eyes are lively; it climbs along the walls, and even along the glass, lives upon flies and other insects, and watches with great patience for an opportunity of catching them. It lays eggs that are small and round like

 peas,

peas, having a white and yellow shell, as the eggs of pullets. I have seen some of these lizards so tame, that they would come and take sugar out of a person's hand. Far from being mischievous, they are on the contrary, very useful. Some very beautiful ones are to be seen in the woods, of an azure, and changeable green, marked with crimson on the back, like Arabic characters.

Most insects here are food for spiders, who devour them in great quantities. Some of these spiders have bellies as big as a nut, with large paws, covered with hair. Their webs are so strong, that even small birds are catched in them. They are of use, in destroying the wasps, scorpions, and centipedes. There is a little white louse, that harbours in fruit-trees, and destroys them; and a bug, whose bite is more dangerous than that of the scorpion, and is succeeded by a tumour as big as a pigeon's egg, which continues for four or five days.

Indeed, the temperature of this climate, peculiarly tempting to the inhabitants of Europe, is so favourable to the propagation of insects, that in a short time, the fruits would be eaten up by them, and the island itself become uninhabitable; but the fruits of these meridional countries, are clothed with a thick rind, and afterwards with a skin, a very hard shell, or an aromatic bark, like the orange or citron, insomuch that the flies can introduce their worms into very few of them only. Many of these noxious animals are at

perpetual

perpetual war with each other, as the scorpion and the centipied. The *Formicaleos* lays snares for the ant; the green fly pierces the *Cancrela*; the *lizard* hunts the *butterfly*; the *spiders* spread nets for every insect that flies; and the hurricane which rages once a year, annihilates at once a great part, both of the prey, and of the devourers.

Port Louis, Dec. 7, 1768.

LETTER X.

OF THE OCEAN.

THE sea and its productions shall be my present subject. You will then know at least as much as the first Portugueze that landed in this island. If I can add to this a metereological journal, you will by degrees be acquainted with the whole natural history of this country; from hence we shall go on and treat of the inhabitants, and of the course they have taken for the improvement of their country, where, as in every other part of the world, good and evil are mingled together. Plutarch would have us deduce harmony from these contrarieties; but though good instruments, are very common, good musicians are found but rarely.

To windward of this island, especially about September, whales are seen. This is the time of their coupling. I have observed many this season, that kept themselves upright in the water, and came very near the coast. They are smaller than the northern ones. There is no whale fishery, but the Negroes are not unacquainted with the method

method of harpooning them.* Sea Cows are sometimes catched here: I have eaten of them, their flesh is like beef; I never saw any of this fish.

A blackish fish, and in form and taste a good deal like the cod, is the *Vieille*. One extraordinary circumstance, is, that the fish on the windward-side of the island is never unwholesome. Those then that attribute this poisonous quality to the Madrepores are mistaken; the island being on all sides surrounded by banks of coral. I should rather think it occasioned by some venomous tree falling into the water, which conjecture is the more probable; because at one season, only, some particular species of gluttonous fish are subject to this inconveniency. Moreover that species of pigeon whose flesh occasions convulsions in the eaters of it, proves that the poison is in the island itself.

A number of white ones are suspicious, with a large belly, and a great head, such as the Captain and the Carangue. These two sorts are of an indifferent taste Those that have their mouths paved, that is to say, a rugged bone in their palates are thought to be never dangerous.

* Whales are in such plenty upon the equally southern coast of Brazil, that they constitute the greatest part of the food of the Negroes, belonging to the Planters near the sea; as I have been informed by a person who lived several years in that country.

And Herodotus in Lib. 4, says, that in the Borysthenes, in his time there were whales. *E.*

It is commonly remarked the smaller the fish, the greater the danger.

A sort of turbot, called the water mullet, is the best of all the fish catched here,—the fat is green.

We see variety of parroquets, that are not only green, but have yellow heads, white and crooked beaks, and go in a body like the birds of that name.

The hog-fish is small and oddly shaped; its head is like a pike, upon its back are seven points nearly long as its body, the prick of them is venomous; they are united by a membrane like the wing of a bat: it is streaked with brown stripes, which begin at the muzzle, exactly as those of the zebra at the Cape. The fish is square like a trunk, which name it bears, and is armed with two horns like a bull; there are many species of them: they never grow large.

Eels here are mostly of the conger sort, and very tough, some of them are seven or eight feet long, and as thick as a man's leg. They harbour in the creeks of the rivers, and sometimes devour those who are imprudent enough to bathe within there reach.

Lobsters or cray-fish of a monstrous size, abound also, their paws are not large, they are blue, marbled with black. I have seen here a species of lobster that is smaller and of a beautiful form; it was of a sky-blue; it had two little claws, divided

divided into two articulations, like a knife with the blade shutting into the handle.

Of crabs there is an endless variety. The following seemed to be most worthy of notice.

Such as are rugged with tubercules and points like a madrepore; others that have on their back the impression of five seals; others with something in the shape of a horse-shoe at the end of their claws; a sort covered with hair, that has no claws, and that adheres to the sides of ships; a crab marbled with grey, the shell of which though smooth and polished is very uneven. Many irregular and strange figures are observable among these, which are notwithstanding perfectly alike upon each crab; that with its eyes at the end of two long tubes like telescopes, which when it is not using them, it deposits in grooves along the side of its shell.

A crab with red claws, one much larger than the other; a small crab with a shell thrice as big as itself, in which it is covered over as by a buckler, so that its claws cannot be seen when it walks.

Along the shore and several feet under water are sometimes found a multitude of large *Boudins de Mer*, red and black. In taking them out of the water they emit a white and thick slime, that immediately changes into a number of small and glutinous threads. I believe this animal to be an enemy of the crab species, among which it is to be always met with. Its viscuous gleet is very fit to entangle their claws, which otherwise could have no hold upon its elastic hide, and cylindrical form. The seamen give it a very gross appellation which I will render in Latin *mentula monachi*. The Chinese hold it in high esteem, looking upon it as a powerful aphrodisiac.

Among the shell-fish we may call a shapeless mass, soft and membraneous, in the middle of which is one single flat bone that is a little arched. In these species the usual order seems to be reversed, the animal is on the outside of the shell.

We deem it a great singularity, that all univalves of which there are many, are turned from left to right, in looking at the shell when lying on its mouth, and the point towards ones-self: There are very few exceptions to this rule. What law can have determined them to begin their motion on the same side? Is it the same that has caused the sun to turn from West to East? In this case the sun may in some degree be the cause, as it is of their colours, which are the more beautiful the nearer to the line. There is much ingenuity and variety in the hinges of shell-fish, and our artists might improve by attending to the construction of them.

The oyster named the *tulier* is common here, and is of the same sort as those that are used as holy water pots in the church of St. Sulpice, at Paris: and is perhaps the largest shell which the sea produces: some of them are found at the Maldivia Islands, which are not to be drawn by two

two oxen without difficulty. It is rather extraordinary that this oyster is found in Normandy as a fossil, upon which coast I have seen it.

Shell-fish do not seem to live peaceably together, any more than other animals do. Many of them are found broken to pieces on the shore; those that are taken whole are always pierced. I too have seen a snail armed with a pointed tooth, with which it pierced the shells of muscles: It was brought from the Streights of Magellan.

The whole island is surrounded with Madrepores, a kind of vegetation of stone formed like a plant or shrub. They are so very numerous that the rocks seem formed of them only.

Of such as adorn and diversify the bed of the sea and adhere to it by their roots, are, the cauliflower; the cabbage, whose appearance is very like that plant; it is of the large sort, as well as another madrepore, the stages of which grow spirally; it is very brittle; another, that by the high shooting of its head and the robustness of its branches, resembles a tree; a very beautiful species, which I called the sheaf; it seems formed of several bunches of ears of corn; the pencil or pink,—at the centre of each opening, there is a little piece that is green.

A beautiful madrepore, growing in the form of an island with its shores and mountains; another, like an icicle; another, the leaves of which are digitated like a hand; the stag-wood, with horns very detached and brittle: the bee-hive, a large

large shapeless mass, the whole surface of which is full of regular holes; the pale blue coral, which is rare,—within, it is of a deeper blue; the jointed coral, black and white, containing a small piece of red coral which has not yet been seen here; vegetations of coral, blue, white, yellow and red, so brittle, and so much pierced that one cannot send any of it to Europe.

We observe among the *Litophites*, a plant like a long straw without leaves, buds or buttons; a vegetation like a forest of trees; their roots are very much interwoven, and have each a small nosegay of flowers; the substance of this *litophite* is of the nature of wood, and burns like it in the fire; it is notwithstanding classed among the madrepores.

I have seen our three sorts of sea star-wort, which is all we have, but which discover nothing remarkable. Formerly ambergrease was found upon the coast, there is even a little island to windward called by that name. It is sometimes brought from Madagascar.

The madrepores are allowed to be the work of an infinity of small animals, though they have a perfect resemblance of plants; I was pleased to be experimentally convinced of this, it being delightful to me to look upon the Universe as peopled. Besides I conceive so regular a work can only be carried on by some agent endewed with intelligence and a love of order. These vegetations resemble ours so much, the component matter apart, that I am even much induced

duced to believe our vegetables also to be* the labour of a multitude of living animals combined together for that purpose. I had much rather look upon a tree as a republick, than as a machine without life, and actuated by I know not what laws of hydraulics. I could support this opinion by many curious observations, for which I may perhaps some future time have more leisure. These researches may be useful, but when not employed to a good purpose, do but divert our attention from the more laudable pursuits on which we should be employed, and habituate us to fix upon any thing trifling that presents itself. Our histories are frequently made up of calumnies, our moral treatises, of satires. and our societies and academies of slander and epigrams. And after all this, men lament that friendship and confidence no longer exist; not considering its impossibility; among persons, each of whom carries a shield upon his heart, and a pcignard under his cloak.

Garulity spoils every thing—let us talk little, or let us form systems, *Tradidit mundum disputationibus*. Let us dispute then, but without being angry.

Port, Jan. 12, 1769.

* See letter 29 where this subject is discussed.

METE-

METEREOLOGICAL JOURNAL.

QUALITIES OF THE AIR.

JULY, 1768.

THE winds blew all this month from the south-west, as it usually does all the year. There is a strong breeze all day, and at night it is calm. Though it is now the dry season, yet it frequently rains, with violent squalls, that last but a short time. The air is very sharp; insomuch that cloth clothes are indispensably necessary.

AUGUST.

It rained almost every day. The mountains are covered with vapours like smoke, which descend upon the plains with gusts of wind. These rains often occasion rainbows upon the sides of the mountains, which, however, are not the less black on that account.

SEPTEMBER

Is the season for harvest. If heat and moisture are the sole causes of vegetation, why does nothing shoot at this time? It is no less hot than in May

May in France. Can there be any spirit of life attending the return of the sun? The Romans paid honours to the western wind, and fixed the period of its arrival at the 8th of February. They call it *Favonius*, or the Fosterer. 'Tis the same as the Zephyr of the Greeks. Pliny says it serves as a nusband to all things that draw their existence from the earth.

OCTOBER.

The air is now a little hotter; it is always coldest in the interior part of the island. At the end of this month they sow their wheat, and in four months after is their harvest; they then sow maize, which is ripe in September. Thus have they two crops on the same land; but these are scarcely a compensation for the other plagues with which this island is pestered.

NOVEMBER

The heats begin to be felt, the winds change, and sometimes get round to the N. W. Storms of rain fall.

No ship from France. No letter. It is grievous at this distance to be in constant expectation of our chief happiness from Europe. Ah! what avails it to repine!

DECEMBER

DECEMBER.

The heats are now almost intolerable. The sun is in the zenith, but the air is tempered by plentiful rains. I think I have felt it hotter in the summer at Petersburg. At the beginning of the month I heard thunder for the first time since my arrival.

The wind blew the 23 in the morning, from the S. W. and seemed to presage a storm. The clouds gathered at the top of the mountains. They were of an olive, or copper colour, and one long range of them was higher than the rest, and motionless. The smaller ones below blew about with a surprising rapidity. The sea broke upon the rocks with a great noise. Many of the sea birds flew for shelter to the land. The domestic animals were very uneasy. The air was gloomy and hot, although the wind was still high.

These are all certain presages of a hurricanè, and every body hastened to strengthen their houses with supporters and props, and to block up their doors and windows.

The hurricane at last about 10 in the evening announced itself by horrible gusts of wind, which were followed by not less horrible intervals of calm, in which the wind seemed to collect new powers. It kept augmenting the whole night; my apartment being very much shaken, I went into another. The good woman I lodged with, wept, and was in despair at the thoughts of her house being

being destroyed. Nobody went to bed. Towards morning the wind redoubled its efforts. I perceived that one side of our pallisade fence was falling, and that part of the roof of the house was raised at one corner; I got some planks and cords, by means of which I prevented the damage that would else have happened. In crossing the yard to give directions about this work, I frequently thought I should have been blown down. Some walls at a distance were falling, and some roofs were torn to pieces, the timbers of which were blown away as if they had been cards.

Some rain fell about eight in the morning, and the wind not at all abated, blew it horizontally along with such violence, that it entered like so many *water-spouts* at every the smallest opening. It spoiled several of my papers.

The rain fell in torrents at eleven. The wind subsided a little, the ravines in the mountains formed prodigious cascades on every side. Large pieces of the rocks broke off with a noise like that of cannon; and as they rolled down, cleared to themselves a path among the woods. The rivulets overflowed into the plain, which by this time was like another sea, neither banks nor bridges being any more to be seen

By 1 o'clock the wind veered round to the N. W. and drove the surf of the sea in large clouds along the land. The ships in the harbour were run ashore, and kept firing guns as signals of distress, but in vain, for no succour could be sent to them. By these repeated gusts, the buildings were acted upon

upon the contrary way, and with nearly equal violence. About noon the wind shifted to the E. and then to the W. Thus it went quite the circle of the horizon in the four-and-twenty hours, as usual—after which a perfect calm succeeded.

Trees were every where blown down, and bridges carried away. Not one single leaf remained in our gardens. Even the herb dogs-tooth, so remarkably hardy, seemed in some places to be cut to the very edge of the ground.

While the tempest raged, a worthy man, whose name is *Le Roux*, a joiner, sent his blacks and workmen to help those who might want their assistance, and this without any gratuity. Good actions should never be passed over without notice—especially in this place.

We had an eclipse at four min. past five on the 23, but the bad weather prevented its being seen.

Such terrible blasts, it seems, come regularly every year in December, and sometimes in March. As the winds make the tour of the horizon, there is not a cavern in the island unfilled with the rain, which destroys a great number of rats, grass-hoppers and ants—they are not seen again for some time.

The ravages made by this dreadful visitation of the Almighty, are more to be apprehended than all the calamities even of winter. That of 1760 will be long remembered. A shutter was seen lifted into the air, and then darted like an arrow upon a roof at some distance. The lower masts of a sixty-four gun ship were twisted round and broken off. No tree in Europe could withstand the force of these whirlwinds. How the trees of the country are protected, we have seen above.

JANUARY, 1769.

A great deal of rain, the weather hot and gloomy; great storms, but little thunder. The gales of wind blowing very hard in this season, all navigation is at a stand from December till April.

All the pleasurable parts of the island recover their verdure, the earth presents a most delightful prospect, but the sky a dismal one.

FEBRUARY.

We have still much stormy weather, and violent gusts of wind. The Happy, a passage-boat sent to Madagascar, and the Favorite, a ship, are both lost.

The clouds gathered together on the 25, by a N. W. wind, formed themselves into a long range from the Flag Mountain to the Isle of *Tonneliers*. It is motionless: claps of thunder innumerable proceed from it. The storm lasted from six in the morning till noon, during which time a number

ber of thunderbolts fell; one of them killed a grenadier, and another a negro woman; an ox upon the Island of *Tonneliers* had the same fate: a gun in an officer's house was melted. The people here say, that the thunder never falls within the town; for my part I never heard any so loud, and could not help thinking it very like a bombardment. I am of opinion that if they had fired one cannon, the explosion would have dispelled the motionless clouds from whence the thunder issued.

MARCH.

The rains are somewhat abated, the atmosphere more serene and clear, and the winds always from the S. W. The heat is now tolerable.

APRIL.

A charming season, the herbage becomes every where dry, and should it now be set on fire, the landscape would be totally black for seven months to come.

MAY.

The winds, as is customary, are turned in the end of this month to N. W. We have now the dry season. I was in the plains, called *Williams Plains*, and found the air of a temperature perfectly pleasant and refreshing.

JUNE.

JUNE.

Now we have no winds but from the S. E. and the showers of small rain again begin to fall.

This country has no peculiar malady, but the people have all those we have in Europe, as the apoplexy, small-pox, pleurisies, and obstructions in the liver; which last, I should imagine, proceed rather from vexation, than from the bad quality of the water, as is the general opinion. I have seen a stone taken from a negro of the place, which was bigger than an egg. Violent gouts and paralytic disorders are common.

Worms ot a singular species are here very troublesome to the blacks and children, the former have in the venereal disease dreadful chops, or clefts in the soles of their feet. The air is as good as in Europe, but has no medicinal virtues; and I would by all means dissuade gouty persons from coming here, having seen some people keep their beds for six months together.

The vicissitude of the seasons very sensibly affects the constitution of the inhabitants. They are liable to bilious fevers, and the heat occasions ruptures, but temperance and bathing will keep a man in health. I cannot however but observe, that in cold countries the people are more healthy, and their spirits more vigorous, and it is worthy of remark, that history mentions no celebrated man that was born between the tropics, except Mahomet.

LETTER XI.

WHITE INHABITANTS.

THIS Island remained uninhabited till discovered by Mascarenhas. The first French people that established themselves here were some husbandmen from Bourbon. They brought with them simplicity of manners, good faith and confidence, a love of hospitality and even an indifference with respect to riches.

Monsieur de Bourdonnais, who was in some measure the founder of the colony, brought workmen into it that were good sort of men, and some others whom their parents sent from home for misconduct, and whom by his discipline he made good and useful members to society.

Having rendered the island respectable by the labour he exerted for its encouragement, it was thought a proper place to touch at, in the way to India. People of all ranks then poured in upon it. Among these were the persons sent out by the India Company. The principal employments on the island being vested in their hands, they lived in a state equal to that of the nobles in Venice, and to their aristocratical manners joined something also of a spirit of financing, which

which is always prejudicial to the spirit of agriculture. Every appointment was at their disposal, and their power was alike absolute in judicial matters, as in matters of trade. Some of them cleared the lands, and erected buildings, which they sold again at an exorbitant rate to those who came thither to settle. An outcry was raised against the oppressors, but so great was their power, that no redress could be obtained.

Seafaring people established here, for a long time, could not understand that the dangers and fatigue of the trade to India was to them, in proportion as the honours and profits of it were to those for whom they laboured. This settlement so near to the Indies raised great expectations on their first coming. But before their establishment was effected, they became discontented and much more so afterwards.

A military force was sent out, among whom were some officers of high birth. These had no idea of degrading themselves so far as to rank or connect with men who had formerly been merchants clerks; except to receive their pay of them: they liked the seamen as little as the merchants,—their manners were too blunt and unpolished. Thus their pride standing in the way of their fortune, they continued as poor as when they left France.

A few of the King's troops touched here, and staid some time. Some officers tempted by the serenity of the climate and a love of ease continued. Every thing and every body being subject to the company only, the subaltern did not however meet with the distinction and respect paid to him in garrisons, and which were so flattering to his vanity.—Being without employment he was looked upon as an alien among the mercantile people, each of whom had his own particular interest to attend.

Other settlers, were the Missionaries of St. Lazarus, who availing themselves of the simplicity of the first inhabitants, had exercised a dominion over them uncontroled: but when the body of the people increasing very fast, divided and dispersed itself, they were content to attend to their pastoral functions, and to some of the better sort of families who countenanced their visits.

Some merchants were the next inhabitants who brought money with them, though to no great amount. In an island without trade they added to the abuses of brokerage already practised, and introduced besides monopolies of every kind.

These soon became odious to the other inhabitants, who wanting the means of imposition, were themselves imposed upon, and gave their oppressors the epithet of *Banians*, a name there held in as much abhorrence as that of Jew in France. They also affected to despise the distinctions of rank, looking upon every man after his having crossed the line, to be the equal of his neighbour.

But the late war in India, inundated upon the Isle of France, the scum of Europe and of Asia; bank-

bankrupts, ruined libertines, thieves, and wretches of every kind, who driven from the former by their crimes, and from the latter by the bad success of our arms, attempted to re-establish their fortunes upon the ruins of the public. On the arrival of this set of men, the complaints both general and particular of the inhabitants were augmented; every character was traduced with an Asiatic ingenuity, hitherto unknown to the calumniators of our climate; no woman was now looked upon as chaste, nor any man as honest: all confidence and esteem, were at an end. Thus by vilifying all mankind, they thought to reduce all to their own level.

They had no hope but in a change of the administration, and they at last affected their design. The company in 1765 yielding up to the King, a colony which had cost them so much trouble and expence;—Order and peace were now expected to resume their seat, but it was found that this change had added new leaven to the fermentation; for a number of persons were sent by authority from Paris to make their fortunes in an island, uncultivated and without any settled trade, and where paper is the only currency. These then were malcontents of another sort.

Such as were grateful enough to continue their attachment to the company, saw with grief, the introduction of the royal jurisdiction. The other party that had reckoned upon the new government, seeing that none but œconomical plans were adopted, felt their disappointment the more

 severely,

severely, on account of the expectations they had formed.

These dissentions were enhanced by those from other bodies of men, who were at continual variance even in France,—the departments of the marine,—the pen,—and the sword;—In short, the mind of every individual, being neither occupied by business, nor amused by public entertainments, retired within itself, to brood over its own inquietudes.

The island is such a victim to discord as has entirely extirpated that love of society which might be expected to prevail among Frenchmen banished to a desart, surrounded by the seas, and at the end of the world. Each man is discontented;—each man wants to get a fortune—and to leave the place. To hear them talk one would think the island would be again uninhabited, every man declaring he would go away next year, and some of them have held this intention for thirty years past, yet remain to make the same declaration the year ensuing.

The soldier soon loses here his military ardour. In general he has but little money and is in want of every thing; his house is without furniture; provisions when bought by retail are excessively dear, and he finds himself the sole consumer between the inhabitants and the merchant, who seem to strive who shall impose upon him most. This forces him to act upon the defensive,—he buys by wholesale, and makes the most of all opportunities of getting good bargains, every com-

commodity being of double value after the departure of the ships. The anxiety of providing for his family being at an end, another ensues, he torments himself with the thoughts of being an exile from his native country, and being destined to remain he knows not how long in one destitute of every comfort and convenience, want of employment and company, aided by the hopes of gain, allure him to engage farther in that commerce, which originated in mere necessity.

Some exceptions there doubtless are to this general character of the military, and were they not even numerous, I should recite them with pleasure. M. de Steenhovre, the commanding officer is a pattern of every virtue.

We have many workmen; for the heat is not so excessive as to prevent white people from the regiments working in the open air. Sufficient advantage, however, for the benefit of the colony, has not been made of this circumstance. Among the recruits sent from Europe, there are frequently wretches capable of the most atrocious villainies. I cannot for my part conceive but that the sending of culprits whose crimes have rendered them unworthy to remain in their native country, must be of bad consequence to any colony in an incipient state. These unhappy creatures frequently become so desperate, as to murder each other with their bayonets upon the most trifling occasion.

Though the seamen do but just come and go, they have a powerful influence upon the manners

manners of the inhabitants. Their policy consists in complaining of the places whence they come, as well as of those they arrive at. They would have you believe that their lucky hour has passed them without their making a proper advantage of it.—They speak of themselves constantly as ruined men; they tell you how dear they have bought, and to what loss they have sold. The truth of this matter is, that they think no bargain a good one, unless they get a 150 per cent. by it. A cask of claret costs 150 livres, and every thing else in proportion. One would scarcely imagine that European goods were dearer here than in India, and Indian goods dearer than in Europe. This however is the case. The seamen are much regarded by the inhabitants, who indeed could hardly exist without them. Their murmurings, and perpetual going to and again give the island the appearance, and in a degree the manners of an inn.

From this motley assortment of emigrants in such different conditions, results as it were, a people of opposite characters, and from nations of dissimilar habits, who hate each other most cordially. Probity and honour are in no esteem. The *cunning* man is here the man of wit. It is however in my opinion a character worthy only of foxes; it is certainly not a property natural to the human species, and a wretched society must that be, where it is looked upon as an estimable quality. On the other hand, mistrustful or wary people are much disliked; this may appear a contradiction, but the reason is, that there is less to be got, from persons used to be on their guard, who

who may detect and expose those who would impose upon them. They will flock about a man whom they know to be artful, and will assist him to the utmost in duping the ignorant.

They are altogether without sensibility to the feeling which constitutes the happiness of a generous mind. They have no taste for arts or literature, but deeply regret their absence from the Opera and the women of Paris. Every sentiment of humanity is here depraved, nay, I may say extinct. I was once at the funeral of a considerable merchant, but saw no signs of affliction; his brother-in-law remarked, indeed, that they had not dug the grave so deep as it should have been!

This apathy is extreme and extends to all things about them. The streets and courts are neither paved, nor planted with trees; the houses are mere cabins of wood, which may be easily removed from one place to another upon rollers. The windows have neither glass nor curtains; and the houses have but little furniture, and that little very shabby.

We have the semblance of an exchange, where people meet at noon, and in the evening; here they make their bargains, and rail at, and talk scandal of their neighbours. The married people in the town are very few. Those who are not rich, plead their circumstances as an excuse for continuing single: others say they will not settle till there return to France; but the true reason is, their seldom or ever meeting with a repulse in their

their attempts upon the negro girls. Besides, there are very few good matches for the men, ten thousand franks being a fortune but seldom to be found in this solitude.

Most married people live upon their plantations. The women scarcely ever come to town but to a ball, or to confess at Easter. They are most passionately fond of dancing. No sooner is a ball announced than they come in crowds, brought in palanquins, which are a sort of litter, and carried upon the shoulders of four negroes, four others following as a relay. As many children as there are in the family, so many of these vehicles are there, and each attended as above by eight blacks. The husbands who are prudent and saving, are very averse to these excursions, as hindrances of the business of the plantations; but the roads are so bad, that a wheel carriage here is of no use.

Our females are rather pale, but well made, and in general handsome,—they have naturally a great flow of wit and spirits, and if better educated would be most agreeable companions, but I have known some so ignorant as to be unable to read.

They are reserved and silent at their meetings; each woman brings with her some secret pretensions, either from the fortune, the employ, or the birth of the husband: others reckon upon their youth or their beauty; an European looks with disdain upon a Creole, who as often looks upon the European as an adventurer.

But

But though the tongue of scandal is ever speaking to their prejudice, they are in my opinion far more deserving than the men, by whom they are neglected for the black slaves. Such of the women as are really virtuous, are the more to be commended, that it is by no means owing to their education that they are so. They have at once to combat with the heat of the climate, the indifference of their husbands, and the prodigality and ardour of young officers, skilled in seduction and regardless of repulse; if then Hymen complains, and with justice, of the infidelities of the fair sex, whom can we thank but ourselves, who have introduced the manners of France upon the shores of Africa.

With all their frailties they possess many good and amiable qualities,—are domestic, sober, drink water only, except rarely, neat in their apparel to an extreme, and very cleanly. The dress most common here is of muslin trimmed with rose-coloured taffaty. They are extravagantly fond of their children, who run about the house naked, very soon after they are born; are never put in swaddling clothes, but are frequently bathed, eat fruit as they think proper, live without care, and without study, and soon grow strong and robust. The puberty of both sexes makes a very early appearance. I have known girls married only eleven years old.

Their habit of bringing up children which approaches nearly to a state of nature, and leaves them in an almost utter ignorance; but the vices of the negro women, which they imbibe with their milk, and their caprices, which they are suffered to exercise upon the poor slaves to a degree of tyranny beyond all bounds, adds to their ignorance almost all the depravity incident to society. To remedy this evil, the principal people send their children while very young into France, whence they return with vices perhaps more amiable, but certainly more dangerous.

There are but few planters on this island, not perhaps above four hundred. We have nearly an hundred women of condition, about ten only of whom live in the town. The evening is their visiting time—and for want of conversation, they game, or soon grow tired of each other. At eight o'clock the evening gun fires, and every body goes home.

Adieu, my good friend; I am really grieved to think that in speaking of mankind as they are, has more the appearance of burlesque, or exaggeration, than a real resemblance.

Port, Feb. 10, 1769.

LETTER XII.

BLACKS.

POPULATION.

INDIANS and negroes are necessarily included in my account of our population, the first are the Malabars, or Malayans, a mild and gentle people, who come from Pondicherry, where they let themselves as servants for a term of years. They are almost all of handicraft trades, and occupy a suburb, called the Camp of the Blacks. This people is of a deeper hue than the islanders of Madagascar, who are perfect negroes; but have features as regular as a European, and not the frizzled hair. They are sober, thrifty, and much given to women. They wear on their heads a turban, are clothed in long muslin gowns, and carry large rings of gold in their ears, and silver bracelets on their wrists. Some of them let themselves to the rich people, and are called *Pions*, a kind of domestics like our running footmen, who execute every commission, with the most profound gravity; and by way of distinction, carry a cane in their hand, and a poignard on their girdle. It were to be wished, that a great number of Malabars

bars were established here, especially as labourers; but I never saw one of them fond of farming work.

Our ground is tilled by Blacks from Madagascar; where a slave may be bought for a barrel of powder, for a few musquets, linen, or especially for piastres; the greatest price paid is * fifty crowns, and that rarely.

These have neither so flat a nose, nor so black a skin as the negroes of Guinea. Some of them are only to be called brown, and some, as the *Balambous*, have long hair, of a brown, or carrotty colour. They are active, ingenious, have a quick sense of honour and of gratitude, far less mindful of injuries done to themselves personally, than of those offered to their family—which last, they deem an insult of the highest degree. When in their own country, they make a variety of things with much art and industry. Their *zagaye*, or half-pike, is very well forged, though they have nothing but stones for both anvil and hammer. Their linens, or *pagnes*, which are weaved by women, are very fine, and beautifully coloured. Their manner of throwing this garment round them, is extremely graceful. Their head-dress is very regular, in rows of curls and braids, nicely ranged one above the other; this is also the work of women. They are passionately fond of dancing and music, and play upon an instrument called a *Tamtum*, which is a kind of bow, with a gourd bottle fitted to it. The sound of it is very soft,

* 7l. 10s.

and is a pleasing accompaniment to their songs, of which love is always the subject. The girls dance to the songs their lovers compose, while the spectators beat time, and applaud the performance.

Their hospitality is exemplary. A Black who is travelling, enters, though unknown, into the first cottage he comes to; sits down with the inhabitants of it, and partakes of their repast, without being questioned, whence he comes? or whither he is going? This custom is general.

Such is the simplicity they bring with them to the Isle of France, where they are landed with a rag round their loins. The men are ranged on one side—and on the other, the women, with their infants, who cling for fear, to their mothers. The inhabitant having examined them, as he would a horse, buys what he finds for his purpose. Brothers—sisters—friends—lovers—are torn asunder, and bidding each other a long farewell, driven—weeping, to their respective situations. Sometimes they turn desperate, fancying that the white people intend eating their flesh, making red wine of their blood, and gun-powder of their bones.

Their treatment makes me shudder only to recite it. At break of day, a signal of three smacks of a whip calls them to work, each of them betakes himself with his spade to the plantations, where they work almost naked in the heat of the sun. Their food is maize, bruised, and boiled, or bread made of Manioc *, and their clothing, a single piece of linen. Upon the commission of the most trivial offence, they are tied hand and foot to a ladder; the overseer then comes with a whip like a postillion's, and gives them fifty, a hundred, or perhaps two hundred lashes upon the back. Each stroke carries off its portion of skin. The poor wretch is next untied, an iron collar with three spikes put round his neck, and he is then sent back to his task. Some of them are unable to sit down for a month after this beating, which punishment is inflicted with equal severity on women as on men.

When they return home at eve, they are obliged to pray for the prosperity of their masters; and before they go to rest, they wish him a good night.

A singular law in their favour is yet in force, called the *Code Noire*, which ordains, that they shall receive no more than thirty lashes for any one offence—that they shall not work on Sundays—that they shall eat meat once a week—and have a new shirt every year; but this law is not observed, because the practice of it is not enforced. Sometimes, when grown too old to labour, they are turned out to get their bread where they can. One day I saw a poor creature, who was nothing but skin and bone, cutting off the flesh of a dead horse to eat;—it was one skeleton devouring another!

* A root, for which the English have no name. 'Tis poison, if eaten raw, but wholesome and good, if boiled. *E.*

A stranger,

A stranger, who seems affected at these sights, is told coldly by the inhabitants, he does not know the Blacks.—That they are such gluttons as to go and steal victuals from the neighbouring houses; —so idle, that they take no manner of care of their master's business, nor do what they are set about; that the women are totally inattentive to family affairs, and so little concerned about children, that they had rather procure an abortion, than bring them into the world.

Who should be surprised were all this true! The negroes are naturally lively, but after having been some time in slavery, become melancholy. Love seems the only passion their sorrows will permit them to indulge. They do all in their power to get married; and if their own choice is suffered to take place, they generally prefer those who have passed the prime of their youth; who, they tell you, *make better soup than the very young ones.* They give the wife all they possess. If their mistress is the slave of another planter, they will go three or four leagues in the night to see her, through ways one would think impassable. When under the influence of this passion, they are alike fearless of fatigue or of punishment. Sometimes they appoint a rendezvous in the middle of the night, and perhaps, under the shelter of a rock, they dance to the dismal sound, of a bladder filled with peas: but the sight of a white person, or the barking of a dog, immediately breaks up the assembly.

These unfortunate creatures are, however, indulged with dogs; but it is an undoubted fact,

 that

that these animals know perfectly, even in the dark, not only a white man, but a dog that belongs to a white man—both of whom they fear and hate; howling as soon as they approach.

Dogs of white people seem, on their parts, to have adopted the sentiments of their masters; and at the least encouragement will fly with the utmost fury upon a slave, or upon his dog.

Blacks are not unfrequently unable to endure their hard lot, and give themselves up to despair. Some—hang or poison themselves; others will get into a little boat, and without sails, provisions, or compass, hazard a voyage of two hundred leagues, that they may return to Madagascar, where they have been sometimes seen to land; and have been taken, and sent back to their masters.

For the most part they secrete themselves in the woods, where they are hunted by parties of soldiers, and by other negroes with dogs. Some of the inhabitants form partie of pleasure for this purpose—put up a negro as they would a wild beast, and if they cannot hunt him down—will shoot him—cut off his head—and bring it in triumph to town upon the end of a stick. Of this I am an eye-witness every week.

A *Maron-Negro* when catched, is whipped, and one of his ears cut off: the second time, he is again whipped, the sinews of his hams cut across, and he is put in chains: for the third offence he is hanged; but is kept in ignorance of his sentence, until put in execution.

Some

Some of them are even hanged and broken alive. They went to execution with joy, and suffered without a cry. I once saw even a woman, throw herself from the top of the ladder. They believe that they shall find more happiness in another world, and that the Father of Mankind is not unjust, as men are.

When baptized, they are told they become, by that means, the brethren of the white people, and will go to heaven. But they are hardly to be made believe that the Europeans can ever be instrumental to their going to Paradise; saying, that on earth, they are the cause of all the sufferings they endure. They say, that before Europeans landed in their country, they fought with sticks headed with iron; that they now, taught by us, kill each other at a great distance with fire and balls; that in order to procure slaves at a cheap rate, we foment continual divisions and wars among them; that formerly they followed the impulse of Nature, without fear of those grievous distempers, with which we have poisoned the constitutions of their women: that we suffer them to languish, without clothes, and without nourishment, and beat them inhumanly without reason.

Of all this, I have seen frequent instances. A female slave came one day, and throwing herself prostrate at my feet, told me—that her mistress made her rise so very early every morning, and sit up every night so late, that she was almost totally without sleep; and that when overcome with fatigue, she did chance to drop asleep, her mistress caused her lips to be rubbed with ordure, which if she did not lick off, she underwent a whipping. A relief from this intolerable grievance was what she begged I would intercede for. —I did so; and obtained my request.

Intercessions of this kind, are sometimes complied with, and the punishment is redoubled a few days after. I was a witness to this conduct, in a counsellor, whose Blacks complained of him to the Governor, and who assured me, that on the morrow he would have them flayd from head to foot.

Not a day passes, but both men and women are whipped for having broken earthen ware—for not shutting the door after them, or some such trifling reason; and when almost covered with blood, are rubbed with vinegar and salt to heal their wounds.

On the key, I have sometimes seen them so overwhelmed with grief, that they have been unable even to utter a cry—others biting the cannon to which they are tied. My pen is weary of writing this recital of horrors; my eyes of seeing, and my ears of hearing their doleful mournings.

Happy you, who when tired of continuing in town, can retire to a country where fertile plains are seen, with rising hills, villages, harvests and vintages, the plenty of which cheers the hearts of a people who accompany their labours with dancing

dancing and singing.—Signs these, at least, of happiness.

The sights I see, are poor negro women bent over a spade, the companion of their labour—their children flung at their backs—negroes who pass trembling and shrinking before me—sometimes I hear the sound of their *tambour* afar off; but far more frequently, the smack of the whips, that echo in the hills like the report of a pistol, and cries of—"Mercy, Master, mercy!" which at once strike my ears and pierce my heart.

From these shocking scenes I often retire, and find a country, almost every where barren, rugged and rocky; mountains, whose summits, inaccessible, retard the course of the clouds, and breaking them, form torrents that rush into abysses equally horrible and tremendous. The winds that roar in the deserts, the hollow, dismal sound of the waves dashing upon the breakers, the sea before me, vast, and extending to regions unknown to the human race, all combine to depress and deject my spirits, and to furnish me with ideas fit only for an exile and an outcast.

Port, April 15, 1769.

P. S. Whether coffee and sugar be really essential to the comfort of Europe, is more than I can say, but I affirm—that these two vegetables have brought wretchedness and misery upon America and Africa. The former is depopulated, that

 Europeans

Europeans may have a land to plant them in; and the latter is stripped of its inhabitants, for hands to cultivate them.

We deem it more our interest to have plantations for cultivating ourselves the commodities we want, than to purchase them of our neighbours. But since carpenters, bricklayers, masons, and other workmen from Europe, can work in the open air, and exposed to the sun, why should not white men be employed in all sorts of labour? But what then is to become of the proprietors of these lands? I answer, they would become the richer by this means. An inhabitant would live at his ease, were he to employ twenty farmers—possessed of twenty slaves, he struggles in vain with an insurmountable poverty. The number of slaves here are computed at 2000. A yearly recruit of an eighteenth part of that number, is found absolutely necessary. Hence we see that the colony left to itself, would in eighteen years be extirpated. So true is it, that without liberty and property, population must decrease—and that injustice and good husbandry are incompatible.

The law mentioned above, or the *Code Noir*, is said to be made for relief of the slaves. Be it so—yet does the cruelty of the masters exceed the punishment it permits, and their avarice withhold the food, the rest, and the rewards it decrees. If the poor wretches complain of this infringement, to whom do they seek for redress? To judges, who are perhaps the tyrants, under whose oppression they languish:

But

But these people, it is alleged, are not to be restrained, but by severities. Punishments must be inflicted, iron collars with three points, whips, fetters for their legs *; and chains of iron for their necks must be made use of—they must be treated like savage beasts, or the white people could not live like men. From this principle, so

* I cannot help attempting to describe in this place, a sort of IRON MASK, or as it is more properly called, a MUZZLE, great numbers of which, I am told, were formerly kept by several wholesale ironmongers, more especially in the sea-port towns of France, to supply the orders of merchants and planters in the West-India islands.—I have seen one of them at the house of a gentleman as well known for his universal benevolence, as for his particular perseverance in behalf of the African Negroes, and who uses it as an IRON argument against the toleration of slave-holding. It is fastened round the neck of the wretched culprit, by a collar, from which rise some bars of iron, forming the mask and head-piece;—before the mouth is a round plate of iron, wherein are bored holes, to allow a small portion of breath to the wearer. There is also a place for his nose. A flat piece of iron goes into the mouth, and acts upon the tongue and glands, as a slavering-bit does upon those of a horse. Worn by a man working beneath the scorching rays of the sun, in the torrid zone, it soon attains a violent degree of heat, which with the constant flowing of the saliva, in a little time excoriates the nose, mouth, and chin, and must occasion a TORMENT, the very idea of which it would give me pain to convey to the reader. In England, we put upon a vicious *horse*, or a mischievous *dog*, a muzzle of LEATHER—this—self-preservation dictates; but what cogent motive can urge the slave-holder, to put upon his fellow-creature—upon a MAN—A MUZZLE OF IRON. I will tell the reader——'Tis to prevent him, when at work, from sucking, or eating of the sugar-canes, herein denying him that indulgence which the ALMIGHTY GOD charged the Israelite, by the remembrance of his own slavery in Egypt, to shew to HIS BEAST, when treading out the corn—or from putting an end to his wretched existence, by cramming himself with the dirt of the ground.——A practice to which the despairing wretches are frequently driven, by the merciless treatment of their worse than Egyptian taskmasters.

grossly

grossly unjust, no consequences can be deduced, but what are equally unjust and inhuman; nor does it suffice, that these poor negroes are victims to the avarice and cruelty of the most depraved of men, but they must also be the sport of their sophistical arguments.

Missionaries tell them, that the slavery of their present life, will ensure to them a spiritual liberty in heaven. But the greater part are bought at an age too late to learn French, and our Missionaries do not understand the language of the country. Moreover, those who have been baptized, are not a jot better treated than the rest.

It is also an allegation of their masters, that the negroes merit the vengeance of heaven, for the traffic they carry on. Are we then to take upon us to be their executioners! Let us leave the destruction of kites to vultures.

Alas! that our philosophers, who enter the lists with so much alacrity to combat other abuses, scarcely speak of this slavery of negroes, beyond a degree of pleasantry. Indeed, it is a subject they seem desirous of avoiding. They speak of the massacre of Paris, and of the Mexicans by the Spaniards, as if the crimes of our days, and in which the half of Europe are concerned, either as principals or accessories, were not equal to them. Can they believe the iniquity of murdering a number of people, of a different persuasion from ourselves, to be greater than that of bringing misery and torment of the severest nature upon a whole nation, to whom we are indebted for

for those delicacies which our luxury has rendered necessary to us? Those beautiful rose and flame-colours, in which our ladies are dressed, cotton, of so general use, coffee and chocolate, now the only breakfast admitted to polite tables; the rouge with which the pallid beauty gives new bloom to her complexion—all these are prepared by the industrious hand of the enslaved and oppressed negro!

Ye women of sensibility and sentiment, who weep at the affecting story of a novel, or the representation of a tragedy, know, that what constitutes your chiefest delight, is moistened with the tears, and died with the blood of men!

LETTER XIII.

CULTURE.

MOST of the plants, trees and animals, I am about to describe, have been brought here by order of government. Some of the inhabitants have contributed their endeavours for this purpose; among others, Messrs. de Cossini, Poivre, Hermans, and Le Juge. I wished to have learnt the names of the others, that I might have mentioned them with the respect which is their due. The gift, or introducing of a useful plant, being, in my opinion, of more consequence, than the discovery of a gold mine, and a monument more durable than a pyramid.

The following is the order of my remarks; first, the plants, which being once sown, ever after sow themselves, and are, as it were, naturalized in the country; secondly, those that are articles of cultivation in the country; thirdly, the produce of the kitchen-garden; fourthly, of the flower-garden. I shall pursue the same method with the trees and shrubs. Of these I know, I shall omit none. Whatever Nature has not disdained

dained to form, we certainly ought not to think too insignificant to describe.

In some of the plains round the town is found, a kind of indigo, which I apprehend to be foreign to this island. It is of no use.

In sandy places we find the purslain; I take this to be natural here, being reckoned among that class of plants, which when rotten, manures the ground, and which Nature seems to have made the growth of dry and sandy soils, to facilitate vegetations of other kinds.

Every rivulet abounds with water-cresses. They have been brought here these ten years. The dandelion and wormwood grow spontaneously in rubbish, or ground newly opened: but above all, the mullen expands its large downy leaves, and shoots up its girandole of yellow flowers to a surprizing height.

Bulrush, not the Chinese, is a grass about the height of well-grown rye. It extends itself daily, and choaks the plants that grow near it. It is apt to be tough when dry, and should therefore be cut before ripe. It is green for five months only in a year, and it is afterwards set on fire, notwithstanding the burning of it is prohibited. The flames of it burn and parch up the out-skirts of the woods.

White-grass, so called from the colour of its flower, was brought here as forage, but no animal will eat it; the seed resembles that of cherville.

It

It multiplies so fast, that it is become one of the plagues of husbandry.

Brette, signifies in the Indian language, a leaf good to eat, and is a species of the morell. There are two sorts of it; one called the *Brette* of Madagascar. Its leaf is rather prickly, but of a pleasant taste, and is purgative. The other is commonly served up to table as spinage, and is the only food of which the Blacks may eat at discretion, and grows all over the island. The water in which it is boiled becomes very bitter. In this liquor, mingled and still more imbittered by their tears, the negroes steep their cassave.

The cassave root is among our exotics. It grows in dry soils; its juice has lost the poisonous quality it formerly had. It is a shrub, whose leaf is like that of hemp, with a root as thick and as long as a man's arm; when rasped, and unpressed, they make cakes of it, that are heavy like dough. Three pounds of this are allowed for the food of a negro for one day. This vegetable grows and spreads very fast. M. de la Bourdonnois brought it from America. It is a useful plant, being easily sheltered from the hurricanes, and ensures a certain subsistence to the negroes, for the dogs will not eat it.

We have nothing more beautiful than the maize or Turkish corn. It is a precious grain; turns to good account, but will not keep more than a year, as the mites get into it: this, I think, a good reason why the cultivation of it should be encouraged in Europe, as it cannot be with-held long from market

market It serves as food for the slaves, the fowls, and the cattle. The inhabitants speak highly of the excellence of maize and the manioc, but never eat of either. I have seen little cakes of them in a desert, and when they are made with a great deal of sugar, of wheat-flower, and yolks of eggs, they are very palatable indeed.

We have plenty of wheat, but it does not grow to any great height. They put the seed into the ground by single grains, because of the rocks; they cut it with knives, and thresh it out with small sticks. It will not keep so long as two years. Pliny tells us, that in Barbary and Spain, it was put in full ear into holes in the earth, taking care to introduce a proper quantity of air. Varro says, that it would keep by this means for fifty years, and millet, for a whole century. Pompey found at Ambratia some beans preserved in this manner, since the time of Pyrrhus, which was near 120 years. But Pliny will not admit of the cultivation of the earth by slaves of any kind, whose work, he says, is never done effectually. Though the meal of the wheat that grows here is not so white as that from Europe, yet I prefer the bread of it to that of European meal, which either grows vapid, or ferments during the voyage.

The most wholesome of all aliments, and the best rice, thrives very much. It keeps longer than the wheat, and yields more plentifully. A wet soil agrees with it best. There are above seven different species of it in Asia, one of which grows best in a dry soil; it were to be wished, that

that this grain were cultivated in Europe, on account of its extraordinary fertility.

Millet, especially the smaller kind, yields abundantly. It is seldom given but to the blacks and the beasts. Oats thrive exceedingly, but the cultivation of them, or of any thing else, which the blacks or the beasts only derive benefit from, is very little attended to.

We have no good tobacco. None is planted save by the Negroes for their own use.

Fatigue, is a grass, bearing large leaves, of the nature of a small rose-tree. They import it from Madagascar, and make of it the most delightful artificial meadows.

All our experiments have been without success, to make saint-foin, trefoil, hemp, flax, and hops grow here.

Our vegetables for the most part degenerate, and those who wish to have them good, are supplied every year with seed from Europe, or the Cape of Good-Hope. The small peas are tough, and tasteless; the French beans are hard; there is a sort larger, and more tender, called Cape-peas; it is worth transplanting to France. Another sort of beans which they barrel, they chop the husks to pieces, and dress them as peas. There is another kind of bean ftill, with a pod a foot long, which they plant and form arbours of. The grain is very large, but of no sort of use.

We

We have a sort of artichokes, whose leaves are very large, and the fruit but small. The *Cardoon* * is always tough here; but being also very prickly, and growing to a great height, it makes very good hedges.

A pumpkin called Giromon is not so large as ours, and if possible, of a more insipid taste. The cucumber is smaller, and not so plentiful as in Europe. The melons are good for nothing, though much boasted of on account of their scarcity. The *Pasteque*, or water-melon, is something better than the other. The climate suits these fruits very well; but the loominess of the soil is against them. Gourds grow here to an enormous size, and are of particular utility; they serve the Blacks for plates and dishes.

The *Briugella* or *Aubergine*, is of two sorts; the one bears a small, round and yellow fruit, and has a very prickly stem; it comes from Madagascar. The other, which is known in Paris, is a violet-coloured fruit, of the size and form of a large fig. When this fruit is well seasoned and boiled, it is not bad eating.

There are two sorts of pepper; that known in Europe, and another natural to this place; it is a shrub bearing very small fruit, that shine like so many grains of coral upon the most beautiful green foliage imaginable. The Creoles use it in all their ragouts. It is stronger than any other

* A kind of thistle, one sort of this plant is used in salad. *E.*

kind of pepper, and will burn like a caustic. They call it mad pepper.

The pine-apple, the most beautiful of all fruits, for the variegated colouring of its scaly rind, for its purple crest, and for its fragrant smell, which is like that of a violet, never ripens here perfectly. Its juice is very cold, and prejudicial to the stomach. Its bark is on the contrary very hot, and tastes like pepper; perhaps as corrective of the juice. Nature frequently contrasts the qualities of the same subject;—the bark of the citron is of a hot nature, the juice of a cooling;—the rind of the pomegranate is astringent, the seeds are laxative, &c.

Strawberries begin to thrive in the cool parts. They have neither the fragrancy nor the sweetness of ours; they yield but sparingly, any more than the rasberries, which are much degenerated. There is a species of them from China, very beautiful, and in great plenty, which grow to the size of cherries, but have neither taste nor smell.

Spinage is scarce here. Garden cresses, sorrel, cherville, parsley, fennel, and celery, have stringy stems, and are raised with great difficulty. Leeks, lettuce, endive, and cauliflowers, are smaller, but not so tender as ours. Cabbage, the most useful of all vegetables, and which is found in all parts, thrives very well here. Burnet, purslain, and sage, grow in abundance; but especially the *Capucine* which grows upon large espaliers, and is very long lived.

Asparagus

Asparagus is hardly so great as a packthread, and has degenerated in taste as well as in size, and so have carrots, parsnips, turnips, sassafras, and radishes, which are of a biting taste. There is, however, a radish from China, that grow, very well here The beet-root grows beautifully, but is very sticky. Potatoes, *selanum Americanum*, are not bigger here than nuts. The Indian ones, called *Cambar*, frequently weigh above a pound a-piece; their skin is of a beautiful violet-colour, but within they are very white and tasteless; they, however, serve for food for the blacks. They increase very fast, as well as the Jerusalem artichoke, some sorts of which are preferable to our chesnuts. Saffron is an herb that tinges the ragouts with yellow, as do the stamina of the European kind. Our ginger is not so hot as that of India. What is called here, the Pistachia-nut, which is not the fruit of the pistachia-tree, is a small almond, that grows in the ground in a wrinkled shell. It is pleasant eating when roasted, but is hard of digestion. They cultivate it here, in order to extract oil for burning. This plant is a sort of phenomenon in botany, it being uncommon for vegetables that yield fruit of an unctuous nature, to bear them below the surface of the ground.

Chieves, leeks, and onions are all inferior to those in Europe, and even those in the Isle of Bourbon, which is so near.

Of vegetables in the flower-garden, I shall speak first of our own, and then of those in Asia and Africa.

The large daisy of China, tuberose and larksfoot, pinks of a small species, flourish here as in Europe; large pinks, and lillies bear a number of leaves, but seldom flowers. The anemony, ranunculus, Indian-pink, and rose, do not thrive with us, any more than the July-flower, or poppy. I saw no other flowers that we know of in Europe among the curious, except the above-mentioned. Many people have attempted, but in vain, to transplant hither, thyme, lavender, the field-daisy, violets, and wild-poppy, the red of which, with the azure of the blue-bell, so beautifully decorate our golden harvests. Oh! happy France! a corner of whose fields, is, in my eyes, more desirable, than the most beautiful garden this island affords.

Of those in Africa, I know but one, the *belle-immortelle* of the Cape, the seeds of which are as large and as red as strawberries, and grow in a cluster at the top of a stem, the leaves of which are like pieces of grey cloth; another *immortelle*, with purple flowers, grows all over the island; a reed, the size of a horse-hair, which bears a group of leaves, white in the inside, and violet-coloured without: at a distance, that bouquet appears in the air, it comes from the Cape, as does also a sort of tulip, bearing but two leaves, which lie upon the ground, and seem to adhere to it: a Chinese plant that sows itself, and bears little flowers like roses; upon its stem there are five or six, variegated alike, from a deep blood-red to the brightest scarlet. None of these flowers have any smell, and those which are known to have

have it in Europe, lose it on their being transplanted hither.

We have aloes in abundance. Their leaves turn to good account,—the sap of them afford a medicinal gum, and the threads are very fit for a manufacture of cloth. They grow upon the rocks, and in the parts scorched by the sun. The one grows out in leaves, strong, thick, and as large as a man, and is armed with a long shaft: from the center grows a stem as high as a tree, furnished with flowers, from which drops gum-aloes in a perfect state. The others are upright, like tapers, several spans high, and have a number of very sharp prickles about them: these last are marbled, and resemble serpents that crawl upon the ground.

Africans and Asiatics seem treated even by nature as barbarians, to whom she gives at once magnificent, yet monstrous vegetables, while we are dealt with as beings capable of sensibility and society. Oh! when shall I breath the perfumes of the honeysuckle? again repose myself upon a carpet of milk-weed, saffron, and blue-bells, the food of our lowing herds? and once more hear Aurora welcomed by the songs of the labourer, blessed with freedom and content!

Port, May 29. 1769.

LETTER XIV.

EXOTIC SHRUBS AND TREES.

HEDGES are made of the Rose-tree here, so well does it thrive, but the flowers are not so tufted, nor is the smell so fine as ours; there is of different sorts, among which, a small one from China, is in bloom all the year round. The jessamines of Spain and France are perfectly naturalized in this soil; those of Asia, I shall speak of in their place. There are pomegranate-trees with a double flower, and with fruit upon them, but they are good for little. The myrtle does not grow so beautiful here as in Provence. These are all the shrubs from Europe.

Asia, Africa, and America, give us the *Cassis* * with a scalloped leaf; it is not at all like ours, is a large shrub, overgrown with yellow flowers of a strong smell, that looks like small tufts: it yields a bean, with the grain of which they dye black. Being prickly, it makes good hedges.

Foulsapatte, signifies the *shoemaker's flower*; its flower rubbed upon leather, stains it black.

* Black currant bush. *E*

The

The foliage of this shrub is of a beautiful green, and larger than that of the yoke-elm; in the middle of which glitter the flowers like pinks, but of a deep red. They have nurseries of this shrub, of which there are various sorts.

Poincillade, is from America. It is a species of bramble, bearing girandoles of yellow and red flowers, from which shoot tufts of a flame-colour. This flower is very beautiful, but soon fades; it yields a bean. Its leaves are divided like that of all leguminous shrubs.

Jalop produces a flower in shape of a funnel, of a crimson red; they blow only in the night, and have a smell like the tuberose. I have seen two sorts of them.

Of the rattan from Madagascar they make cradles; it gives a yellow flower. Its downy leaves seem as if covered with meal.

Mougris is a jessamine, with a flower like the orange-tree. Some have double, and some single flowers, of a very agreeable smell.

Franchipanier is also a jessamine, that grows in the form of stagwood: from the extremity of these horns sprout bunches of long leaves, in the center of which are large white flowers, shaped like a funnel, and of a charming smell.

We grow the Indian *Lilach*, which dies soon; its leaf is scalloped, and of a beautiful green. It is loaded with clusters of flowers, which have a

 pleasant

pleasant smell enough, and turn to seed. This shrub rises to the height of a tree, and in a handsome form; its green is finer, but the flowers not so beautiful as those of our lilac, which does not grow here.

Our *Pepper-tree* is a rattan, or *lianne*, which creeps along the ground like ivy; it shoots well, but yields no fruit. It is not yet known whether the soil will agree with the tea-tree, which has been brought hither from China, as well as the rattan,—this last is used as commonly in India, as the osier is in Europe.

The *Cotton-tree* grows in most dry parts of the island, like a shrub, it bears a pretty yellow flower, to which succeeds a pod, containing the flocks. Cotton is not cultivated here, for want of mills to grind it: and till ground it is not an article of commerce

We have a species of the *Sugar-cane* which ripens in perfection; the inhabitants make an indifferent sort of liquor of it, which they call *flangourin*. There is but one sugar-house in the whole island

By far the most useful plant, of any that grows here, is the coffee-tree. It is a species of jessamine, its flower is white, leaves of fine green, shaped like laurel leaves, and are opposed to each other. Its fruit is a red olive, like a cherry, which separates into two beans. They plant them at seven feet and a half a-sunder, and when they grow as high as six feet, they crop them. It lives seven years

years only, and when three years old is in its prime. The annual produce of each tree is valued at one pound of berries. A black can attend to one thousand feet of these in a year, exclusive of what else he cultivates for his own subsistence. The island does not yet produce coffee enough for its own consumption. The inhabitants reckon it to be next to the Mocha coffee in quality.

The fir, the pine, and the oak from Europe, grow to a middling stature, and then decay. I have also seen here cherry, apricot, medlar, apple, pear, olive, and mulberry-trees; but without fruit, though some of them had flowers. The fig-tree produces a tolerable fruit. The vine does not succeed upon props; but when in arbours, bears grapes, which, like those in the gardens of Alcinous, ripen one part after another: a good vintage cannot therefore be expected. The peach-tree gives fruit enough, and well tasted, but they are never luscious. There is a white louse that destroys them.

Burying these trees, which are constantly full of sap, in the ground, might perhaps be of use to retard their vegetation. It is as necessary here to protect them from heat, as from the cold in the North of Germany. These trees lose their leaves in what is called the cold season, that is, when it is summer with you; notwithstanding, the heat and moisture are equal to what you have in the spring: there must therefore be some latent cause of vegetation of which we are ignorant.

Such foreign trees, as are brought here for curiosity

riosity only, are the laurel, which thrives very well; as does also the *Agathis* of various sorts, the leaves of which are scalloped; it bears bunches of flowers, white and streaked, to which succeed long leguminous pods. The Chinese frequently represent this shrub in their landscapes.

In Europe the fruits of the same tree are ripe nearly at the same time; here it is quite the contrary, they grow ripe in a regular succession; which causes a remarkable difference in the taste of fruits gathered from one and the same tree.

From India we have the *Polche*, its foliage is tufted, the leaf is in the shape of an heart. It affords a pleasant shade, and answers no other purpose, its fruit being sticky and good for nothing. —It is in the form of a medlar.

At some distance the bambou looks like our willow. 'Tis a reed which grows as high as the tallest trees, and shoots out branches, furnished with leaves like those of the olive: They make the most delightful avenues, in which the wind murmurs incessantly. It grows fast, and its canes may be applied to the same uses as the branches of osier. There are many India pictures in which this reed is badly enough represented

Our fruit-trees are chiefly the *Attier*, whose triangular flower, of a solid substance, tastes like the pistachia; its fruit is like a pine-apple: when it is ripe it is full of a white and sweetish cream, which smells like the orange-flower. It is full of black kernels: the *Atte* is very pleasant, but being very heating, soon cloys, and gives a pain in the stomach to those who eat it.

A very beautiful tree, is the mango: The Indians often represent it upon their painted silks. It is covered with superb girandoles of flowers, like the Indian chesnut. To these succeed a great number of fruits, shaped like a large flat plumb, covered with a rind which smells like turpentine. This fruit has a vinous and agreeable taste; and, but for its smell, might vie with the best fruit of Europe. It is never prejudicial to those who eat it, and I should think, a wholesome and pleasant drink might be made from it. This tree has one inconvenience attending it—being covered with fruit at the time of the hurricanes, which strip it of the greater part

Every where we find the banana-tree. It has no wood, or stock; being only a tuft of flowers, which spring up in columns, and blow at the top in large and long leaves, of a beautiful sattiny green. At the end of a year, their issues from the summit a long stem, all hung with fruit in the form of a cucumber; two of these stems are a load for a black; this fruit, which is mealy, is also pleasant and very nutritive. The blacks are very fond of it; and it is given to them on the first of January, as a new year's gift; they count their years of sorrow by the number of banana feasts they have regaled at. Linen cloth might be made of the thread of the banana-tree. The shape of the leaves like belts of silk, the length of its stem, the upper part of which hangs down from the height of a man, and whose violet-colour at the end, gives it the

the look of a serpent's head, may have occasioned its being called by the name of Adam's fig-tree. This fruit lasts all the year; there are many sorts of it; from the size of a plumb, to the length of a man's arm.

Something like a medlar is the gouyava-tree. Its flower is white, and its fruit smells like a bug. It is astringent, and is the only fruit of this country, in which I have found worms.

We are afforded a very fine shade by the jam rose, though it does not grow high. It bears a fruit of a smell like a rose-bud, and of a sweetish, but insipid taste.

Papa, is a fig-tree without branches. It grows fast, and rises like a pillar, with a capital of large leaves. From its trunk shoots out a fruit like a small melon, of an indifferent taste; the seeds taste like cresses. The body of this tree is of a substance like a turnip The female *Papa* bears flowers, only; in form and smell as agreeable as the honey-suckle.

The form of the *Badamier* seems calculated purposely for shade. It rises like a very fine pyramid, in different stories, distinct and separate from each other. Its foliage is very fine, and it yields almonds which are well tasted.

The *Avocat* is a beautiful tree. It bears a pear which incloses a large stone, of a substance like butter. When it is seasoned with sugar and citron

citron juice, it is not bad to eat; though it is heating.

Jaca exhibits a sweet foliage, but the fruit it bears is abominable. 'Tis as big as a large pumpkin, and has a rind that is green and shagreened all over. It is full of seeds; the outside, which is a white skin, sweet and clammy, is good to eat, but has an ugly smell, like that of rotten cheese. This fruit is aphrodisiac, and our women are passionately fond of it.

Our *Tamarind-tree* has a beautiful head; its leaves are opposed to each other on one side, and close at night, like most other leguminous plants. Its pod contains a mucilage which makes excellent lemonade.

Among orange-trees, which are of many sorts, is one yielding an orange called a *mandarine*. A large kind of *Pamplemousse*, of a red colour, and but middling taste. A citron that bears very large fruit, but with little juice in it.

Our *Cocoa-tree* is a kind of palm, which thrives in the sand. This is one of the most useful trees in the Indian trade, though it affords nothing else than a bad sort of oil, and cables as bad in their kind. It is reckoned at Pondicherry that each cocoa-tree is worth a pistole a year. Travellers speak much in praise of its fruit; but our flax will ever be preferred to cotton, for making cloth, our wines to its liquors, and our filberds to its nut.

It

It prospers so much better near salt-works, that salt is always put in the hole, wherein the fruit is sown, to facilitate the blowing of the bud or shaddock *. The cocoa seems designed to float in the sea, by the wad which surrounds it, and helps to bear it up, and by the hardness of its shell, is impenetrable to the water It does not open by a joint, as our nuts do, but the juice comes out at one of the three orifices which Nature has contrived at its extremity, and has afterwards covered with a cuticle. Cocoa-trees have been found upon the borders of the sea in desart islands, and even upon shoals of sand. This, is the kind of palm which fringes the banks of the rivers between the tropics, as the fir does those of the north, and the date, those of the burning mountains of Palestine.

Am I mistaken in alledging, that the cocoa is calculated to float upon the sea, and to sow itself afterwards in the sands. Every seed has its own peculiar method of propagating itself; but an investigation of this matter, would make me digress too much from the subject. I may, perhaps some day or other undertake it, and when ever I do, it will be with delight. † The studie of Nature

* In those parts of the East-Indies, where fish are plenty, a quantity of the refuse of them is laid about the bottom of every cocoa-tree. But this practice is very prejudicial to the health of the inhabitants;—the island of Bombay was the most unwholesome of all our settlements, till a stop was put to the corruption of the air by this animal putrefaction, and the natives now have recourse to some less pestiferous manure for their cocoa-trees. *E.*

† This may be considered as a promise of what has been since so very ably performed by our author in his masterly *Studies*

Nature compensates for our disappointments in the study of mankind, as we cannot but trace throughout the whole, the harmony with which intelligence and beneficence unite to render the system compleat. But if it were possible that we should be deceived even in this;—if all things by which mankind is surrounded, were combined to distract him; at least, let our errors be errors of our own choosing, and let us give the preference to those which afford consolation, rather than excite disgust.

Such as conceit that Nature, in raising so high the heavy fruit of the cocoa-tree, has lost sight of that law which decrees the pumpkin to creep upon the ground, do not consider that the head of the cocoa-tree is but small, and can therefore afford but little shade. 'Tis under the leaves of the oak, men seek a shelter from the sun's scorching rays. Why not rather observe, that in India, as in Europe, those trees which bear a mellow fruit, are but of a middling height, that in falling they may not be destroyed; on the contrary, those producing fruit of a hard nature, as the cocoa, chesnut, acorn, and nut, are lofty, their fruit being not liable to be damaged by falling to the ground? Moreover, the trees that are furnished

Studies of Nature: a work which, apart from those eccentricities and paradoxes so very characteristic of the genius of his countrymen; for luminous imagry, accurate observation, picturesque beauty, and sublime devotion, has no paralell among the French writers of the present century, posterior to the days, at least, of the good Fenelon, and the romantic Citizen of Geneva. Whoever would view the creation as the genuine vehicle of divine intelligence, will find a rich *fund of sound* instruction in the *Studies of Nature*.

with

with a number of leaves, yield as well in India as in Europe, a desirable shelter without danger. There are some, as for instance, the *Jaca*, which bears fruits of a very great size; but then they bear them near to the trunk, and within reach of the hand: thus, Nature, which man is ever accusing of imprudence, has contrived with equal bounty for his shelter, and his nourishment.

At the foot of the cocoa-tree a kind of crab has been lately discovered to burrow. Nature has provided this animal with a long claw, at the end of which is a nail, serving to extract the substance of the fruit by the holes I have described. It has not the large pincers of other crabs, they would be useless to it. This animal is found upon the isle of Palms, to the northward of Madagascar, discovered in 1769, by the shipwreck of the *Heureux*, which was lost there in going to Bengal.

There is just discovered in the isle of *Sechelle*, a tree bearing double cocoa-nuts, some of which weigh upwards of forty pounds. The Indians attribute great virtues to it. They believe it to be a production of the sea, because the currents formerly threw some of them upon the coast of Malabar. They call it the *sea-cocoa*. This fruit, *mulieris corporis bifurcationem cum natura & pilis repræsentat*. Its leaf, shaped like a fan, will cover half a house. Order is observable in every work of nature—the tree which bears this enormous fruit, bears three or four only at the most: the common cocoa-tree bears bunches of more than thirty; I have tasted both, and think their flavour very much

much alike. They have planted the sea-cocoa in the Isle of France, and it begins to bud.

There are still some other trees, which though curious, are of little or no use, as the *Date*, which seldom bears fruit; the *palm*, which is called here the *Araque*; and that which produces *sago*. The *Caneficier*, and the *Cushoe*, bear flowers, but no fruit. The *Canellier*, of which I have seen whole avenues, has the semblance of a pear-tree in growth and leaves. Its little bunches of flowers smell like excrement. Its cinnamon has very little of the aromatic. There is only one *cacao-tree** in the island; and the fruits of this never ripen. They should bring hither the *muscabine* and the *clove*. Time will decide as to the success of these trees, transplanted from under the line to 20 deg. of latitude.

Not long ago were planted here, layers of the *Ravinesara*, a species of the *muscadiae* of Madagascar; of the *Mangoustan* and the *Litchi*, which are said to produce the finest fruit in the world; the *Vernis*, whence is extracted an oil to preserve furniture; the tallow-wood, whose seeds are impregnated with a kind of wax; a tree from China, which bears citrons in bunches, like raisins; the silver tree of the Cape; and lastly, the *Tecque* wood, nearly equal to the oak for building of ships. The greater part of these trees vegetate on this island with difficulty.

This climate seems too cold for the trees of Asia, and too hot for those of Europe. Pliny ob-

* The tree of whose fruit chocolate is made. *E.*

serves, that the temperament of the air is more necessary for the culture of plants, than the qualities of the soil; and says, that in his time, pepper and citron-trees were seen in Italy, and incense trees in Lybia; but that they merely vegetated. I am however of opinion, that the coffee-tree might be naturalized in the south of France, for it delights in a cool and temperate air. These expensive experiments can scarcely be carried on by any but princes; and yet, the acquisition of one plant unknown before, is a circumstance, by which a whole nation may be benefited. To what purpose have been all the wars upon our continent? Of what consequence is it now-a-days, that Mithridates was once conquered by the Romans, and Montezuma by the Spaniards unless some benefit accrue? Europe might, with reason, weep over her unprofitable trophies; but whole provinces in Germany subsist upon potatoes brought from America, and our fair ladies are indebted for the cherries they eat, to Lucullus. The desert was indeed costly; but for this, our fore-fathers paid. Let us be wiser—let us collect together the good things which Nature has scattered abroad.

Should bodily labour ever become necessary to my health, I will make a garden after the Chinese fashion;—the situation they delight in, is on the banks of a river;—they chuse an irregular piece of ground, on which are old trees, large rocks, and rising hills. They form round it a boundary of rugged rocks, placed upon one another, so that their junctures cannot be perceived. Hereon grow clumps of *scolopendria*, tendrils with blue and

and purple flowers, and borders of moss of different colours. A stream of water meanders among these vegetables, whence it escapes in cascades. Health and enjoyment are diffused over such a spot as this, while the European's garden presents with no other view but that of a dreary brick-wall.

They turn all the hollow grounds into pieces of water, which they stock with fish, surrounded with banks of turf, and plant with trees. They are particularly careful that no level spot or strait line shall appear; nor any masonry; How often does the fancied skill of the artist, mar the simplicity of Nature's handy work?

Tufts of flowers, and walks of green sod, in which fruit-trees are planted, diversify the plain. The sides of the hills are variegated with clumps of shrubs, some bearing fruit, others flowers; the summit is crowned with trees, whose spreading branches afford a pleasing retreat from the parching rays of the sun.

No strait walks in these delightful gardens force upon every object at once; but winding paths which throw open to your view in an agreeable succession, are every where preferred. Nor are their objects, statues, or vases, useless, as they are large;—but a vine bending under a load of ripening grapes, and adorned with rose-bushes, and other flowers: the mind is at the same time delighted with a sonnet or epigram upon the bark of an orange-tree—or a philosophical maxim upon a piece of broken rock.

My garden is not an orchard—a park—a lawn—but an agreeable assemblage of them all;—It is itself a country, with hills, woods, and plains, where each object contributes to the perfection of the whole. A Chinese has no more idea of a regular garden, than he has of cutting a flowering shrub into the squared form of a chest of tea.

There is no leaving, it is said, these delightful retreats, but with a kind of regret; for my part, I would enhance the pleasures of them, by the society of an amiable woman, and by having in my neighbourhood such a friend as yourself.

Port, July 10, 1769.

LETTER XV.

ANIMALS IMPORTED.

FOR the improvement of this colony, even foreign fish have been imported; the *Gourami* comes from Batavia, it is a fresh-water fish, like a salmon, but of a finer flavour, being reckoned the best fish that is eaten in India. The Chinese goldfish is brought here, but loses its beauty as it increases in bulk. These two species breed very fast in the ponds and lakes.

We have attempted, but without success, even to bring frogs here, that they might eat the eggs which the musquito lays upon the surface of the standing waters.

A bird, however, from the Cape, is of infinite service. They call it the gardener's friend. It is brown,—the size of a large sparrow, and lives upon worms, snails, and small serpents, which it not only eats when pressed by hunger, but makes an ample store of them, by sticking them upon the prickles of the hedges. I have seen but one of them; which, though deprived of its liberty, retained the manners of its kind, and suspended

 the

the meat which was given it, upon the wires of its cage.

The martin has multiplied very fast in the island. It is a species of the Indian *sansonnet**, with a yellow beak and claws, It differs but little from ours, except in plumage, which is less spotted. In chirping, however, as well as in an aptitude to talk, and to mimic other birds, it perfectly resembles the European. It will perch upon, and peck at beasts without fear; but the prey it pursues with an unwearied perseverance, is the grass-hopper, numbers of which species are destroyed by it. The martins always fly in pairs, and assemble constantly at sun-set in flocks of some thousands. After a general chirping, the whole republic fall asleep, and at day-break, again disperse by pairs to the different quarters of the island. This bird is not fit to eat; yet they are sometimes shot, though shooting them is prohibited. Plutarch relates, that the lark was adored at Lemnos, because it eat and destroyed the grass-hoppers eggs: but we are not Grecians.

Many ravens have been let loose in the woods to destroy rats and mice. Three cocks are all that are left of them. The people accused them of killing their fowls, and in this were at once accusers, judges, and executioners.

* Called by some the Starling, by others the Fiskin. *E.*

The

The Cape-bird does much execution, it is a species of small *tarin**, and is the only inhabitant of these forests that is heard to sing. They were brought here first as curiosities, but some of them escaped to the woods, where they breed very fast, and live upon the spoils of the harvest. Government gives a reward to any body that kills one.

We have a beautiful titmouse, with a number of white specks on the wings; and the cardinal, whose head, neck, and belly, at a particular season, are of a lively red; the rest of its plumage is of a pearl-coloured grey.—This bird comes from Bengal.

Here are three sorts of partridges, all smaller than those of Europe. The cry of the male resembles that of a cock when hoarse; they roost at night upon the trees, for fear of the rats.

Some *pintadoes*†, and Chinese pheasants, are put in the woods, and into the lakes some geese and wild ducks: They have also tame ducks here, especially the Manilla ones, which are very beautiful; and European barn-door fowls; a species of fowl from Africa, whose flesh and bone are black; a small species of fowl from China, the cocks of which are very fierce and bold, and for ever a fighting with the

* A kind of lark,—a bird well known in France, and admired for its song, and aptitude to talk. *E.*

† So called by the Spaniards, from the beauty of its plumage, which seems as if painted. It is believed by some to be the *Storm Bird*, or *Procellaria Capensis*. *E.*

Indian cocks. I saw one of them attack a large Manilla duck, which seized the little champion with its beak, and smothered it with its belly and claws: and although the cock is sometimes drawn half dead from this perilous situation, it will return to the charge with redoubled fury.

Some folks make a great deal of money of their poultry, on account of the scarcity of other provisions. Pigeons succeed well, and are the best birds of flight in the island. They have also brought two species of turtles, and of hares.

Wild goats, wild hogs, and especially stags, are found in our woods, which had multiplied to such a degree, that whole squadrons were supplied with venison for provisions. Their flesh is very good, especially during the months of April, May, June, July and August. Some of them have been taken when young, and brought up tame; but they will not breed in that state.

Our domestic quadrupeds are sheep, that fatten and lose their wool, goats that thrive prodigiously, and oxen of the Madagascar breed, that have a great wen upon their neck; the cows of this breed give but very little milk; those from Europe give much more, but their calves degenerate. I saw once, two cows and two bulls from Bengal, which were no bigger than an ass. This breed did not succeed.

We

We can seldom get any butchers meat. Pork is the substitute on these occasions, and is better than ours in Europe; notwithstanding which, it will not salt to keep, on account of the salt's being too sharp or acid. The female of this animal, is subject in this island to bring forth monsters. I was once shewn a little pig, preserved in spirits, the snout of which was produced in the manner of an elephant's trunk.

Our horses are by no means fine, and very dear. A common horse cannot be bought for less than a hundred pistoles. They fall to decay very soon at the Port, from the excessive heat. They never are shod, though the island is so rocky. Mules are rarely seen. The asses are small, and but few in number. The ass would be a truly useful animal in this country, as it would lighten the severe labours of the poor negroes. Every load, how heavy soever, is carried on the heads of the slaves.

A little while ago, two beautiful wild asses were brought from the Cape, a male and female, —they were of the size of a mule, and striped on the shoulders like the zebra, from which, however, they differed in other respects. These animals, though young, were not to be tamed.

Cats degenerate greatly on this island, they grow lean and thin flanked. The rats scarcely fear them,—the dogs are therefore the rat-catchers, and my favorite has often distinguished

himself

himself in this service. I have seen him strangle the largest rat of the southern hemisphere. The dogs at the long run, lose their hair and their sense of smelling; but it is said they never go mad!

Port, July. 15, 1769.

LET-

LETTER XVI.

TOUR THROUGH THE ISLAND.

IT was proposed to me some time since by Monsieur de Chazal, counsellor, and M. le Marquis d'Albergaty, both of them fond of natural history, to go and see a famous cavern about a league and a half from hence. We embarked upon the Great River, which, like the other rivers of this island, is not navigable for sloops, above a musquet shot from its mouth. A small settlement is established there, consisting of an hospital and a few store-houses; and here also begins the aquæduct that supplies the town with water. Upon a little height, in the form of a sugar-loaf, there is a kind of fort to defend the bay.

Having passed the Great River, we took a guide, and walked through the woods westward, for near three quarters of an hour. It was not long before we came to the entrance of the cavern, which seemed like the hole of a cave, the vault of which had fallen in. Many roots of the *mapou* grow perpendicularly down it, and bar up a part of the entrance. The head of an ox was nailed in the center.

 Before

Before we descended this abyss we thought it prudent to breakfast. After which, we lighted flambeaux and candles, and furnished ourselves with tinder-boxes to strike fire, if necessary.

Upon going about a dozen paces down the rocks at the mouth of it, we found ourselves in a vast, and far more spacious cave than I had ever seen before.

It is an immense vault, formed of a black rock.

The width of it was about thirty feet, and its height twenty.

We found the soil to be solid, very adhesive, and covered with a fine earth.

By each side of the cavern, about breast-high, extends a large fillet with mouldings, which I suppose to be the work of the waters, which flow down in the rainy season, of different heights; the land, as well as river shells that we saw here, confirm this conjecture. Yet the country people fancy it to be the ancient crater of the volcano. It rather appeared to me as having been the bed of some subterranean river.

The roof is vaulted on a great scale, and covered with a sort of dry shining varnish, or stony concretion, which extends itself to the sides, and in some places, even to the floor of the cave, and forms thereon ferruginous stalactites,

tites, which broke and crackled under our feet, as if we had been walking upon frozen snow.

As we walked on for some time, we found the soil perfectly dry, except at about three hundred paces from the entrance, where a part of the roof is mouldered away. The water had oozed through in this place, and had settled in different parts of the ground beneath.

The roof gradually lowered from thence, till we were at length obliged to go upon our hands and knees; being almost stifled with heat, I would go no farther. My companions being more curious, more active, and in a proper deshabille, continued their route.

I discovered on our return a plant about the size of my finger, which hung to the roof by very small filaments. It was more than ten feet long had neither branches nor leaves, nor did it appear to have ever had either. It was unbroken at both ends, and was filled with a kind of milky juice.

We came back to the entrance of the grotto, and sat down to breathe the fresh air, and in a little time I heard an inarticulate noise, and then by the light of the flambeaux carried in the Negroes hands, saw my fellow-travellers returning in their caps, shirts, and drawers, so dirty and so red, that they looked like so many actors in an English tragedy. They were bathed in sweat, and all besmeared with this red earth, over which they had crawled upon their bellies, without

without being able to go much farther than I had done.

Such a commodious cavern as this, which chokes and fills up daily, might surely be turned to use. Methinks, magnificent store-houses might be constructed, by making partition-walls to keep out the water.

On the evening we returned home. This excursion made me desirous of another. I had been invited on my first arrival by Monsieur de Messin, who lives about seven leagues from Port-Louis, upon the Black River, to spend some days at his house. As his pirogue came every week to Port-Louis, I took the opportunity of going in her on her return.—The pirogue is a kind of boat cut out of a single piece of wood, and goes either with oars or sails.

We sailed at midnight, and in about half an hour got out of the harbour. The sea ran high, and dashed with great violence upon the breakers, over which we were several times driven by the surf, without knowing it. The night being very dark, the master told me he would land, as he thought it dangerous to proceed till day-light.

We scarcely had gone a league and a half, when the blacks carried me to shore on their shoulders; after which they took two pieces of wood, one of *veloutier*, the other of *bambou*, and kindled a light by rubbing them together. This practice is very ancient; Pliny tell us, it was in use among the Romans, and that nothing is so fit for

for the purpose of striking fire, as a piece of ivy-wood rubbed against the laurel.

These poor creatures with great good humour seated themselves round the fire, smoaking their pipes, which are a kind of crucible at the end of a long reed, and which they hand to one another as they sit. I gave them some *eau-de-vie,* then wrapping myself in my cloak, went to sleep on the sand.

They called me by five in the morning to go on board again. The day breaking, I saw the tops of the mountains covered with thick clouds, which blew along at a great rate; the weather was hazy, and the wind drove the fog along the vallies; the main sea grew white with foam, and the pirogue, carrying both her sails, made great way

When we came to that part of the coast called *flicq-en-flacq*, about a league and a half from land, we found a prodigious short and broken sea, with squalls of wind, so violent as to oblige us to down both our sails. The master said to me in his Patois jargon, "*C'a n'est pas bon, Monsié.*" I asked him, if there was any danger, he answered me twice, "*Si nons n'a pas gagné matheur, ça bon.*"—In short he told me, that a fortnight before, the pirogue had overset, and drowned one of his comrades.

We were now on a lee-shore, so covered with rocks, that there was no possibility of landing; and had we passed the island, we could not have made

made it again without the utmost difficulty. As we could not carry sail, the men took to their oars. The sky grew more and more lowring, which made it necessary to hasten as much as possible. The men having drank some *eau-de-vie*, pulled stoutly, and by dint of arms, and at the risk of being twenty times overset, we once more got into tolerable smooth water, and coasted along between the shore and the breakers.

The blacks were as easy and unconcerned during the whole storm, as if they had been safe on shore. Their belief in predestination, and their indifference for life, gives them a tranquillity, which all our boasted philosophy can never attain.

About nine in the morning I landed at the mouth of the Great River: M. de Messin was agreeably surprized at the arrival of his pirogue, which he did not expect that day, and received me with the utmost cordiality. His estate includes all the valley through which the river flows. It is imperfectly described in the chart drawn by the *Abbé de le Caille*; he has omitted a branch of the mountain, on the right-hand shore, which extends towards the promontory *du Tamur*. Moreover, the course of the river is not so strait as he represents it, for at a short league's distance from the mouth, it turns to the left hand. This learned astronomer having given us a description of the out-line only of the island, I propose to make additions to his plan*, according as the

* I wish the author had furnished us with this plan *E.*

information

information I procure in these excursions may furnish me with opportunity.

Great plenty of every thing is found at Black River; of game, venison, and both fresh water and sea-fish. While we were at dinner one day, a servant came to tell us that some *lamentins** were seen in the bay, we ran down immediately; they cast nets across the entrance, and when drawn ashore, we found a great quantity of the sword-fish, of skait, two sea-turtles, and other kinds of fish; but the lamentins were escaped.

Much good order prevails in this, as in every other plantation I have been at. The negroes cabbins are ranged in lines, like tents in a camp. Each man has a small piece of ground allotted him for growing tobacco and gourds;—flocks and poultry, are bred in great numbers upon these plantations. The harvests are plentiful, but receive great damage from the swarms of grass-hoppers.

Commodities from thence to the town, is inconvenient and hazardous, it being impossible for a carriage of any burden to get along by land, the roads are so bad; and the wind being in general contrary on the voyage from thence to the Port.

Having tarried only a few days, I determined to return to town by a tour over the plains *de Villiams*; for this purpose my host furnished me with

* A kind of sea-cow.

a guide, and a pair of pistols, lest I should meet with any of the * Maron negroes.

In the afternoon I set out for Palma, the plantation of M. de Cossigni, about three leagues off, where I proposed to lay that night: there being none but foot-paths over the rocks, I was obliged to walk. When I had gone over the mountains of Black River, I found myself in a vast forest, through which a narrow path only is grubbed up, and which passes close by a lonely house, the solitary retreat of a man, who in France had squandered a considerable fortune, and who now drags on a wretched and miserable life in this gloomy desart, without property; the land round his house not being his own, and without society, except that of a few negroes, his slaves. As I passed, he was sitting at his door, in his shirt and drawers only, with his legs naked and his sleeves tucked up, diverting himself with rubbing a monkey with the juice of red mulberries, himself being all over smeared therewith.

* The Dutch who came here in the year 1638, upon forming a settlement, found themselves in want of slaves, for the cultivation of their lands, and applied to the French, who were settled on the island of Madagascar, to supply them with some of the natives from thence for this purpose. The French complied, and sold them fifty, whom they had taken by force from among the inhabitants. These, exasperated at the outrage, attacked, and massacred the invaders.—The poor people who had been sent to the Mauritius, fled from their servitude to the woods, from whence they made such continual incursions upon their former masters, that at length they determined to quit the place, rather than be subject to the dangers which constantly attended them. The slaves were now the sole occupiants of the island; such of their progeny as escaped the vigilance of Monsieur de la Bourdonnais, are the Maron Negroes.

About

About half an hour's walk from thence brought me to the side of Tamarind River, whose waters flowed with a loud noise over a bed of rocks. My black found a ford, and carried me over upon his shoulders. I saw before me the mountain of three paps, which rose to a very great height, and on the other side was the plantation of Palma. My guide persuaded me to go along the side of this mountain, assuring me that we could not fail of finding the path that led to the top. We got quite round it, after having walked above an hour: but seeing the man was at a loss, I returned immediately, and again reached the foot of the mountain, before the sun was set. I was much fatigued, and very thirsty, and could I have got water, would have passed the night there. But I determined otherwise, and though there was no sign of a path, began to ascend the mountain through the woods, being sometimes forced to clamber over huge rocks, or to drag myself along by the trees, and at others, being supported by my black servant, who came after me. I had not walked half an hour, before night came on, and was then without guide, except the steepness of the mountain. Not a breath of wind was stirring, the air was intensely hot, and ready to faint with heat, fatigue, and thirst, I lay down several times, determining to stay all night where I was. At length, after an infinite deal of trouble, I perceived that I ascended no longer. Soon after, a breeze from the south-east refreshed me exceedingly, and the appearance of some lights at a distance, afforded me an additional comfort. The side I had quitted was inveloped in total darkness.

Descending I frequently slid down upon my back, without being able to prevent it. The noise of a rivulet was my only guide, and I at length reached it, very much bruised. Though in a violent perspiration, I drank heartily; and having felt herbage under my hand, had the additional good fortune to find some water-cresses, of which I ate several handfuls. I continued to approach the fire I saw before me, carrying my pistols ready cocked in my hand, fearing I might find an assembly of Maron negroes; but it proved to be a part of the wood that was lately cleared, in which there were several trunks of trees still burning. No body was near. I halloo'd, and listened, in hopes at last to hear the barking of a dog,—but in vain, no other sounds were to be heard, than the distant murmurs of the brook, and the whistling of the wind among the trees.

The black with my guide kindled some brands, by the light of which we walked over the ashes of this burning wood, towards another fire a little farther. Here we found three negroes watching some flocks, that belonged to a neighbour of M. de Cossigni. One of them conducted me to Palma. It was now midnight, and every body was fast asleep. A negroe, whom our noise had awakened, informed me that his master was abroad; he, however, offered me all the accommodation the house afforded. I rose early in the morning, intending to go to Mr. Jacob's, who lived about two leagues off upon the high grounds of Williams-plains; a fine broad road being cleared all the way to his house, I soon arrived there, and was received with his usual hospitality.

Here

Here the atmosphere is so much colder than at the Port, and the place I had just left, that I found the fire-side the best situation towards evening. This part is the best cultivated of any in the whole island, and is watered by several rivulets, some of which, especially one they call the Deep River, runs in beds of a depth frightful to look down. The road from hence to town running close by the side of this river, on my return I observed it particularly, and suppose I could not be less than three hundred feet above its channel. The sides are covered by five or six stories of very large trees, rising one above another; a sight which gave me a violent swimming in my head.

The nearer we approached the town, I perceived the heat of the air increase, and the herbage insensibly lose its verdure, till I reached the Port, where every thing is dry and barren.

Port, Aug. 15, 1769

LETTER XVII.

JOURNEY ON FOOT OVER THE ISLAND.

A MILITARY gentleman had proposed to me a tour round the island on foot, but just before we were to have set out, excused himself from going—I therefore determined to go alone.

I placed the utmost confidence on *Côte*, one of the King's blacks, who had accompanied me before; he was little, but he was very strong, of approved fidelity, sober, of few words, and fearless of danger.

A slave, whom I had recently bought, I called by your name, hoping it would be an omen in his favour. He could not speak French, nor was his constitution healthy; but he was well made, and of a very decent appearance.

My dog I took with me by way of guard in the night, and to look out for game in the day time.

Aware

Aware I should be very often alone, and that these woods were without inns, I provided every thing which I thought might be necessary for myself or my people. My baggage weighed two hundred pounds, and consisted of a kettle, some plates, a quantity of rice, biscuit, maize, a dozen of wine, six bottles of *eau-de-vie*, some butter, sugar, citrons, salt, tobacco, a small hammock, linen, a plan of the island, some books, a sabre, and a cloak.

These were divided into four packs, two of sixty pounds, and two of forty; and got them tied to the ends of two very strong reeds. *Côte* took the heaviest, and *Duval* the other. I, for my part, was in my waistcoat, and carried a double-barrelled gun, a pair of pistols in my pocket, and my *couteau de chasse.*

My plan was to begin my course on the leeward-side of the island, proposing to keep constantly close to the shore, that I might form a a judgment of its defence, and to make observations upon any objects of natural history which might present themselves.

With his usual good-natured complaisance, M. de Chazel offered to accompany me as far as his estate, situated five leagues from the town, in the plains of *Saint Peter*, and M. le Marquis d'Albergati, agreed to do the like.

It was early in the morning of the 26 of August we set out, and we went all the way along the shore. From *Fort-Blanc*, to the left of the Port, the sea washes a sandy strand, that is not at all steep, till it gets to the point of a plain, on which *Paulm* battery is raised; though this shore is level, a descent would be impracticable, on account of a long bank of rocks, which run along shore at two musquet-shots distance, and form a natural defence. From this place the shore becomes steep, and the sea runs so high, that it would be impossible to land hereabouts; and it would be equally impossible for cavalry or artillery to make good their landing upon the plain, because of the rocks with which it is covered all over. There are no trees, except a few *mapous* and *veloutiers*. The shore is no longer steep at *Little-River Bay*, where there is a small battery.

At this stage we dined with M. de Seligny, a man of singular merit. He shewed us the plan of a machine, by which he cut a canal to the Neptune, a ship that was run aground here in the hurricane, in 1700. They were two iron rakes, put in motion by two large wheels that were supported upon barges; and whose effect was increased by levers, again supported by rafts.

He also shewed us a cotton-mill of his own invention, which was worked by water. It was formed of a number of small metal cylinders, in a parallel position to each other. Children are taught to hold the cotton to two of these cylinders, the cotton passes and the seed remains. This same mill answered the purpose of a pair of bellows to a forge—to grind meal, and to make oil. He informed us, that he had discovered a vein of coal, some iron ore of an earth very proper for making crucibles,

crucibles, and that the cinders, which are called *nymphea,* burnt with coal, produced glasses of a variety of colours. In the afternoon we took leave of this useful and unrequited member of society.

The tract we pursued was about a musquet-shot from the shore, and having forded the river *Belleisle,* whose mouth is very narrow, after walking about a quarter of a league we entered a wood, which leads to M. de Chazal's house. This estate, which is called *St. Peter*'s *Plains,* is still more rocky, than the rest of the way. In many places, the negroes were obliged to lay down their burdens, and to assist us to clamber. When we were within half an hour's walk of our journey's end, *Duval,* being no longer able to stand under his load, was obliged to lay it down. We were much perplexed by this accident; for night was coming on, and the other negroes were gone before. How was he to be found again if we left him in these woods? I struck a light with the lock of my gun, and kindled a fire with some straw and dry sticks; after which we left *Duval* there, and when got home, we sent some blacks to seek for him, and bring his packs.

Between the *Little River* and *St. Peter*'s *Plains* the shore is very steep and craggy. My companions found among the rock the purple-fish of Panama, and a variety of other shell-fish.

We rested the whole day, August 27. This stony soil is well enough adapted to the culture of cotton, the thread of which is but short. The coffee that

that grows here is of a good quality, but yields very little, as usual, in dry places.

We set out at 8 o'clock the 28, in the morning, and in the course of our journey forded the rivers *Dragon* and *Galet*, at the last of which the shore ceases to be steep; and we had from thence the pleasure of walking upon a fine sand by the sea-side, along a large plain, which leads as far as the bay of *Tamarinds*. It may be about a quarter of a league broad, and more than a league long. Nothing grows upon it: but I think cocoa trees might be planted to advantage, as shey thrive in a sandy soil. To the right, there is a stream of bad water, running the length of the whole wood.

In such parts as the sea has left dry, we found some fossil madrepores, which prove that the sea once washed over this shore. We dined upon the right-side of Tamarind Bay, and then my companions left me, and returned back.

I had but a short league from Black River to M. Messin's, and therefore resolved to sleep there that night. I forded the bay of Tamarinds, and from thence kept along the shore with more difficulty and fatigue than I expected: being very steep and craggy all the way 'till we got to Black River. Among these rocks I found many sorts of *crabs*, and the same kind of *boudins* that I have spoken of before.

This bay is bottomed in sand, and a landing might be effected here, if the situation at the entrance

trance did not subject those who attempted it to a cross-firing. A battery at the point of the sand, on the right shore of the Black River, would be of great service.

I continued the 29 and 30 my walk along the shore at low water. I found the great *conch*, and a fish called the *faux-amiral.*

I set off the 31 at six in the morning, and passed the Black River at a ford, near the house; after this, attempting to cut across a kind of island covered with wood and stones, I bewildered myself in the grass, and had some difficulty to find the path again; at last, however, I did, and it brought me to the sea-side again. All along this shore the oysters stick to the rocks in great numbers: *Duval*, my new servant, in walking across one of the mouths of the Black River, got a very deep cut in his foot, by one of their shells. We made a halt about eight o'clock in the morning, and I gave him some *eau-de-vie* for *Côte* and himself to drink, and to bathe his wound. As they were heavily laden, I thought it proper to make two halts in a day, to confine my walks to the morning and evening, and to give them all the refreshment I could. This little indulgence gave them strength and spirits—they would have followed me to the end of the world.

A stag, pursued by hounds and hunters, came strait towards me, between the two mouths of Black River. The poor beast wept and panted: as I could not save it, and was unwilling to kill it, I fired one of my charges in the air. He then took

took to the water, and was overtaken and killed by the dogs. Pliny observes, that this animal, when pressed by the hounds, will fly for protection to a man. I stopped at the first rivulet I came to, after having passed the Black River; it runs into the sea opposite to a little island, called *Tamarind*'s *Isle*, which is not described upon the chart; one may get to it on foot at low water, as also to the little island, called *Morne*, where vessels sometimes perform quarantine.

Here every thing was provided for dinner, but something to eat. Seeing a pirogue of a Malabar fisherman pass along the coast, I asked them if they had any fish on board; they sent me a very fine mullet, but would not let me pay any thing for it. I made my kitchen at the foot of a *tatamague-tree*; I lighted a fire, while one of my negroes went in search of wood, and the other of water, that where I was, being brackish. I made a hearty dinner of the fish, upon which I also regaled my servants.

Some pieces of the rocks here were obviously ferruginous, and abounding in ore. There is a ridge of rocks, extending from the Black River, as far as the promontory of Brabant, which is the most leeward point of the island. There is but one place to land at behind the little island, called *Tamarind*'s-*Island*.

I set out again about two o'clock P.M. but walked with more circumspection than before. I had now twenty leagues to go through a desart part of the island, where there are no more than two

two inhabitants, except the Maron negroes, who harbour thereabouts. I ordered my men to keep close; and my dog, who used always to run before, now kept very near me, and at the least noise pricked up his ears and stopped: he seemed sensible that we were not among men. Thus we continued our walk in good order, following the shore, which forms an infinite number of small bays, To the left we had the woods, where the most profound solitude reigns. Behind these, runs a tract of hills, the tops only of which we could see; the soil here is but poor, notwithstanding which, by the *polchers*, a species of tree, brought from India, and some other signs, it was evident that a settlement had been attempted. I had the precaution to take some bottles of water with me, and it was well I did so, for the rivulets marked in the plan, were entirely dried up.

My negro's wound bled incessantly, which made me very uneasy. I walked very slowly, and at four o'clock made another halt. As night approached, I would not attempt to go round the promontory, but cut across the wood, over the isthmus which joins it to the other mountains. This isthmus is a hill of a middling height. Upon this eminence I met a black belonging to M. le Normand, whose house I was going to, and from which I was not above a quarter of a league. This man went on before, while I stopped, and looked with delight upon the prospect of the two seas. A house built here would be in a charming situation, if any fresh water were near. As I descended the hill, a black came and brought me a jug of water, and told me, that I was impatiently

tiently expected at the house. I got there. It was a long building of pallisadoes, covered with the leaves of the *latanier*. Eight negroes belonged to the plantation, and there were nine persons in family; the master, the mistress, five children, a young lady related to the family, and a friend. The master was abroad: all this I learnt from the negro as I went along.

The whole house consisted but of one large room; in the middle was the kitchen; at one end they kept their stores, and here also lay their servants; at the other was the bed where lay the master and his wife; it was covered with a cloth by way of tester, upon which was a hen sitting with eggs;—under the bed were some ducks;—pigeons harboured among the leaves of the roof;—and at the door were three great dogs.

All the implements both of the husbandry and housewifery hung up against the walls. What was my surprise at finding the mistress of this wretched dwelling, to be a very handsome genteel woman. Both she and her husband were of good families in France. They had come here several years since, to seek their fortune; and had quitted their relations, their friends, and their country, to pass their days in this desert, where nothing is to be seen but the sea, and the frightful cliffs of the promontory of Brabant; but the air of contentment and good-nature about this young mother of a family, seemed to make every body happy who came near her. She gave suck

suck to her youngest child, while the four others stood round her, playful and contented.

Every thing the house afforded was served up at supper with the utmost propriety.—This meal appeared a very agreeable one to me. I could not help being struck with the sight of the pigeons fluttering about the table, the goat-kids and the children at play together, and such a variety of animals in perfect agreement with this amiable family, and with each other. Their peaceful sports, the solitude of the place, the murmuring noise of the sea, all combined to present to my imagination, a picture of those times when the children of Noah, descended upon the new earth, began afresh to partake of the domestic enjoyments they had so long been strangers to.

I was shewn afterwards to my lodging-room, which was a little hut, newly built of wood, at about two hundred paces from the house. The door was not yet put up; but I closed the opening with the boards of which it was made. I laid my arms in readiness, the Maron negroes being very numerous in this part. A few years ago, about forty of them retired to the promontory, and began to make plantations. An attempt was made to take them; but sooner than suffer this, they all threw themselves into the sea.

The master of the house having returned home in the night, Sept. 1, persuaded me to defer my journey till afternoon; promising to accompany me part of the way. It was no more than three short leagues to Bell-ombre, the last plantation, or or house, that I should find. Madame de Normand herself, prepared a remedy to apply to the wound of my poor negro. She made over the fire a kind of Samaritan's Balsam, with turpentine, sugar, wine, and oil. His wound being dressed, I sent him on before with his comrade. At three o'clock, I took leave of this hospitable house, and of the amiable and excellent mistress of it. Her husband and I set out. He was a very robust man; and his arms, legs, and face were exceedingly sun-burnt. He worked himself in the plantation, as well as in cutting down and clearing away trees. Nothing gave him concern, he said, but the ill-health his wife brought upon herself by bringing up her children; and that she had lately added to the fatigue, by taking upon her the charge of an orphan. He told me only his grievances, for he could not but perceive how sensible I was of the happiness he enjoyed.

Near the house, we passed a rivulet, and walked upon the green sod as far as point Corail. Here the sea runs up into the iſland, between two chains of perpendicular mountains: we followed this chain through broken and rugged paths, and sometimes swinging by the rocks. Our greatest difficulty was on the ſide of the bay, in doubling what they call the Cape. I saw several negroes passing it; they scrambled along the side of the rock, and had they made one false step, must have fallen into the sea. In bad weather this passage is impracticable, the sea beating in, and breaking among the rocks in a most frightful manner. In a calm, small vessels can come into the bay, at the end of which, they load with wood.

Luckily for us, the King's *Senau* the *Desire*. was then in the bay, and we borrowed her boat to cross it. M. le Normand went over with me, and we then took leave of each other, and parted.

Having walked for three hours over a green sod, I reached the other side of Point St. Martin. Sometimes I walked upon the sand, and sometimes upon the turf, which grew in thick tufts like moss. Here I found a pirogue, in which M. Etiene, partner in the plantation of Belle-ombre waited for my coming. We soon got to his house, which was situated at the entrance of the river Citroniers, on the left shore of which they were building a ship of two hundred tons.

From M. le Normand's all the way, the coolness of the air and the verdure of the ground is delightful. It is a savannah, without rock, lying between the sea and woods, which have a beautiful appearance.

I observed a large shelf of coral, above fifteen feet high, just before I passed the Cape. It is a kind of breaker, which the sea has abandoned; at the foot of it, there is a long piece of fenny ground, which might be easily converted into a bason for small vessels.

My negro being almost cured of his wound, by the remedy Madame de Normand had applied to it, I fixed my departure for the afternoon of Sept. 2. In the morning I went out in the pirogue between the breakers and the coast.

 The

The water was clear to the very bottom ; and one might see a forest of madrepores of five or six feet high, like trees, some of them with flowers growing upon them. Different sorts of fiſh, and of all colours, swam about among their branches ; in some parts were numbers of beautiful shell-fiſh, and in others tunny-fiſh, equally beautiful, which meandered about, as the motion of the pirogue disturbed and frighted them. I might have made a valuable collection, but I had no diver here, nor any proper iron pincers, to raise up the plants from this maritime garden, or to root up those trees of stone. However, I brought away with me some of the rock called, the Ear of Midas, the Golden Cloth, &c. &c.

Two Gentlemen from aboard the Desire dined with us, who, with Monsieur Etiene, agreed to accompany me as far as the arm of the sea *de la Savanne*, three leagues off. Nobody lives there, but there are some huts made of straw. We had sent the negroes foward in the morning ; and after dinner I followed them by myself.

I now reached *Post Jacotet* ; a part where the sea runs up into the land, forming a circular bay, in the middle of which is a small triangular island ; this creek is surrounded by a rising ground, that gives it the appearance of a bason. It is open only at the entrance, where the sea-water enters ; and at the other end, receives a number of rivulets, that run over a fine sand, from a piece of fresh water above, in which, were plenty of fish. Round this piece of water are several little hills, rising one above another in the form of an amphitheatre,

 and

and crowned with clumps of trees, some shaped like pyramids or yews, and others like an umbrella—behind, and far above all these, were the towering tops of a wood of palm-trees, whose bending branches looked like so many plumes of feathers. This huge mass of verdure, rises out of the middle of the green turf, and is joined to the forest, and to a branch of the mountain leading to the Black River. The murmuring of the springs, the beautiful greenness of the waves, the constant, but gentle whistling of the winds, the smoothness of the plain, with the pleasing umbrage of the high lands, and grateful smell of the *veloutiers*, diffused around me peace and happiness. I regretted my being alone; a variety of projects suggested themselves to my imagination; and I would have given up all the universe beside, might I but with some chosen and beloved objects, have spent my days to come in this delightful place.

This pleasing prospect I relinquished with reluctance. Before I had gone two hundred yards from it, there met me a troop of negroes armed with fusils; upon their nearer approach, I perceived them to be a party sent out by the police of the island; they stopped when they came up to me. One of them had got in the shell of a gourd, two puppies just whelped; another of them led a woman tied by the neck with a cord made of rushes; this was the booty they had taken from a camp of Maron negroes, which they had routed. They had killed one man, whose *grisgris* they shewed me. It was a kind of talisman made like a rosary. The poor negro-woman seem-

 ed

ed overwhelmed with grief. I asked her some questions, but she did not answer me She carried upon her back a bag made of *vacoa*, I opened it, and was shocked beyond measure, at finding in it the head of a man. The country before me seemed no longer beautiful in my eyes, but was converted to a scene of horrors, from which I fled with precipitation.

As I was with some difficulty going down a declivity, towards the arm of the sea *De la Savanna*, my companions rejoined me. It was now night, and we seated ourselves under some trees at the bottom of the bay; where we supped by the light of flambeaux.

We naturally talked of the Maron negroes, for they as well as I, had met the party with the poor woman, who was carrying, perhaps, the head of her lover! M. Etiene told us, there were troops of them, of two or three hundred in number, in the environs of *Belle-ombre*, and that they elected a *chief*, disobedience to whose orders, was punished with death. They are forbidden to take any thing from the houses in the neighbourhood, or to go to the side of the frequented rivers to seek for fish or other food. In the night, they go down to the sea-side and fish; and in the day-time drive the deer or stags to the interior parts of the woods, with dogs trained to great perfection for this purpose. When there is but one woman in a party, she is reserved for the chief; but if there are many, they are in common. Their children when born, are immediately killed, lest their cries should discover their retreat. The whole morning

is

is spent in casting lots to presage the destiny of the ensuing day.

Being a hunting one day last year, he told us that he met a run-away negro, whom he pursued and presented his gun at—it missed fire thrice. He was then going to knock him down with the but-end, but was prevented by two negro-women, who came out of the wood, and weeping, threw themselves at his feet. The black seized the opportunity and escaped. He brought the two generous creatures home with him; he had shewn us one of them in the morning.

By clearing away some of the beds of coral, *Post-Jacotet*, I had just observed, the chearful place above described, might be made a very good harbour for small vessels. The arm of the sea *De la Savanna*, would also serve to load, or land goods from the barges. This part, in general, is by far the most beautiful of the whole island; but it remains uncultivated, a communication with Port-Louis being difficult, on account of the mountains between them, and the wind being so seldom fair for doubling Brabant promontory in returning from the Port.

M. Etiene, and M. de Chezemure, captain of the *Desire*, accompanied me as far as the left-hand shore of *La Savanna*, which is much steeper than the other. Sept. 3. In this place their dogs put up a stag; and here I took leave of them, to go alone the twelve leagues that remained, through a desolate and uninhabited country. I observed as I went along, that the meadows were much

 larger,

larger, and the woods thicker and better grown. The mountains run a long way into the land, and the summits only of the distant ones were to be seen.

A river every now and then opposed me. I forded three different ones in the course of two hours walking, and the second, called the river *Anguilles*, with some difficulty; its bottom being covered with rocks, and the current very rapid. It flows from springs of a ferruginous quality, which cover the water with an oil, the colour of a pigeon's breast.

Here I saw a sparrow-hawk, which makes great havock among the poultry. It was perched upon the trunk of a *latanier*. I presented at him, within a gun's length; both my primes flashed in the pan, without either gun's going off. The bird kept his place, and there I left him. This accident made me look very carefully to my arms, in case of an attack from the negroes.

I made a halt on the left-hand side of the third river, and near the sea, upon a level part of the rocks, under the shade of a *veloutier*. My blacks made me a kind of tent, by throwing my cloak over some branches. Here I dined; and they catched me some perch and conchs—and ears of Midas.

I went on again about two hours after dinner, my guns and people in good order: there was no need to fear a surprize, the plain being entirely open, and the woods at a great distance. As the path was a fine smooth sand,—that I might walk

the

the more at ease, and not have the trouble of taking off my shoes and stockings at every ford, I determined to walk barefoot, as the hunters did in the morning. This is not only the most natural, but the safest way of going here, the foot seizing or griping the angles of the rocks like a hand. The blacks are so expert by constant use, that they can pick up a pin from the ground with their toes. It is not therefore in vain, that Nature has divided this part into toes, and them again into articulations.

While indulging these reflections, having pulled off my shoes and stockings, I walked on and forded the first river; but in coming out of the water, I received a violent stroke of the sun upon my legs; which immediately became red and inflamed. In crossing a second, I cut one of my heels, and one toe, and felt the wounds exceedingly painful, when I put my foot in the water. I gave up my project, lamenting that want of custom had deprived me of one of the advantages a man might enjoy here.

Arriving at the side of the river *Jacotet*, I crossed it upon the back of my negro, at about cannon-shot distance from its mouth. The water makes a great noise in running over the rocks, and is so transparent, that I could distinguish the black snails that stuck to the bottom. I must own I shuddered at passing this stream. It being near sun-set, I determined to go no farther, but walked over the stones along its brink, to get to a shed which I perceived on one of the points of the mouth, and which I found it impossible to reach, the rocks were so very rugged. I returned, and again took the path, which led me to the top of the slope at the foot of which the river runs. On my left-hand, in a recess, I saw a little clump of branches of trees and *liannes*, but could not penetrate it. A thought struck me, to cut a way into it with a hatchet, and lay down as in a nest, thus assuring myself of a place to sleep in. But some drops of rain falling, a roof, though ever so bad a one, appeared to be the better shelter. I went down the recess towards the sea, and was very happy to find on my right-hand, the shed I had seen from the opposite shore. It was nothing but a mere roof of leaves of *latanier*, built out from the rock; on my right, was the passage I had in vain attempted, and on the left, that I had descended by,—and before me was the sea.

All things here seemed combined for my safety and convenience: They made me up a bed of dry leaves, upon which I lay down. My two paniers were laid one on the right, the other on the left side of me, one of my blacks at each entrance, my pistols under my head, my gun at my side, and my dog at my feet.

Scarcely were these dispositions made, when a shivering seized me. This was the consequence of the stroke of the sun, which is generally succeeded by a fever.

My legs became very much inflamed and painful. They made me some lemonade, and by the light of a candle I made notes of my observations during

during this journey, and corrected some errors in the chart.

From the æstuary *la Savanna* the whole coast is steep and inaccessible. The rivers that empty themselves here have steep banks.—It would be impossible for cavalry to get along at all, and the march of an enemy might be impeded with great ease, every river being a ditch of a depth absolutely frightful. As to the country, it is by far the most beautiful in the island.

The fever left me about midnight, when I fell asleep. At half past three o'clock, my dog waked me, by running from under the shed, and barking as loud as he could, I called to *Côte*, who rose; we went out, but could see nothing but a starry sky. My black returned in a few minutes, and said, he had heard some body whistle twice, as if in the wood. I ordered them to light a fire and keep watch, and placed Côte, armed with my sabre, as a centinel.

The waves of the sea came up almost as far as my cottage. The noise of its breaking among the rocks, added to the darkness of the night, inclined me to rest, but my apprehensions would not suffer me. I was five leagues from any house, and if the fever should again attack me, no assistance could be had. I had no fears about the Maron negroes; my servants were both resolute men, and my situation was such as would enable me to stand a siege. All things considered, I thought myself very happy that I did not take up my lodging in the thicket.

I gave

I gave a glass of *eau-ae-vie* about day-break to my body-guards, and renewed my journey Their burdens were much lightened, by the constant consumption of our provisions.

It was half past five when I set off, Sept. 4, resolving not to stop till I got to a house. We presently came to the side of a small river, and a little farther on to a rivulet almost dried up. After an hour's walk, the beautiful turf I had walked on from the promontory of *Brabant* ended, and the soil became stony and covered with rocks, as in the other parts of the island. The grass here is of a finer verdure, and of a large blade,—very proper for pasture.

Here we forded an arm of the sea called *du Challon*, over a sand-bank. The description of it in the plan is not a good one. The sea runs deep into the land, through a narrow channel, across which gratings migbt be put, and there would then be a fine reservoir for fish. On the left shore there was a shed, in which I rested myself.

Half a league from thence the path divides, I took that to the left, which leads into the woods. It conducted me to a wide road, marked with a track of wheels,—an appearance that pleased me very much, as it was a sign of my being near a house of some note, and the print of a horse's hoof was at that time a much more desirable sight than a foot-step of a man. We soon arrived at a house, but the master was out; I therefore went back, and struck into a path, that led through the

the woods to the plantation of M. Delaunay. I got here in good time, for my leg were so terribly inflamed, that I could scarcely walk. He lent me a horse to carry me two leagues off to a plantation occupied by some priests.

The rivers *de la Chaux*, and *des Crecles* I crossed successively, three quarters of a league from the last, I crossed one of the bays to the south-east of the Port, in a pirogue.

All the shores here are covered with mangliers. The views are every where delightful, the country being hilly, and covered with plantations, interspersed with a great number of clumps of orange-trees. It was six o'clock when I arrived at the house of the priest, who had the management of the plantation. My legs were bathed with elder-flower water, and I slept with great comfort.

I was, Sept. 2, but one league from the Great Port. The good priest lent me a horse, and I got to the town about ten o'clock. It consists of about a dozen houses. The most remarkable buildings are, a large mill nearly fallen to ruins, and the governor's house in little better condition. Behind the town is a high mountain, and before it the sea, which forms a bay, two leagues deep, including the rocks at its entrance, and four leagues long from point *Cocos* to point *Diable*. I alighted at the house of the curate

I was charmed, Sept. 6, 7, and 8, with my host, and with the country I had seen; but neither he, nor his parishioners drank any thing except

cept water. It is frequently a month's voyage from hence to Port Louis, and the inhabitants are upon these occasions in absolute want of every article that comes from Europe. I gave part of my provisions to M. Delfolie, my host, who was a good sort of man.

Of this place the south-east port was formerly inhabited by the Dutch, one of whose ancient buildings is now used as a chapel. There are two ways to enter the Port, one at point *Diable*, for small vessels; the other, which is much wider, is by the side of an island towards the middle. At each of these is a battery, and at the bottom of the bay, is a third, called the Queen's battery.

Had my present indisposition permitted me, I should have examined the variety of strange bodies thrown ashore by the sea, in order to have formed some opinion of the lands to windward of the island; but I could not undergo the fatigue, for my legs were very painful, and the skin peeled off entirely.

Here follows all I could learn:

About the south-east port whales are often enough observed, where it would be very easy and safe to harpoon them. Fish is very plentiful upon this coast, especially shell-fish, of the most beautiful kinds. They gave me some oysters of a violet colour, from the mouth of the river *La Chaux*, and a species of crystallization from the neighbouring river, *Sorbes*.

Three

Three nights successively I have seen a comet, which first appeared a fortnight before, the nucleus was pale and nebulous, its tail white and very long, the rays diverged but little. I drew the position of it in the sky, which was a little below the three kings. Its course was eastward, and consequently its tail in a westerly direction. At half past two on the morning of the 6, its elevation was about 50 deg. above the horizon—my observation could not be very accurate for want of the proper instruments.

Here the air was cool and refreshing, and the country beautiful and fertile: but the inhabitants are so few, that during a whole day, I saw but two negroes pass through the street.

I now found myself able to continue my journey, especially as the part I went through was inhabited. I determined to stop for the night at four leagues distance from the mouth of the Great River, which is something broader than that of the same name, near Port Louis.

By six in the morning we were in readiness and set out, following the course of the shore, which is broken in several places by bays, on the sides of which grow *mangliers* in abundance. It is not impossible but that the seeds may have been brought by the sea from some land to windward. We went along the side of a range of high mountains to our left—they were covered with wood. The country is divided into small hills, on which grows a very fine grass; the provender of cattle, bred

bred here in great numbers. It is a pleasant part of the island, but very fatiguing to travel over.

We were not long in spying upon an eminence a fine house built of stone. Here I stopped to refresh myself; it belonged to a wealthy inhabitant, whose name was V*** He was abroad.— His wife was a raw-boned Creole, who, according to the custom of the country, went barefoot. I found her in a room, with five or six girls about her, and as many mastiff dogs, who immediately attacked my dog, and were very near strangling him. She turned them all out of the room, and placed at the door to keep them out, a negro wench, who had nothing on but a ragged petticoat. I begged leave to stay in her house during the heat of the day. The first compliments were scarcely ended, before one of the dogs found means to get in among us again, and the uproar was renewed. Madame de la V—— held in her hand the prickly tail of a dried thornback, with which she gave the poor negro a cut across the bare shoulders, which were marked immediately with a long wheal, and then she gave a back stroke to the dog, who ran howling away.

She had narrowly escaped, as she told me, being drowned in going in a pirogue to harpoon turtles among the rocks. She seemed to value herself much upon going to hunt the Maron negroes in the woods; but the governor, she said, had deprived her of her favourite sport, which was stag-hunting, and added, "I should have been better pleased, if he had stuck a dagger in my heart."

I left

I left this negro-hunting Bellona at four o'clock in the afternoon, and took a path, which went across point *Diable*, so called by the first navigators on this coast; because it is said, that their compass varied without their being able to account why it did so. We crossed the mouth of the Great River in a canoe—it is navigable for nothing larger, on account of a sand bank, which runs across it, and a cataract formed by it, about a quarter of a league from hence.

We kept along an earth redoubt on the left shore, at the beginning of the road that leads to *Flacq*, the rocks being so rugged here as to render it impassable. Here we once more entered the woods, which are very fine, and abound in orange-trees. A quarter of a league from hence I came to a house,—the master of it was not at home; I stopped notwithstanding.

We had been on our legs full two hours and a half in the morning, and as long in the afternoon, which rendered an opportunity of resting very acceptable.

We travelled on the direct road to *Flacq*, till we got about a quarter of a league beyond the river *Seche*, which we forded as we had done the rest: then taking a path on the right-hand, I came to the sea-shore at *Eaudouce* bay, where there was a post of thirty men.

The shore was now very passable which we chose to walk on. *Côte* carried me over an arm of the sea, which was rather deep. The sand is almost

almost every where covered with rocks, except a long meadow of dog's-tooth grass, of the same sort I had seen at Belle-ombre. All this part is dry and barren; the woods are low and thin, and extend as far as the mountains which are seen at a distance: this plain, over which are three roads, is not good for much; it reaches as far as a settlement called *Quatre Cocos*. There is no other water but a brackish well, dug in the rocks, full of veins of iron ore.

Having dined, a path on our left hand led us into the woods, which were very stony. We came to the brink of the river *Flacq*, at about a quarter of a league from the mouth, and crossed it upon planks. In going along the side of this river, I passed several plantations, of which there are many hereabouts, and came down to a store-house on the left, where there is a post, commanded by M. Gautier, the Captain of a company. He desired me to lodge there that night.

I laid by all day Sept. 11. This part, which is called *Le Flacq*, is the best cultivated in the island; rice grows in great plenty. There is a creek in the rocks, by which barges can come and load with the greatest convenience.

Sept. 12. My host next day, accompanied me part of the way; we went in a pirogue to post Fayette, as far as which the coast is entirely covered with rocks and mangroves. Near the landing place, we saw the trace of a turtle in the sand; this induced us to land in search of it, but we found nothing but its nest. We forded the bay *des Aigrettes*,

Aigrettes, which is a large arm of the sea. I was upon the shoulders of *Côte*, when the sea became so deep towards the middle of the passage, that I feared he would not be able to keep his feet; the water came up to his neck, and wetted me very much. A little farther on, we came to another æstuary, called the *Bay de Requins.* I observed many parts of the rock pierced with a number of round holes, of about a foot diameter. Some of them were as deep as my cane —and I imagined that the lava of some volcano, having formerly flowed through the wood, had consumed the trunks of the trees, and left the print of the place they had grown in.

The meadow is continued from the post of *Fayette* to the river *Du Rempart.* This part is also well cultivated, and here we dined. I then crossed the river, and went on alone, till I came to the river *Des Citroniers.* The sun was just setting, when I perceived an inhabitant at a little distance, who invited me very kindly to his house —his name was Le Sieur Goule.

In the morning of Sep. 13, he offered me his horse to go to the town, which was but five leagues off. I would willingly have gone round the whole island, but there remained still four leagues of the way totally without inhabitants, or water; besides, from point *Des Canoniers*, to the Port was a part of the coast that I already knew.

The offer mine host had made me, I now thought it prudent to accept, and left this quarter, which is called *La Poudre d'Or*, on account say they, of the colour of the sand, which however, appeared to me to be white, as in other places. I crossed the river, which is called by the same name as the quarter, and then entered a large wood, the soil of which is good, but without water. In the quarter of Pamplemousse, which was the next I came to, the land seem quite exhausted, the inhabitants having cultivated them for thirty years, without ever laying dung upon them *. I forded this river, and the rivers *Seche*, and *De Lataniers*, and in the evening arrived at the Port.

The most fertile soils I had seen on my tour were all mixed with stone, except some parts of Pamplemousse.

Not a single monument worthy of remark fell under my notice the whole of this journey. There are three churches in the island; one at Port-Louis, the second at the south-east port, and the third and handsomest at Pamplemousse; the two others being smaller than the churches of a little country village. They had built one at Port Louis, upon a very handsome plan, but the roof being too much raised, the walls were insufficient to bear its weight, and resist the force of the hurricanes. What remains of it is now used as a store-house, of which there are but few in the island, and the greater part of these built of wood, a material by no means proper for public buildings,

* The author calls it *fumer*—smoking them. Saturn was called *Stercutius* by the ancients, for having taught them this method of improving their lands. *E.*

especially

especially here, where the strongest beams will only last forty years, if the worms do not destroy them sooner; besides, stone is found every where in great abundance, and the island is surrounded with coral, for lime. The greatest difficulty is in laying the foundations, for which, the rocks must be blown up with gunpowder; and yet, all things considered, I do not think, that a building in stone would cost one third more than one of wood. The latter is soon built, and as soon decays. Those who are too eager for enjoyment, never enjoy any thing to perfection.

The whole isle is reckoned to be about forty-five leagues in circumference. It is watered by a number of rivulets, which run in deep channels from the center of the island into the sea. Although we were now in the dry season, I crossed above four-and-twenty flowing with fresh and wholesome water. I suppose that about half this island lays fallow, one quarter of it consists of plantations, and the remainder of pasture grounds, of various kinds.

LETTER XVIII.

COMMERCE, AGRICULTURE, DEFENCE.

ALL that may be said upon these three subjects, which are boundless, cannot easily be compressed into one letter.

I do not know a corner of the earth whose wants are supplied from so many, or so distant parts. Their dishes aud plates come from China; their linen and clothes from India; their slaves and cattle from Madagascar; their provisions, or part of them, from the Cape of Good Hope; their money from Cadiz, and their government and laws from France. M. de la Bourdonnais wished to have made it the staple of the trade to India—a second Batavia.

Like all projectors, however, with the view of great genius, he had also the weakness of a man: place him but upon a point, and he will make the center of all things.

Staples, for the most part, augment the expences of trade, and should never be established but

but when absolutely necessary. No nation has any staple between the Indies and Europe, but where the trade is immediately concerned. Batavia is a spice island.

This place is looked upon as a fortress, which assures to us our possessions in India; with equal reason Bourdeaux might be deemed the citadel of our American colonies. The Isle of France is fifteen hundred leagues from Pondicherry. Suppose a garrison, ever so numerous, were to be maintained here, yet a squadron must rendezvous in a port, where the worms will totally destroy a ship in three years. Neither pitch, tar, cordage, or mast-timber are found here; nor is the wood of a proper sort for any other branch of building.

After all we must at last run the risk of a sea-engagement. If beaten, we cannot succour the place; if victorious, our soldiers, carried suddenly from a temperate to a very sultry climate, will be unable to endure the fatigue of the service.

Half the money sunk here, expended upon some part of the Malabar coast; or at the mouth of the Ganges, in lieu of the Isle of France, might have secured us a respectable fortress in India itself, and the troops would have been seasoned to the climate; nor would the English, in this case, have been masters of Bengal. From them we may learn how to form a settlement, and protect it when formed. They have an army of three or four thousand Europeans upon the very banks of the Ganges; besides a number of distant islands under their dominion: they have no-

 thing

thing now to do but to establish themselves on the western side of Madagascar: but in all their enterprizes, they never, while pursuing the means, lose sight of the end. A flock of sheep would be in a dangerous situation, were the dogs, their protectors, at fifteen hundred leagues distance from them.

Ah! why then do we keep this Isle of France? To supply us with coffee, and as a port for harbouring our ships occasionally.

The spot which sends us this small quantity of coffee, has wants enough to engage all its attention to them alone. This must be entirely supplied from France for some time, or the colony will never arrive at a state to be of the least real use to the mother-country. Our commodities, our cloths, our linens, our manufactures are in plenty, and the cotton-works of Normandy are far better than those of India with which they clothe the slaves. No money but our own should circulate here. A paper currency is set on foot, but is of no great credit; at the best rate of exchange, thirty-three, and frequently fifty per cent. is lost by it. Indeed it is impossible that this paper money can lose less; It is payable in France six months after sight, it is six months upon the voyage thither, and six months on the return. This is eighteen months. Ready money is reckoned here to produce thirty-three per cent. in eighteen months, if employed in the maritime trade; and therefore whoever gives paper for piastres, justly looks upon himself as running risks of more sorts than one.

Every

Every thing bought for the king, is sold to him at one third less than its real worth. The corn of the inhabitants—all buildings erected for him—stores, and expeditions of every sort. You may have a store-house built for 20,000 francs, ready money; * if you pay in paper, the price is 10,000 crowns—and upon a matter of this kind, there never is any dispute.

He is paid, however, only in this paper-money. It was once thought it never would have gone out of the island; but now not only this goes, but the piastres also, and never to return; the colony would else be in want of every thing.

The only one, of all the places to which it trades, that is indispensibly necessary at present to its existence, is Madagascar, for slaves and cattle. These islanders were formerly content with the wretched fusils that were offered them in barter, but they must now have piastres, and those milled at the edges.—All the world is rising into perfection.

Were there besides the most distant prospect of this island ever becoming a flourishing seat of trade, the port must be cleared out without delay, there being now seven or eight hulks of ships each forming an island, which is every day increased by the madrepores growing round them.

None should be allowed, on any pretence, to possess lands situated conveniently for the port, but what should pay for them accordingly. Nor should any person procure for himself extensive

* A franç, or livre, is 10½*d.* English.

grants of the finest lands in the island, to sell them again to others. This abuse is expressly prohibited by the laws; but the laws here are not put in execution.

Breeding beasts of burthen should be an object, and especially of asses, so useful in a mountainous country: An ass will carry twice the load that a negro can stand under. The black is of a little higher price, but the ass is the strongest and the happiest of the two.

Various laws, relative to the planting business, exist. No people in the world know their own interest better than the inhabitants of the isle of France, nor what is best suited to the soil they possess.

Many soldiers here are entirely useless,—these men might have lands alotted for cultivation, and assistance for clearing them, and might marry the free negroes. Were a plan of this kind adopted, in ten years the whole island would turn to profit in one way or another; and we should have an established nursery for sailors and soldiers to serve in India. This idea is so very simple, that I do not at all wonder it has been rejected as contemptible.

Means for alleviating the severities of the poor negroes, I leave to men abler and of more influence than me;—some abuses are too enormous to admit of mediation.

Talk of defence proper for this island, and a sea officer will tell you a squadron should be kept here

here constantly; an engineer would have it fortified; a brigadier is persuaded that a few regiments would best answer the purpose; and the inhabitants think the island will of itself, defend itself. The three first of these objects depend upon the will of the administration, and may partly be dispensed with, though in some respects necessary. I shall inlarge upon the last, as I wish you to be acquainted with some of the œconomical views of the people here.

It struck me, in my tour round the island, that it was almost entirely encircled at some distance from the shore, by a belt of rocks: and that in those parts where the belt was not continued, the coast is formed of rocks high and inaccessible. This disposition, so excellent for its defence, could not fail to astonish me; but it is nevertheless certain, the island would be totally inaccessible, but for some clefts in the rocks which afford a passage; of these I counted eleven. They are formed by the currents of the river.

In these passes, properly secured, consists the defence of the island from without—some of them might be shut up by means of floating chains, and others by batteries raised upon the shore.

In the navigable part for boats between the rocks and the shore, small armed sloops might be used with good effect, when the pass is not within cannon-shot of the coast.

The shore, behind the rocks, is very accessible; the landing being upon a level. These parts, however,

however, might be rendered impracticable by art, as those of the bays of the South East port are by nature. Nothing need be done but to plant *Mangliers*, a sort of tree which, growing far out into the sea, form forests absolutely impenetrable. This expedient is so very easy, that nobody has yet thought of it.

If where the surf runs high, such of the rocks, as are found accessible, being no where of much extent, might be defended by raising a wall or line; by keeping *chevaux-de-frise* to throw into the water, or by *Raquettes* which will grow in the driest places; but the *Manglier* will grow if there is ever so little sand by trees, prickly shrubs, &c. They have besides, this advantage, they cost but little; and time, the destroyer of every other fortification, increases and strengthens what I am recommending. So much for the defence against attacks by sea.

This island may be viewed as a circle, and the rivers flowing from the centre, as so many raddi of it. The shores might be cut either perpendicularly or with a talus, or raquettes and bambos might be planted upon the sides towards the town, and the opposite shore laid open for three hundred toises. By this means the ground between every two rivulets is rendered a strong fortified place, and the channel of each rivulet a very dangerous ditch. Every attempt to pass, on whatever side it is made, must be perceived by the inhabitants, who would be enabled thereby to act for their defence accordingly; nor could any enemy arrive at the town but through a thousand

sand difficulties and obstructions. This system of defence might be adopted in all small islands, whose waters constantly flow from the centre to the circumference.

There is need of little fortification between the two wings of the mountains which encompass the town and port, except, perhaps, in that part towards the sea. Upon the isle of *Tonneliers* should be built a fort, with batteries placed in a kind of covered ways to infilade each other. These should be mounted with a number of mortars,—so terrible to shipping. To the right and left, as far as the ends of the promontories, the land should be protected by strong and respectable lines. Nature has already done her part towards the defence of the right side,—the river *Latanier* running the length of the whole front.

At the back of the town, a deep valley is formed by the mountains, and includes a vast extent of ground, whereon all the inhabitants of the island and their slaves might be assembled. The other side of these mountains is inaccessible, or might be easily made so, at a trifling expence.

One advantage peculiar to this place, ought not to be overlooked: In the very highest part of the mountain, at a place called *Le Pouce,* there is found a large piece of land planted with trees, among which run two or three rivulets of very fine fresh water. There is no ascending thither from the town, but by a very intricate path. It has been attempted, by force of mines, to make a wide road of communication with the interior part of the island; but the back of the mountains are of so prodigious a height and steepness, that scarce any thing, except a negro or a monkey, can scramble over them Four hundred men, in this post, if furnished with provisions, could never be driven from it; and there is space enough for the whole garrison.

To these natural means of safety, if we add those which should be furnished by government, a squadron, and proper troops, an enemy would have the following obstacles to surmount:

I. He would be under the necessity of hazarding the event of an engagement by sea.

II. Supposing him victorious, our squadron might still obstruct, with success, his descent, by making him bear to the windward of the island in the course of the engagement.

III. Even then the difficulties of a disembarkation would remain to be encountered. The coast can be attacked only at particular points, and no where upon a front of any extent.

IV. The enemy's passage, however strong, over each rivulet would be attended with an engagement to his manifest disadvantage; if, by the method I have proposed, the one side of the rivulet should be laid quite open.

V. The siege of the town could only be formed on a side where there is but little room: The enemy would also have to sustain the fire from the promontories,

promontories, which command this place; and open his trenches among rocks.

VI. Were the garrison even driven out of the town, they could still retire to the adjacent heights, a secure retreat, well provided with water, and where they might be constantly supplied with succours from the interior part of the island.

Here I might have spoken of the defence of the neighbouring island of Bourbon; but am yet a stranger to it. I know only that a landing is impracticable; that it is well peopled, and grows more corn than it can consume; yet does every one contend that the fate of Bourbon depends upon that of the isle of France. Is this, * because the military chest is kept here?

* The author has suppressed some observations relative to the Isle of France, lest, what he proposed as a means of its defence, might be of advantage to an enemy about to attack it. This ought to have occurred to those who have published plans and charts of our colonies, of which our enemies have more than once availed themselves to our disadvantage. The Dutch will permit no plans of their islands to be engraved. Manuscript ones are given to each master of a vessel, who, at his return, delivers them again into the proper office at their admiralty.

END OF THE FIRST PART.

PART

PART II.

LETTER XIX.

RETURN—BOURBON—HURRICANE.

BEING permitted to sail again for my native country, I prepared to embark on board *L'Indienne*, a ship of 64 guns.

To *Duval*, the slave who bore your name, I gave his freedom; but lent him to a good man of the country, until he had discharged a debt he owed to the administration. Had he spoken French, I would have brought him to Europe. His tears testified his regret at parting with me, of which he seemed more sensible than of the pleasures of liberty. I proposed to have bought the freedom of *Côte* also, if he would have attached himself to my fortune, but he declared there was a girl in the island whom he could not part with. The situation of the King's slaves is very easy. Here he found himself happy, which was more than I could promise, he should be, if he went with me. I should

I should most gladly have brought back my favourite to his own country, but some months before I left the island my poor dog was taken from me; in losing him, I lost a faithful friend that I frequently regret.

A little previous to my departure, I revisited *Autouru*, the islander of Taiti, who had been brought thus far on his way home from Europe.* On his passage from his own country to France, he was open, gay, and a little of the libertine; on his return, I observed he was reserved and polite; he had studied the graces. He was enchanted with the opera at Paris, and imitated the airs and dances he had heard and seen there. He had a watch, upon which he described the hours by the several employments of each; he shewed the hour of rising, of eating, of going to the opera, of walking, &c. &c. This man was very intelligent, and expressed, by signs, whatsoever he pleased. Though the men of Taiti pass for having had no communication with other nations before the arrival of Monsieur Bougainville, I observed, however, one word in their language, and a custom which they have in common with other people; *Matte*, in the language of Taiti, means to kill. The *Mattè* of Spain, and the *Mat* of Persia, bears the same signification. They are also used to paint their skins, as was done by many people of the old and new world. They knew what iron is, though they have none of it; they call it *aurou*, and ask for it with eagerness.

* He was brought from Otaheitic by Monsieur Bougainville, in 1769—and staid eleven months in Paris. *E.*

But

But all these analogies tend little to the tracing of the original of a nation. Follies, wants, and evils of human nature appear naturalized among all people. A more certain mode of distinction is the knowledge of their languages. All nations in Europe eat bread; but the Russians call it *Gleba*, the Germans *Broth*, the Latins *Panis*, the inhabitants of lower Britainy, *Bara*.

This man was greatly chagrined at his long stay in the isle of France. He walked, but always alone. I perceived him one day in a profound meditation, looking at a black slave at the door of the prison, round whose neck they were rivetting a large chain. It appeared a strange spectacle to him, that a man of his colour should be thus treated by white people, who had loaded him with benefits and presents when at Paris. But, alas! he was little aware that, by their passions, men are carried across the seas, and that the morality by which they are influenced in Europe, within the tropics, actuates them no longer.*

When I embarked, Novem. 9, 1770, many Ma-

* To corroborate this opinion of the author's, I beg leave to insert an extract from the history of the conquest of New Spain, published at Madrid in the year 1632, by Castillo.— "We bought three ships of the governor of Cuba, who proposed that we should pay him for them with slaves, which we were to bring from the small islands between Cuba and Honduras.—We rejected this proposal, telling him, that neither God nor the King had ordained these people, by nature free, to be enslaved." Castillo afterwards engaged with Cortes, and accompanied him in his expeditions to Mexico, during which, there is no doubt, but he got rid of those scruples which occasioned the above spirited answer to the governor of Cuba. *E.*

layans accompanied me to the sea-side, and with tears, desired my speedy return. These good people never lose the hope of seeing again those who have done them service. I recognized among them a master carpenter who had bought my books of geometry, although he could scarcely read. He was the only man in the island who would have them.

A calm detained us in the road eleven days. The evening of the 20, we set sail, and at three in the afternoon of the 21, anchored in the road of St. Dennis, Bourbon

The island of this name is 40 leagues to the leeward of the isle of France. It is one day's sail only to Bourbon, but a month is frequently spent in returning. It appears afar off, like a part of a sphere, with very high mountains, the land of which is cultivated to the height of 800 toises.—They reckon 1600 perpendicular toises to the summit of the three Salasses, which are three inaccessible pikes.

Here is a very proud shore; the seas roll with a great surf, preventing all but pirogues from approaching the land without being dashed to pieces. At St. Dennis, a draw-bridge is contrived for the unlading of sloops, which projects more than fourscore feet over the sea, and is sustained by iron chains. At the end of this bridge there is a rope-ladder, up which those who would land, must climb. There is this one place only in the whole island, where any body can land, without first jumping into the sea.

The

The *Indienne* was to stay here three weeks to lade coffee, and several of the passengers proposed passing some days on the island, and even waiting at St. Paul, seven leagues to leeward, till the ship should go thither to compleat her cargo.

I, the Captain, and several officers of other vessels, joined with them in this plan, as we were rather short of provisions on board.

I embarked the 25 in the afternoon, alone, in a little yawl, and, notwithstanding the breakers ran very violently, by keeping the boat's head to the sea, I disembarked at the bridge. We were an hour and an half making this trip, which was not half a league.

On the commanding officer in this place, I deemed it my duty to wait on our first landing. He told me there was no inn at St. Dennis, nor in any part of the island, and that strangers lodged with such of the inhabitants as they had concerns with. Night came on and having no traffick here, I prepared to return on board, when this officer offered me a bed.

My next respects were paid to M. de Cremon, *commissaire ordonateur*, who invited me to his house while I staid on shore. This was the more agreeable to me as I wished to see the volcano of Bourbon, to which I knew M. de Cremon had once made an excursion.

No opportunity, however, of this kind, now offered.

fered. The way is very difficult,—few of the inhabitants know it; and a journey would require an absence of seven or eight days.

The swell was so great from 26 to the 30, that few of the boats used in the harbour came to land. Our captain availed himself of a fortunate minute to get on board his ship, whither his affairs called him, but the bad weather prevented his re-landing.

At six in the morning, this breeze, which always comes from the S. W. rises and ends at ten at night. While I staid, it blew with equal violence day and night.

The wind fell Decem. 1, but there rose from the open sea a monstrous gale, which blew upon the shore with such violence that the centinel on the bridge was obliged to quit his post.

Clouds, very thick and motionless, cover the top of the mountains. The wind continued to blow from the S. W., but the sea ran from the W. Three large waves beat successively over each other, and appeared along the coast like three ranges of little hills. From the upper part of them issued several water-spouts which fell down again in white surf, and rushed violently upon the shore, forming an arch, which, rolling as it were round itself, foamed to a height more than fifty feet perpendicular.

So very close and heavy was the air, that we breathed with difficulty; the sky was dark, clouds of of sea fowls came from the main and took refuge on the land. The birds and animals on shore seemed disturbed. Even men were seized with an inward horror at seeing a dreadful tempest in the midst of a calm.

The wind fell entirely on the morning of the 2, and the swell increased. The rolling waves were more numerous and came from a greater distance. The shore, beaten by the sea, was covered with a white moss, like snow, which heaped together like packs of wool. The vessels in the harbour rode very hard at anchor. There was now no doubt but that the hurricane approached. The pirogues which were on the Galet, were drawn a great way upon land, and every one hastened to secure his house with cords and ropes.

L'Indienne, Le Penthievre, L'Alliance, Le Grand Bourbon, Le Gerion, a Gaulette, and a little boat, all lay at anchor. The shore was lined with people, drawn thither by the spectacle the sea presented, and the danger of the ships.

The sky loured prodigiously about noon, and the wind began to freshen from the S. E. We began to fear that it would turn and blow from the W. and run the vessels ashore. From the battery, the signal was given them to depart, by hoisting the flag, and firing two guns with shot in them. Immediately they cut their cables and set sail. The Penthievre not able to ship her boat, left it behind. *L'Indienne* being anchored farther at sea, went before the wind with her four prin-

 cipal

cipal sails. The rest got out as fast as they could. Some blacks who were on board a shallop, took refuge on board the L'Amitie. The little boat and the Gaulette, were already in the rolling waves, in which they were every now and then lost to the eye; they seemed fearful of putting to sea, but at length, they also hoisted sail, exciting uneasiness and prayers for their safety in all who beheld them. At two hours end, the whole of this fleet disappeared in the N. W. being inveloped in a gloomy horizon.

The hurricane announced itself by a most tremendous noise, about three in the afternoon; the wind blew from all quarters successively. The sea, beaten and agitated to the greatest degree, threw upon the land clouds of foam, sand, shells, and stones. Some boats refitting at fifty paces from the water-side, were buried under the surge. The wind carried away a sheet of lead from the roof of the church, and the colonade from the governor's house. The hurricane lasted all night, and till three in the morning.

The two first ships that returned to anchor on the 6, were the little boat and the Gaulette; they brought a letter from the Penthievre, which had lost her top-gallant-mast. Themselves had met with no accident; the lowest stations are often the least liable to misfortune.

The Gerion appeared the 8,—she had been driven so near the isle of France that she put into the harbour, where she learnt that the Garronne Pink foundered while at anchor.

We had tidings of all the ships, except the Amitié and the *L'Indienue*, by the 18. The size and strength of the *L'Indienne* seemed to secure her against all events, and we did not doubt but that she would continue her voyage to the Cape of Good Hope, there take in provisions, and go from thence to France. Besides I knew this to be the captain's intention.

On the morning of the 19, a signal was made that a ship was in sight; it was the Normande, Pink; she passed by St. Dennis, and anchored at St. Paul. She came from the Isle of France, and was going to the Cape for provisions. This opportunity was too favourable a one to be neglected by me and an officer with me. Monsieur and Madamoiselle Cremon provided us with beds and linen for the voyage, we got horses and guides to go to St. Paul, and were accompanied thither by a relation of Monsieur Cremon.

All my luggage being on board the *Indienne*, I was destitute of every thing except linen, which I had brought on shore with me.

On the 20, at eleven in the morning, we set out, we had seven leagues to go. The Pink was to sail in the evening, and therefore having no time to lose, we took leave of our hosts.

By zig-zag paths paved with sharp stones our horses began forthwith to climb the mountain of St. Dennis. They were very strong, and sure footed, and, according to the custom of the country, were unshod.

A dinner, M. D. Cremon had kindly caused to be provided for us, we found at two leagues and a half from St. Dennis, under some citron trees at the brink of a rivulet.

Having gratefully finished this welcome meal, we descended and came to the *Grand Chaloupe*. It is a frightful valley formed by two mountains that are very steep. We walked part of the way which the rain had rendered dangerous, and at the bottom we found ourselves between the two mountains, in the strangest solitude I had ever seen; we were in a manner between two walls, the heavens only being over our heads: we crossed the rivulet and came at length to the shore opposite to the *Chaloupe*: at the bottom of this abyss, there reigns an eternal calm, however the winds blew on the mountains.

From St. Paul two leagues, we entered into a large plain of sand, extending as far as the town, which is built like St. Dennis. There are large lawns encompassed with hedges in regular rows, and in the middle is the house were the family lives. These towns have the air of large villages.

This place is situated by the side of a great lake of fresh water, of which a port might, I apprehend, be easily constructed.

We did not arrive till night, were much fatigued, and knew neither where to lodge, nor where to get bread, there being no baker at St. Paul.

The

The Captain of the Normande, whom I luckily found on shore, I immediately addressed. He told us he would not venture to take us on board without an order from the Governor of the Isle of France, who was then at St. Dennis, and that he should not sail till next morning.

I wrote to the Governor instantly, and to Mademoiselle Cremon. I gave my two letters to a black, promising to reward him if he returned by eight o'clock next morning. It was then ten at night, and he had fourteen leagues to travel on foot.

My comrades, who were supping at the storekeepers, who lodged all of us in a house belonging to the King, unfurnished, except with chairs, of which we made beds. We were up betimes. At nine o'clock the answers to my letters were brought by a black whom my messenger had sent in his room. What was our astonishment, when we read that the Governor had left the master to his discretion.

After many negotiations, much hesitation, and we had given him bills of payment for our passage, he agreed to take us, and the departure of the ship was deferred till next day.

All I could collect relative to Bourbon is what follows: It is well known that the first inhabitants were pirates, who cohabited with negro women from Madagascar. They fixed here first about the year 1657. The India Company had also at Bourbon a factory, and a governor who lived with them in great circumspection. The Viceroy of *Goa* came one day to anchor in the road of St. Dennis, and was to dine with the Governor. He had scarcely set his foot on shore before a pirate ship of fifty guns anchored along side his vessel, and took her. The captain landed forthwith, and demanded to dine at the Governor's. He seated himself at table between him and the Portuguese Viceroy, to whom he declared that he was his prisoner. Wine and good cheer having put the seaman in good humour, Monsieur Desforges the governor asked him at how much he rated the Viceroy's ransom. "I must have" said the pirate "a thousand piasters." "That's too little," said Monsieur Desforges, "for a brave fellow like you, to receive from a great Lord like him,—ask enough, or ask nothing." "Well, well, then I ask nothing," replied the generous Corsair, "let him be free."

This expediated the Viceroy's departure, who instantly set sail, happy at having escaped on such good terms. This piece of service of the Governor was recompensed ſhortly after by the Court of Portugal, who presented his son with the order of Chriſt.

Sometime afterwards this same pirate settled on the island, and was hanged, a considerable time after an amnesty had been published in favor of his companions, and in which he had failed to get himself included. This injustice was the work of a * *Conseillor*, who was desirous of ap-

* In the French courts of judicature, the judges are called *Conseillers* Counsellors, and the Barristers, are called *Avocats* Advocates. *E.*

propriating

propriating his spoils to his own use. But this last villain, a little while after, came to nearly as wretched an end, though the justice of men did not reach him.

The last of these same pirates, whose name was Adam, is said to have died but lately, aged 104 years.

More peaceable occupations having by degrees softened their manners, there remained among them a spirit only of independence and of liberty, which corrected itself still more in the society of many worthy people, who established in Bourbon for the purpose of cultivation. Sixty thousand blacks are reckoned to live in Bourbon and only five thousand inhabitants. This island is thrice as populous as the Isle of France, on which it depends for its export traffick. It is also much better cultivated, having produced twenty thousand quintals of corn, and as much of coffee, besides rice and other provisions for home consumption. Herds of oxen are not scarce there. The King pays * fifteen livres per cwt. of corn, and the inhabitants sell † a quintal of coffee for forty-five livres in piastres, and seventy livres in paper.

St. Dennis is the principal place in the island. It is the residence of the governor and council. Nothing worth remark is to be seen here, except a redoubt built of stone, but situated too far from the sea,—a battery before the governor's

* About thirteen shillings sterling.

† A quintal is equal to a cwt. English. *E.*

house,

house, and the drawbridge before-mentioned. Near the town is a large plain called Le Champ de Lorraine.

Here the soil seemed still more sandy than at the Isle of France: it is mixed at some distance from land, with the same kind of small pebbles with which the sea shore is covered,—a proof that the sea has withdrawn itself, or that the island is risen out of the ocean. This I think might be the case, if we may judge from the mountains, which are full of chasms, and very rugged and broken in their interior parts. When we speculate upon nature, opposite opinions always present themselves with a nearly equal appearance of probability.—The same effects frequently result from different causes. This observation might be extended very far, and should induce us to be very moderate in our decisions.

I was assured by a man of eighty years of age, that he had been one of those who took possession of the Isle of France when the Dutch abandoned it. Twelve Frenchmen were detached for that purpose, who landed in the morning, and in the afternoon of the same day, an English ship anchored there, for the same purpose.

The first inhabitants of Bourbon seem to have been very simple in their manners, the greater number of the houses were not made to shut,—a lock was a curiosity. Some people even put their money in a tortoise-shell over their door. They dressed in blue cloth, went bare-footed, and lived upon rice and coffee; they imported but little

little from Europe, content to live without luxury so they lived without want. They joined to this moderation the virtues which ever attend it: good faith in commerce, and generosity in their proceedings. As soon as a stranger appeared, the inhabitants came to him, and as a stranger offered him their houses.

A very great change in their manners seems to have resulted from the last Indian war. The volunteers of Bourbon distinguished themselves in it by their bravery; but the stuffs of Asia and the military distinctions of France, thereby got footing in their island. The children, richer than their parents require to be treated with more consideration. They have now no enjoyment of an unnoticed good-fortune, but seek in Europe, pleasures and honours, in exchange for domestic happiness, and the quiet of a country life. The attention of the fathers being chiefly fixed upon their sons, they send them to France, whence they seldom return. Hence it is, that in their island there are more than five hundred marriageable girls, who are likely to die without husbands.

It was the 21 in the evening that we got aboard the Normande. We found a case of wines, of liquors, coffee, &c. which Monsieur and Mademoiselle Cremon had caused to be put on board for our use. We were received at their house with the hospitality of the ancient inhabitants of Bourbon, and the politeness of Parisians,

I am, &c.

Bourbon, Dec. 21, 1770

LET-

LETTER XX.

DEPARTURE—BOURBON—CAPE.

THE bay of St. Paul we left about ten at night. The sea here is calmer, and the anchorage safer than at St. Dennis, the road of which is spoiled by a vast number of anchors left there by ships. Their cables cut presently. Yet the seamen prefer St. Dennis.

It is very difficult to clear the bay of St. Paul, when the wind blows directly into it, and if a vessel should run on shore, she must certainly be lost; the sea breaking upon a very high sand.

Of this island we lost sight the 23. The services we had received from Monsieur and Madamoiselle de Cremon while we staid, the fair winds, a good table, and the company of Monsieur de Rosbos, our captain, condoled us for our disappointment in not finding the *Indienne*.

Alas! for the unfortunate passengers on board of her, who had to undergo at once, very bad weather, and want of provisions.

It

It is about ninety leagues from Bourbon to the Cape. On Jan. 6, 1771, in the morning we saw Point Natal ten leagues a head of us. In three days we hoped to be on board the *Indienne*. We went before the wind all the way till Monday. It fell calm in the evening, and was sultry hot. At midnight it lightened prodigiously, and the horizon was every where covered with large and heavy black clouds. The sea shone with the fishes which played round our ship.

A contrary wind sprung up at 3 in the morning from the W. with such violence that it obliged us to make for the Cape under our mizen. The tempest drove on board of us a little bird like a titmouse. The coming of land birds on board of ships is always a sign of bad weather, as it proves that the violence of the storm extends far over the land.

We perceived the third day of this storm that our mizen-mast was sprung four feet above the yard—we reefed the sails, strengthened the mast with ropes and slices of wood, and stood for the Cape under a mainsail.

The horizon was wholly hid from us by a tremendous sea. We were much surprized to see within cannon-shot a Dutch vessel steering as we did. It was impossible to speak with her; the fifth day the wind abated. The mizen-mast was examined, and found absolutely broken through. This accident caused us to redouble our efforts to reach the Cape.

The

The way we necessarily lost by boisterous weather, the calm now prevented our recovering.

We again saw the Dutch ship on the 12, and spoke to her. She very warily came up to us with her matches alight, and her guns run out: she came from Batavia, and was going to the Cape.

The Cape appeared at last over our starboard quarter, Jan. 17. We beat about all night. In the morning a violent gale blew. The air was darkened with a thick fog, which totally hid the land. We were near missing the entrance of the bay, when we perceived in a part which cleared up for a moment, a corner of the Table Mountain. We directly loughed up, and about noon found ourselves near the coast, which is very high. It is entirely bare of trees; the higher part rises to a point, formed by the declivities of parallel rocks; it resembles the walls of an old fortification with their talus.

At night we found ourselves behind the Lion Mountain, which at a distance appears like a lion couchant. The head is formed by a great rock, and detached from the body, which is composed of the ridges of different hills. From the head of the lion, they give signals to ships.

We were here quite becalmed, being sheltered from the wind by the lion. In order to enter the bay, we were forced to pass between the island of Roben, which we saw before us on our left, and a neck of land called the point, which is found

at

at the foot of the lion. We were within two cannon-shot, and our impatience redoubled. From hence we could perceive the ships in the road, and the *Indienne* could not be the least remarkable among them.

The tide making, we observed at length from the tops, twelve vessels successively appear, which were lying at anchor. But none of them had French colours. It was the Dutch fleet.

In the chops of the bay we thought proper to anchor. At three in the afternoon, the Commandant came on board, and assured us that the *Indienne* had not appeared.

We had at the bottom of this bay a fine view of Table Mountain, which is the highest land on this coast. Its top is level, and steep on all sides, like an altar: the city is at the foot of it, upon the edge of the bay. There frequently gathers upon the table a thick fog, heaped up as it were, and white as snow. When this happens, the Dutch say, the cloth is laid.

A flag is hoisted by the commandant of the bay as a signal for the vessels to be upon their guard, and a prohibition of the sloop putting to sea. From this cloth descend whirlwinds mingled with fog, like long flakes of wool. The earth is covered with clouds of sand, and ships are often forced to set sail. This gale seldom rises in this season but at about ten in the morning, and lasts till evening Sailors are very fond of the land at the Cape, but are afraid of the road,

road which is most dangerous from April to September.

Here the whole India fleet perished at anchor in 1722, except two ships. Since that time no Dutch ship is allowed to anchor there after the sixth of March. They go to False-bay, where they are under shelter.

Some years ago an attempt was made to have formed the road into an harbour with only one opening, by joining the point *Aupendus* to the isle of Roben; but it did not succeed.

It was my wish, not altogether without hope, to have landed that evening, but I was prevented by a breeze from off the land.

The Normande anchored early in the morning near the town.—It is composed of white stones in straight rows, which at a distance look like houses built with cards.

Three shallops very prettily painted came on board us about sun rising. They were sent by the town's people, who invited us to land and lodge among them. I went on board a shallop of a German, who assured me that for my money I should be well accommodated at Monsieur Nedling's.

I now reflected in our way across the road, upon the singular situation I was in; to find myself, without clothes, money; or acquaintance, among Hollanders, at the very extremity of Africa.

But

But my reflections were interrupted by a spectacle quite new to me. We passed by a number of sea calves, lying at their ease upon floats of sea-weed, like the long horns with which shepherds call their flocks together: penguins swam quietly within reach of our oars; sea fowls came and perched upon the shallop, and on my landing upon the sand I even saw two pelicans at play with a large mastiff, and taking his head into their great beak.

Of a land, in which hospitality and good-will shewed themselves so conspicuously, even among the brute creation, it was impossible not to conceive a good opinion.

Cape of Good Hope, Jan. 10, 1771.

LETTER XXI.

CAPE CONSTANCE—TABLE MOUNTAIN.

ALL the streets here are very strait, some of them are watered with canals, and most planted with chesnut-trees, It was very pleasing to see them covered with leaves in the month of January. The front of the houses were shaded by their foliage, and at the two sides of the doors were seats of brick or turf, on many of which sat ladies with clear and ruddy complexions. I was rejoiced at once more seeing the countenances and the architecture of Europeans.

In company with my guide, I walked through some parts of the place, to Madame Nedling's, a fat Dutch woman, who was very sprightly. She was drinking tea among seven or eight officers of the fleet, who were smoking their pipes. She shewed me a very neat apartment, and assured me that every thing in her house was at my service.

Perhaps one Dutch town is no bad sample of all—the order of each house is alike. The custom

custom of Madame Nedling was this: there was always company in the parlour, and a table covered with peaches, melons, apricots, raisins, pears, cheese, fresh butter, wine, pipes and tobacco. At eight o'clock tea and coffee is ready for breakfast. At noon they have game and fish in plenty for dinner—at four—they drink coffee and tea—at eight they have a supper as plentiful as their dinner.—These good people are eating from morning till night.

Boarding, even in this liberal manner, was formerly no more than half a piastre, or fifty French sols, a trifle more than two shillings per day, but some French officers of the marine, in order to distinguish themselves from other nations, raised the price to a piastre, which is now commonly paid.

When we consider the great plenty of provisions, this is an exorbitant price; it is true, that more elegance is to be found here than in our best taverns. The servants of the house are at your command; you may invite whom you please, and may pass some days at your landlord's country-house, and have the use of his carriage, without any additional expence.

Having dined, I went to see Monsieur Tolbac, the governor, a man of eighty years of age, whose merit procured him this government fifty years ago. He invited me to dinner the next day. I had apprized him of my situation, of which he seemed very sensible.

 The

The company's garden afforded me an agreeable walk; it is divided into four quarters, and watered by a rivulet. Each quarter is bordered by a row of chesnut-trees, twenty feet high. These pallisadoes shelter the plants from the wind, which always blows hard; they have even had the precaution to defend the young trees of the avenues, by a screen of reeds.

Here I saw the plants of Asia and Africa, but particularly the trees of Europe, covered with fruits at a season when I had never before seen leaves on them.

It was now I recollected that an officer in the king's service, named the Viscount du Chaila, had at my leaving the Isle of France, given me a letter for Monsieur du Berg, Secretary of the Council. This letter was in my pocket, having had no time to put it among my other papers on board the *Indienne*, I therefore waited on Monsieur du Berg, and delivered it to him.

My reception with him was very cordial, and as he made me an offer of his purse, I made use of his credit for such things as I absolutely wanted. I asked him if I could not procure a passage on board an India ship, six of which were then going away, and the other six were to go in the beginning of March.

But this was perfectly impracticable, as he assured me, the Dutch India Company had absolutely forbidden it. Indeed the governor had told me as much. I was therefore reduced to the necessity

cessity of staying at the Cape, till some other opportunity offered of getting away.

I was obliged to an unforeseen accident for having brought me hither, and I hoped for another that should carry me away.

An amiable society, however, of a good tempered and happy set of people, added to the plenty of every sort of provisions, made my confinement very supportable.

I was much solicited by Monsieur de Berg's son, to go to Constance, a famous plantation of vineyards, situated about four leagues off. We slept at his country-house, behind the Table-Mountain, at two short leagues distance from the town. We walked thither through a beautiful avenue of chesnut-trees. We saw there—vineyards, ripe for vintage—orchards, chesnut-groves, and a very great abundance of fruits and vegetables.

We continued our route next day to Constance; It is a little hill, rising to the north, which is here the side of the sun at noon. On our approach, we passed through a wood of silver trees, *Arbres d'Argent*. They resemble the pine-tree, have a leaf like the willow, and are covered with a white down which is very shining.

Nothing could be more beautiful than this forest, which seemed to be all of silver. When the wind blew them about, and the sun shone, each leaf glittered like a plate of metal. We walkeo through these groves, so rich and so delightful, in order to look at the vines, which though less splendid in appearance, are of far greater utility.

An avenue of old chesnut-trees, very broad, conducted us to the vineyard of Constance. Over the front of the house we saw a vile painting of a strapping girl, and ugly enough, reclining on a pillar. I took it for a Dutch allegorical figure of Chastity: but they told me it was the portrait of a Madame Constantia, daughter of a governor of the Cape He caused this house to be built, with deep ditches round it, like a fortification. He proposed to raise it a story or two higher, but was prevented by orders from Europe.

The master of the house we found smoking his pipe in his night-gown. He carried us into his cellar, and made us taste his wine. It was in little casks, called *alverames*, containing about ninety pints, ranged very regularly under ground. There were thirty of them. This vineyard, in common years, produces two hundred. He sells the red wine at thirty-five piastres per *alverame*, and the white for thirty. The estate is his own, conditionally, that he shall reserve some wine yearly for the Company, who pay him for it. This he told us himself.

After tasting his wine, we went into his vineyard. The taste of the muscadine grapes was perfectly like that of the wine. The vines are not upon espaliers, and the grapes are but a little way

way from the ground. They let them ripen till the fruit is about half preserved by the sun. We tasted another sort of raisins, which are very sweet, but not muscadine. They make a wine of them, which is of an extravagant price, but is a very fine cordial.

The wine here derives its quality from the particular nature of the soil. They have planted the same stocks, and treated them in the same manner at a place called Lower Constance, a quarter of a league hence, but they have degenerated, as I perceived when I tasted them. The price, as well as the taste, is very inferior, it being sold for twelve piastres the *alverame;* there are some knaves at the Cape, who sometimes are too sharp for strangers in this particular.

A garden of immense extent is situated near the vineyard. I saw in it most of our fruit-trees, in hedges and espaliers, loaded with fruit. They are rather inferior to ours, except the grape, which I prefer. The olives here are not pleasant.

On our return from our walk, we found a plentiful breakfast; our landlady overwhelmed us with kindness; she descended from a French refugee *, and seemed in raptures at the sight of one of her countrymen. Her husband and she shewed me a large hollow chesnut-tree, before the door of the house in which they sometimes dined. Their

* The Abbé de la Caille says, that the French tongue was no longer spoken among the descendants of the Refugees,— except by the few then alive, who were the immediate children of those who left France, between the years 1680 and 1690. *E.*

union

was like that of *Baucis* and *Philemon*, nor were they less happy—except that the husband had the gout, and the wife cried when any body spoke of France.

You travel from Constance to the Cape through an uncultivated plain, covered with shrubs and plants. We stopped at Neuhasen, one of the Company's gardens; it is laid out as those in the town are, but is more fertile. All this part is not exposed to the wind, like the territory of the Cape, where so much dust is blown up, that most of the houses have double sashes to the windows to secure them. In the evening we arrived at the town.

A short time after, my landlord, Monsieur Nedling, invited me to his country-house, near that of Monsieur du Berg. We set out in his voiture, *whether coach or cart does not appear*, drawn by six horses. We passed many days there in the most delightful tranquillity. The ground was strewed with peaches, pears, and oranges, which nobody gathered; the walks were shaded with most beautiful trees. I measured a chesnut-tree, which was eleven feet in circumference; it is said to be the most ancient tree in the whole country.

My host proposed, to some Hollanders, to go upon Tableberg, a steep mountain, at whose foot the town appears to stand. I was of the party. We set out at two o'clock in the morning, on foot. The moon shone very bright. We left on our right a rivulet, which runs from the mountain, and directed our course to an opening in the middle, and which appeared from the town like a chasm in an old

old wall. On our way we heard some wolves howl, and fired several guns to disperse them. The way is rugged to the foot of the mountain, but from thence upwards, is much more so. The seeming aperture in the table, is an oblique separation, of more than musquet-shot wide at its lower entrance; above, it is not more than two toises. This cavity is like a very steep stair-case, filled with sand and loose pieces of rocks. We climbed it, having to the right and left, precipices two hundred feet high. Great massy pieces of stone project, and are ready to roll down. The water drops from the cracks of the rocks, and nourishes a variety of aromatic plants. We heard, during this excursion, the howlings of bavians, a sort of large monkeys, resembling bears.

It was not till after three days and a half's fatigue, that we reached the top of the table. The sun rose over the sea, and its rays enlightened on our right-hand, the steep summits of the Tiger, and of four other chains of mountains, the most distant of which seemed the highest. On our left, and a little behind us, we saw, as upon a plan, the Isle of Penguins, then Constance, False-Bay, and the Lion-Mountain: before us was the Isle of Roben. The town was at our feet. We distinguished even the smallest streets of it. The vast squares of the Company's garden, with its avenues of chesnuts, and its lofty espaliers, appeared but as a parterre, with borders of box; the citadel as a little pentagon, the size of one's hand, and the India ships as walnut-shells. I felt a kind of pride at the thoughts of my elevated station,

station, till I saw eagles hovering above me, so high, that they were nearly out of sight.

It would have been impossible after all, to have thought, but with contempt of such trifling objects, and especially of men who appeared to us like ants, if we had not felt the same wants as ever. We were cold and hungry. A fire was kindled, and we breakfasted. After breakfast, our Dutchman hoisted a cloth at the end of a stick, as a signal of our arrival: but in about half an hour they took it down, lest it should be mistaken for a French flag. The summit of Tableberg, is a plain flat rock, which I take to be about half a league long, and about a quarter broad. It is a species of white quarry, covered here and there with about an inch or two's depth of black mould, mixed with sand and white gravel. We found some little pools of water, formed by the clouds, which frequently are stopped here.

I could find no fossils in this mountain, the strata of which are parallel. The lower rock is a kind of brown free-stone, which turns to sand if exposed to the air. Some pieces of it resemble pieces of bread, with their crust. Though the soil of the summit has so very little depth, it grows a prodigious number of plants.

Of the *immortals* I gathered six species, some small myrtles, a filex, which smells like tea, a flower like the imperial, of a fine purple-colour, and many others whose names I did not know. I found there, a plant, whose flower is red, but without

without smell; by its appearance, one would have thought it a tuberose. Each stalk has two or three leaves turned up together, and holding a little water. The most singular of all, because unlike to any vegetable I had ever seen—is a flower, round like a rose, of the size of a shilling, and entirely flat. This flower glitters with the utmost brilliancy—It has neither stalk nor leaf—It grows very thick upon the gravel, to which it is held by imperceptible fibres. When taken up into the hand, nothing can be perceived but a slimy substance,

Five entire plants here seem to affect in this configuration, a resemblance to only one part of what is common to other plants. First the Nostoc, which is only a sap, as it were; secondly, a chevelu, a small root or fibre issuing from another root, which grows upon the tops of nettles; thirdly, a lichen, or moss, resembling a leaf; fourthly, the ingulated flower of the Table-hill; fifthly, the trufle of Europe, which is a fruit. I might add, the root of the groffe, or groffo, of the Isle of France, if it was not an instance by itself.

Very probably Nature may have adopted this plan among animals. I know many, marine ones, especially, which in form resemble the members only of other animals.

I reached in my walk the extremity of the table, from whence I hailed the appearance of the Atlantic, for having doubled the Cape of Good Hope, you are no longer in the Indian Ocean. I did homage to the memory of Vasco de Gama, who dared first to go round this promontory of tempests. All maritime nations should have combined to erect a statue of him at this place, before which I would most willingly have made a libation of Constance wine, in honour of his heroic perseverance. It is however doubtful, whether Gama was the first who opened a commerce with the Indies by the Cape of Good Hope. Pliny says, that Hanno went round from the sea of Spain as far as Arabia, as may be seen, says he further, by the memoirs he has left of that voyage in writing. Cornelius Nepos * declares, he had seen a captain of a ship, who flying from the anger of King Lathyrus, went from the Red Sea to Spain. And long before this, even Cælius Antipater affirmed, that he had known a Spanish merchant who traded by sea to Æthiopia.

Whatever may be in this, the Cape, so terrible to mariners for its tempestuous sea, is a vast mountain, situated sixteen leagues from hence; it gives its name to this town, notwithstanding so far off. It terminates the most southern part of

* Neco, king of Egypt, sent out some Phœnician ships with orders to go down the Red Sea, and having gone round thence to the North Sea—to return home through the Pillars of Hercules. They landed in Africa, sowed corn, waited the harvest, and then again embarked; they did the like the year following, and in the course of the third year landed in Egypt, having passed, as directed, between the Herculean columns, and through the Mediterranean Sea. Herodotus, from whom this account is taken, says—" On their return they related, what, if others give credit to, I confess I cannot, viz. *that* in their way round Africa, the sun was on their right-hand." See HEROD. 4. book, *for the account of this expedition, and of another undertaken by command of Xerxes.* E.

Africa.

Africa. In treaties, it is looked upon as a point, beyond which naval captures are lawful, many months after the Princes have been at peace in Europe.

Here has frequently been seen peace on the right, and war on the left hand between flags of the same nations; but it has been more often seen, that they have maintained a good understanding in these roads, when discord has reigned in every place else throughout the two hemispheres. I could not but behold with admiration, this happy shore, which war has never yet made desolate; and which is inhabited by a people, useful to the whole world, from the resources of its œconomy, and the extent of its commerce. The dispositions of men are not entirely dependent upon the climate they live in; nor is this wise and peaceable nation indebted for their manners to the soil of their country. Piracy, and civil wars, agitate the Regencies of Algiers, Morocco, and Tripoli; but at the other extremity of Africa, the Dutch have established a settlement blessed with agriculture and concord.

These pleasing reflections, so rarely to be made in any other part of the world, were very satisfactory and seducing during a long walk, but the heat of the sun obliged me to seek for a shelter. There is none but at the entrance of the river. Here I found my companions reposing by the side of a spring. As they began to grow tired, they determined upon returning. It was high noon.—We descended, some by sitting down and suffering themselves to slide; others, upon their hands and knees. The rocks and sands gave way when

when we trod upon them. The sun was nearly vertical, and the rays reflected from the collateral rocks, made the heat almost insupportable. We frequently quitted the path, and fled to the shade of some point of the rock to take breath. My knees failed ; and I had a violent thirst upon me : towards the evening we arrived at the town. Madame Nedling expected us, and had prepared refreshments against our return. We had lemonade, with nutmeg and wine in it. Of this we drank without danger, and went to bed. No excursion had ever proved so entertaining to me, nor was rest ever before so welcome.

Cape of Good Hope, Feb. 6, 1771.

LETTER XXII.

AIR AND SOIL.

PLANTS, INSECTS, AND ANIMALS.

HERE the air is remarkably salubrious. It is refreshed by the south-east winds, which are so cold, even in the midst of summer, that cloth is worn here all the year round. Its latitude is, notwithstanding, thirty-three degrees south. But I am persuaded that the south pole is much colder than the north.

Few disorders are incident to the people of the Cape. The scurvy is soon cured, though there are no sea turtles. But the small-pox, on the other hand, makes most dreadful ravages—many of the inhabitants are deeply scarred with it. It is reported to have been introduced here by a ship from Denmark. Most of the Hottentots who caught it, died. Since which time, they are reduced to a very small number, and they seldom come down to the town.

 A sandy

A sandy gravel, mingled with a white earth, constitutes the soil of the Cape. I don't know whether precious minerals are a part of its productions. The Dutch formerly had gold mines at Lagoa, in the streights of Mosambique, and had also a settlement there, but were forced to abandon it, on account of the badness of the air *.

At the house of the Fort-Major, I saw a sulphureous earth, in which were pieces of wood; reduced to a cinder; also true *gypsum*, and black cubes of all sizes, united as it were by amalgamation, without having lost their shape. These last are believed to be iron ore.

The only trees peculiar to the country, are the tree of gold, and tree of silver, the wood of which is only fit to burn. The former differs from the latter in nothing but the colour of its leaf, which is yellow. There are said to be forests of these within land; but in this part, the ground is covered with a variety of flowering, and other shrubs. This confirms my opinion, that they flouish only in a temperate air, their calice being formed to imbibe no more than a moderate heat.

Plants which seemed most worthy of notice, exclusive of those already mentioned, are—a red flower, which resembles a tufted butterfly, with legs, four wings, and a tail. A species of hyacinth, with a long stalk, all the flowers of which are formed at the top, like the buds of the *impe-*

* Bad indeed is that air which will drive a Dutchman from a gold mine. *E.*

rial:

rial: another bulbous flower, growing in the marshes; it is like a large red tulip, in the center of which is a multitude of small flowers.

One shrub, whose flower resembles a large artichoke, of a flesh colour. Another common one, of which they make beautiful hedges. It bears clusters of papillonaceous flowers, of a rose colour. They are succeeded by leguminous grains.

Some of these I brought to plant in France, which stood the winter in 1771, and vegetated in the king's garden in 1772.

Here are several species of insects. Among these is a beautiful red grasshopper, speckled with black; some very fine butterflies, and another very singular insect—it is a little brown scarabæus, and runs very fast. When attempted to be taken, it emits with a noise a wind, followed by a little smoke; if the finger is touched by this vapour, a brown stain ensues, which lasts some days. He repeats this operation many times successively. The inhabitants call it the cannonier.

At the Cape, our humming-bird is not uncommon. I saw one of the size of a walnut, of a changeable green colour on the belly. It had a collar of red feathers, which shone upon his stomach like rubies; its wings were brown, like a sparrow's, and appeared upon his beautiful plumage like a surtout. His beak was black, of a good length, and being curved, was of a proper shape to seek for honey in the bosom of flowers. It had a long and taper tongue. It lived several

 days.

days. I saw it eat flies, and drink sugared water. But as it was attempting to bathe in the cup set for that purpose, its feathers adhered together, and the same night the musquitos devoured it.

We see some birds of the colcur of fire, with a belly and head like black velvet; they become brown in the winter. Some of them change colour thrice a year. There is also a bird of Paradise, but not so beautiful as those I saw in Asia. I did not see one of these alive. The Gardner's Friend, and a kind of *Tarins*, are frequently found in gardens. I wished to have taken a Gardner's Friend to Europe—it would have been of great service there. I observed it to be constantly employed in catching caterpillars, and hooking them upon the thorns on the bushes.

Eagles are also found here, with another bird very near of the same species. It is called the *Secretary*, having round its neck a row of long quills, fit for writing with. It has this particularity, that it cannot stand upright on its legs, which are long, and covered with scales. It lives upon serpents only. The length of its claws renders it very capable of seizing them, and this ruff of feathers round its neck, protects it from their bites. This bird also ought to be naturalized amongst us. The ostrich is very common here; they offered me young ones at a crown each. I have eaten of their eggs, which are far inferior to those of pullets. The *Casoar* is found here, and is covered with coarse hair instead of feathers. There is a prodigious number of sea-birds, of the names and natures of which, I am entirely ignorant. The eggs laid by penguins are thought much of, but I did not think them extraordinary. They have this singular quality, that the white being boiled, continues always transparent

On both sides of the Cape the sea abounds in fish, which I thought better than that of the Islands, but inferior to that of Europe. We find on the shore some shells, the paper-nautilus, the Medusa's head, some *lepas*, and very beautiful lithophytes, which, when arranged upon paper, represent trees, brown, saffron, and purple. They are sold to travellers. I saw a fish here, of the size and shape of the blade of a Flemish knife. It was silvered over, and marked naturally on each side with the impression of two fingers; here are sea-calves, whales, sea-cows, cod, and a great variety of other common fish, of which I shall not speak, my observations having been but few, and my knowledge of ichthyology but slight.

A species of mountain turtle, with yellow shells, marked with black, is very common on these shores, they are fit for no use whatever. There are porcupines, and marmots, which differ from ours in form; stags and deer are in plenty, as also wild asses, zebras, &c. An English engineer, some years ago, killed here a giraffe, or camel-leopard, an animal sixteen feet high, that browzes on the leaves of trees.

A large monkey, called the Bavian here, is made like a bear. The nature of the monkey seems to have an analogy with that of every class

 of

of animals. I remember to have seen a sapajou, which had the head and mane of a lion. That of Madagascar, called maki, resembles a leveret, and the ourang-outang is like a man.

I now every day became acquainted with some animals unknown in Europe—they seem to have taken refuge in those parts of the globe least frequented by men, whose neighbourhood is always fatal to them. The same may be said of the plants, the species of which are the most various, the less cultivated the ground. M. de Tolbac informed me, that he had sent to Monsieur Linnæus of Sweden, some plants from the Cape, so different from plants known in Europe, that this great naturalist wrote to him:—"*You have conferred upon me the greatest pleasure; but you have thrown my whole system into disorder.*"

Horses are good at the Cape, and the asses beautiful. The oxen have a large swelling, or excrescence on their necks, formed of fat, and some small vessels interspersed. At first sight, this excrescence seems monstrous; but one may soon perceive that it is a reservoir, with which Nature, for its support, has furnished this animal, destined to live in the scorching plains of Africa. In the dry season, the beast grows thin, and the swelling diminishes; but recovers itself, and the wen is recruited with supplies, when it feeds on green herbs. Other animals, under this climate, have the same advantages. The camel has a bunch, the dromedary has two, in the form of a saddle. The sheep has a large tail, made *en capuchon*, or *poake*, which is but a lump of suet, of several pounds weight.

Even

Even the very oxen here are taught almost to run with the carts to which they are harnessed.

So plentiful are beef and mutton, that the heads and feet are thrown away, which draws the wolves of a night into the very town. I frequently hear them howling in the environs. Pliny observes, that the European lions found in Romania, are more active and strong than those of Africa; and the wolves of Africa and Egypt, he adds, are but small, and not very strong. In fact, the wolves of the Cape are much less dangerous than ours. I might add, that this superiority extends even to the men of our continent. We have more spirit and courage than the Asiatics and Negroes; but, methinks, it would be a commendation more worthy of us, could it be said, we surpassed them in justice, benevolence, and other social virtues.

Here, as every where, the tiger is more dangerous than the wolf; he is cunning as a cat, but wants courage. The dogs attack him fearlessly.

The lion affords very different sport. As soon as they hear his roar, terror seizes them. If they see him, they stand, but will not approach him. The hunters shoot him with guns of a large bore* I have

* Our author not having mentioned the elephant—which is commonly found and frequently hunted at the Cape—I will insert an abstract from the Abbé de la Caille, which I hope will be pleasing to the reader.——" The hunters always seek for the elephant in the neighbourhood of rivers—and attack him in the following manner: Three cavaliers well mounted go out

 together

I have handled one of them, but few, except peasants of the country, can use them.

together—two of them remain at a proper distance in the plain, and the third waits the coming of the beast to quench his thirst at the river—of which he gives notice by a signal to his companions—and then pierces him with a stroke of a launce, while drinking. The animal, enraged at the wound, pursues the cavalier, who retires to the plain. One of his companions hastens to his aid, and attacking the elephant, wounds him a second time. The beast, forgetting his first assailant, pursues the last. The third cavalier then advances, and wounds him also.—The creature now disregards the second, in like manner as he did the first—and follows the third, upon whom he seems desirous of wreaking his fury.——In the mean time he loses blood very fast, and not the less for the violence of his rage — and he sometimes dies exhausted before his first enemy returns to the charge—this, however, is not usually the case, and he is then again attacked by the first man, and so on by the second and third—till he expires." I have here described the chase only of the elephant. The inhabitants have many ways of taking him alive; sometimes by a female put in a park, fenced in for the purpose, and sometimes in toils, of which there are various kinds.

The Abbé then relates a tragical event which happened while he was at the Cape.——" Three brothers, who had been long used to this exercise, were about to return to Holland, but determined to add one more to their many triumphs.—The first brother pierced the beast and escaped; the second wounded him, but in flying, his horse's fore-feet sunk into a mole-hill,—and could not recover before the elephant came up.—The furious beast seized the cavalier with his trunk—tore him from his horse, and whirled him upon the ground,—he then took up the horse also with his trunk, and threw him several yards into the air;—this done, he returned to the poor man, who lay unable to rise from the earth, and having again seized him, cast him with all his might into the air, and held out his teeth to catch him as he came down—the unhappy wretch, falling from a prodigious height upon one of the teeth, it pierced him through the body, and he lay there impaled. The savage beast persisted in holding him for some time in this condition, and seemed to exult over him, by advancing him towards his companions, who, though they saw his distress, and heard the agonizing cries he uttered, were unable to assist him. *E.*

This

This masterly creature, however is seldom found within sixty leagues of the Cape.—He inhabits the forests within land; his roaring, at a distance, sounds like the grumbling of distant thunder. He seldom attacks man; he neither seeks, nor avoids him; but if wounded by a hunter, he will select that man among all the rest, and spring upon him with an implacable fury. The Company allow privileges and rewards for the encouragement of lion-hunting.

The following circumstance was stated to me by the Governor, M. Berg, the Fort-major, and the principal inhabitants, who vouched the truth of it.

Some hundred miles, perhaps, from the Cape, in the uncultivated lands, there is found a prodigious quantity of small Cabris, goats. I saw some of them in the Company's menageries; they have two small horns on their heads; their hair is fallow-coloured, spotted with white. These creatures feed in such vast numbers, that those who go first in the route they take, devour all the pasture, and become very fat, insomuch that their followers, finding no food, grow very lean. Thus they continue their march in vast herds, until stopped by some chain of mountains; they then turn back, and those in the rear, finding in their turn fresh herbage, recover their good plight, while those who were leaders before, lose their flesh, and become lean. Attempts have been made to form them into herds, but they cannot be tamed sufficiently for that purpose. These innumerable armies are constantly followed by troops of of lions and tigers, as if Nature, in creating the former, had decreed a certain subsistence to the latter. It is scarcely to be doubted, from what was declared to me by the Gentlemen I have taken the liberty to mention that, there are lions innumerable in the interior parts of Africa: the account of the Hollanders tallies with history in this respect. Polybius says, that being in Africa with Scipio, he saw several lions placed on crosses, to deter others from approaching the villages. Pompey, according to Pliny, did at one time turn six hundred lions into the amphitheatre, among which there were three hundred and fifteen males. There seems to be a physical cause in the natural system for Africa's being the practical residence of the brute creation. It is to be presumed, that want of water has prevented the increase of the human species, and their forming themselves into great nations here, as they have done in Asia. Vast in extent as this coast is, the rivers are but few, and these small. The animals of Africa can feed a long time without water. I have observed on board of ships, that the African sheep drink but once a week, although their provender is dried herbs.

Here many establishments have been made by the Dutch, for 300 leagues along the coast, and for 150 upon the Straits of Mosambique. They have scarce any at above 50 leagues within land. It is pretended that this colony can put under arms four or five thousand white men, but it would be difficult to get them together. Their numbers would be very soon increased, if the free exercise of religion were permitted. Holland, perhaps upon its own account, fears the aggrandizing of this colony,

lony, preferable in every respect to the mother-country. The air is pure and temperate; all manner of provisions abound; a quintal of corn costs there no more than one hundred sous, ten pounds of mutton for twelve sous. A legre of wine, containing two hogsheads and a half, for one hundred and fifty livres *. They exact considerable duties upon these articles when sold to strangers; but an inhabitant buys at a much cheaper rate.

Various other articles belong to the trade of this country, as the skins of sheep, oxen, sea-calves, and tigers; aloes, salt provisions, butter, dry fruits, and all sorts of eatables † They have tried in vain to

* About six pounds ten shillings sterling.

† In 1771, the Dutch East-India ships homeward-bound, being at the Cape, and not freighted, took on board in bulk some corn, the produce of the country, and brought it to Holland. The wheat is a beautiful berry, thin skinned, white, quite dry, and clean, and in weight exceeds the best English or Zealand, as 140 to 132. The rye is superior to any of Northern growth.—My information of its proportional weight, is not so accurate as that of the wheat; but it was sold at ten or twelve per cent. above the best rye of Prussia. The barley is thin, and much inferior to our Norfolk. It is more like the Zealand barley. The Dutch incline to cultivate this new branch of trade, which promises much benefit. They sell it in small lots at public auction. In 1774, the wheat sold at two hundred and thirty guilders, which is about sixty-four shillings a quarter, Winchester. The heat of the climate at the Cape so effectually dries the grain, that it may be brought in bulk, though the voyage is so long a one, without apprehension of danger from its effervescing.—Why had we not imported to this country, while a defective crop stared us in the face, more especially *now* that it is entirely in our possession, and so little probability of any foreign force intercepting the cargo; as much wheat and other grain as this very fertile colony could spare? *E.*

grow

grow coffee and sugar, the vegetables of Asia will not thrive here. The chesnut-tree grows very fast, but being very soft, is not fit for building. Firs do not thrive. The pine rises to a moderate height. This country might, from its situation, have been the mart for the commerce of Asia; but the North of Europe monopolizes all maritime affairs. The harbour is by no means safe, and the entrance of it always dangerous. I have seen at this season, which is the finest of the year, many vessels forced to hoist sail and go to sea. After all, the people should be thankful to Providence, for having given them every requisite, to supply the real wants of Europeans, without having added those things that serve only to gratify their passions.

Cape of Good Hope, Feb. 10, 1771.

LET-

LETTER XXIII.

SLAVES—HOTTENTOTS—HOLLANDERS.

EVEN among slaves, the plenty of this country abounds. They have bread and greens at discretion. A sheep is allowed weekly for two negroes. They do not work on Sundays. They lay upon beds with matrasses and coverlids. Both men and women are clad with warm clothes. I speak on this subject from experience, having been told by several blacks that their French masters had sold them to the Dutch, by way of punishing them, but that in fact, they had thereby done them a service. A slave costs as much again here as in the Isle of France. Man is therefore doubly valuable in this place. The situation of these negroes would be preferable to that of the peasants of Europe, if there were any compensation for the loss of liberty.

Their liberal and humane treatment has a great influence upon their behaviour; their zeal, activity, and fidelity, are amazingly great. Yet these are the very same islanders of Madagascar, who are

are so inattentive to their masters in our colonies.

From Batavia also, many slaves are imported They are Malays, a nation of Asia, very populous, but little known in Europe. Their language and customs are peculiar to themselves. They are more ugly than negroes, and resemble them in feature. Their stature is lower, their colour *d'ur noín cendré*, their hair long, but thin. These Malays are subject to the most violent passions.

Here Hottentots are the natural inhabitants, and free.—They are not robbers—they do not sell their children, nor do they attempt to enslave each other. Among them adultery is punished with death—the culprit is stoned. Some of them let themselves as houshold servants, for a piastre a year, and serve the inhabitants with so much affection, as to hazard their lives for them. They are constantly armed with a demi-lance, or dart.

Government very wisely seem to make a point of protecting the Hottentots. When they lodge a complaint against an European, they are favourably heard: it being presumed that the party, known to have the fewest desires, and fewest wants, is the most likely to be in the right.

Many of them come daily into the town, driving waggons drawn by eight pairs of oxen. They have whips of a great length, which they use with both hands. The driver, from his seat, flogs with equal address the fore, or wheel horses.

These

These are, for the most part, a simple, pastoral people, and all upon a footing; but in each village they chuse from among themselves two men, to whom they give the title of captain, or corporal, these manage their commercial business with the Company. They sell their flocks very cheap, —so cheap even, as three or four sheep for a roll of tobacco. Although they have such numbers of cattle, they generally wait till they die by accident, or old age, before they eat them.

Such of them as I saw, had a sheep-skin over their shoulders, with a cap and belt of the same stuff. They shewed me how they lay to rest, which was naked, at their length upon the ground, and their cloak serving to cover them.

Their colour is not so strong a black as the negroes. Like them, however, they have a flat nose, wide mouth, and thick lips. Their hair is shorter and more curly, like wool *. I have observed a something very particular in their speech—every word is preceded by a clack of the tongue, the reason, without doubt, of their being called the Choccoquas; which name they have in some old maps, by Monsieur de L'Isle. One would really think they continually repeated choccoq.

* Many different accounts are given of the stature of the Hottentots —Our author is silent on this subject. The Abbé de la Caille says, he measured one who was 6 feet 7 inches ¼ high, and corpulent in proportion; this man came into the town with many others, and does not appear to have been selected for his extraordinary stature—we may therefore suppose these people to be in general larger than Europeans. Had he been remarkable for his size, the Abbé would doubtless have spoken of him accordingly.——*The French foot is to that of England as* 1000 *to* 1068. *E.*

What

What account will satisfy you concerning the apron* of the Hottentot women !—believe me it is a story, which every body affirmed to be false ; It is drawn from Kolben's voyage, which is full of such ridiculous fables.

You very well know Pliny's remark is more to be depended on, that animals are less sagacious, in proportion as their blood is thicker. The strongest animals, by his account, have the thickest blood, and the more cunning the thinnest. I have myself remarked, that on bleeding a negro, his blood curdled very quickly. To this cause I should readily attribute the superiority of white people over the blacks.

You are doubtless aware that, besides their slaves, and the Hottentots, the Dutch retain indented servants. They are Europeans, to whom the Company advance money, and whom the inhabitants take home with them, having first paid the government their disbursements.

These people are, in general, employed to superintend houshold matters. They are diligent enough at first, but good living makes them idle.

Here, the inhabitants do not game, nor do they

* Among variety of contemptible fictions detailed in *Valiant's Travels from the Cape of Good Hope, into the interior parts of Africa*; this especially is attempted to be received, but with circumstances so improbable and gross, that the impostor is much too ridiculous to gain any credit.—And where can such unnatural lies be more wantonly sported, than in a compilation every where crouded with absurdities, and monsters—a mere vehicle of falsehood, extravagance, and blasphemy. *E.*

they visit much. The women look after their servants and houses, the furniture of which is always in the nicest order. The husband manages the business abroad. In the evening the family assembles, they walk, and take the air as soon as the breeze is at an end. The same business, and the same pleasures, are repeated each day.

It is charming to contemplate the harmony that prevails among relations. My hostess's brother was a peasant of the Cape, who came hither from the interior full seventy leagues. This man hardly ever spoke. and was continually sitting and smoking his pipe. He had a little boy with him, of ten years old, who constantly stood by him. The father put his hand to his cheek, and caressed him without opening his lips; the child, as silent as the father, pressed his great hands in his own, looking up to him with eyes expressive of the most filial tenderness. This little boy wore the country habit,—he had a cousin in the house, of his own age, who was very genteely dressed; these children used to walk out together with the greatest intimacy. The little citizen did not look with contempt upon the peasant—he was his cousin.

Though but sixteen years old, Madamoiselle manages without assistance a very respectable family. She receives strangers—attends to the servants—and maintains the most perfect order in the house, and with a countenance always at ease. Her youth—her beauty—her accomplishments and character, gain her the esteem of every body: yet I never observed her pay any regard to the compliments addressed to her. I told her one day, she had a great many friends;—"I have one great one," said she—"that is my *father*."

The supreme delight of this worthy man, when he came home from business, was to seat himself among his children. They jumped round his neck—the little ones embraced his knees; they appealed to him in their little disputes—while the eldest daughter, excusing some—approving others—and smiling upon all, redoubled the joy of the truly parental father. Methought I saw the Antiope of Idomeneus.

Here, a happy industrious people, content with domestic enjoyment, the sure consequence of a virtuous life, do not seek after it, in romances, or upon the theatre. There are no public exhibitions at the Cape, nor are they wished for. In his own house each man views the most pleasing—the most affecting of all spectacles, servants happy: children well brought up:—and wives, faithful and affectionate. These are the delights which the tales of fiction cannot afford. They are a pensive set of people, who chuse rather to feel—than to converse, or to argue. Perhaps the want of subject, is the cause of their taciturnity. But of what consequence is the mind's being vacant, so the heart be full, and actuated by the tender emotions of nature, unexcited by artifice, or unconstrained by unreasonable decorum and unnatural reserve.

Girls of the Cape are no sooner in love, than

they avow it ingenuously. They call it a natural sentiment, a gentle passion, upon which depends the felicity of their lives, and compensates the pains and danger of their becoming mothers; but they, as well as those all over the world—will themselves make choice of the man to whom they make their vows of constancy.

Of their passion, they affect to make no mystery; as they feel it—so they express it. Are you beloved? You are accepted, entertained, and publicly distinguished. I was a witness to a parting scene between Madamoiselle Nedling and her lover. In tears, and with sighs, she prepared the presents which were to be the pledges of her affection—in which employment she neither sought for witnesses—nor did she shun them.

Who must not have observed, that mutual affection is generally productive of a happy marriage. The young men are equally frank in their proceedings. They return from Europe to fulfil their engagements; and bring with them the merit of the dangers through which they have passed. and of a love unaltered by an absence from its object. Esteem and affection are united, and maintain through life that desire of pleasing, which elsewhere shews itself more towards other objects, than towards that to which it is properly due.

Notwithstanding the happiness in which they live here, blessed with simplicity of manners, and a country so rich and plentiful—yet, every thing which comes from Holland, is received among them with transport. Their houses are papered with views of Amsterdam, of its public places,

 and

and environs. They look upon Holland as their country, and even strangers in their service speak of it in that light only. I asked a Swede in the Company's service, how long the fleet would be on its return to Holland—"we shall be at least three months," replied he, "before we get home."

The church is magnificent. Here divine service is performed with great decency. I don't know whether the Dutch think religion an addition to their happiness, but there are men here whose ancestors have sacrificed every thing that they held most dear to the exercise of it. I speak of the French Refugees. At some leagues distance from the Cape, they have a settlement, which is called *La Petite Rochelle*. They are quite in raptures at the sight of a Frenchman, they bring him home to their houses, and present him to their wives and children, as a man, happy in having seen the country of their forefathers, and in a prospect of returning to it again. France is continually the subject of discourse, they admire it, they praise it; yet do they complain of it, as of a mother, whose severity towards them had been too extreme. Thus do they break in upon their enjoyment of the country they now live in—by lamenting their exile from that which they had never seen.

Magistrates, and especially the Governor, are here treated with the utmost deference. His house is distinguished only from others, by the centinel at the door, and by the custom of sounding a trumpet when he sits down to dinner. This piece

piece of respect is annexed to his place. No other pomp attends his person. He goes out without retinue, and is easy of access. His house stands by the side of a canal, shaded with chesnut-trees planted before his door. In it, are the pictures of Ruyter, Van Trump, and some other illustrious persons of Holland. It is small and plain, and suited to the very few people who have affairs to solicit with him: but the Governor himself is so respected and beloved, that the inhabitants do not even pass his door without shewing some mark or other of their respect.

The Governor gives no public entertainments; but what is better, though less practised, his purse is always open for the service of worthy and indigent people. They need pay no court to him. If they seek for justice, they obtain it of the council—if succour, this he takes upon himself as a duty; injustice only can be solicited, but it constantly meets with the merited success.

His leisure, of which he has much upon his hands, he employs for the preservation of peace and concord, being persuaded of their tendency to the well-being of all societies. He is not of opinion that the power of the chief magistrate depends upon discord, and dissension among individuals. I have heard him say, that the best policy was to deal justly and honestly with every man. He frequently invites strangers to his table. Though more than eighty years old, his conversation is lively; he is acquainted with most of our works

works of genius, and is fond of them. Of all the Frenchmen he has seen, he chiefly regrets the Abbé de la Caille, for whom he built an Observatory here. He esteemed him for his learning, his modesty, his disinterestedness, and social qualities. I know nothing more of this learned man than by his works; but in mentioning the respect paid by strangers to his memory, I feel a satisfaction at finishing my account of this estimable body of people, with their eulogium on one of my countrymen *

* The late Dr. Goldsmith is said frequently to have spoke of this chapter, as a master-piece of good sense, and well directed attention and sensibility. *E.*

LETTER XXIV.

CONTINUATION OF MY JOURNAL TO THE CAPE.

MONSIEUR Serrurier, first minister of the church, invited me to go and see the library. The building is handsome and fit for the purpose. I could not help remarking a number of books of theology, which have never yet occasioned any controversies, and indeed the Dutch never look in them. At the end of the company's garden, there is a menagerie containing a great number of birds. The pelicans that I saw upon the beach on my arrival had been boarders in this place; but they were driven away because they eat the young ducks. In the day time they went into the road to seek for fish, and at night returned to roost on shore.

A signal was made, Feb. 10. that a French ship appeared: It was the *Alliance*, that had been forced from Bourbon by the hurricane. She had lost her mizen mast in the storm. She could give us no tidings of the *Indienne*. Having taken in provisions, she continued her voyage to America

 without

without repairing the loss of her mast. The Dutch have a number of them in store, which they keep buried in the sand: but they sell them very dear. A new mizen mast for the *Normande* cost 1000 crowns.

The *Digue*, a pink of the King's, that left the Isle of France a month before, came into the Cape on the 11, to get provisions. I knew the captain, Monsieur le Fer. He told me he should anchor here for a few days only, and then steer for the westward. Despairing to see the *Indienne*, and my effects, any more, and thinking this opportunity a favourable one, I resolved to embrace it.

Monsieur Berg, and Monsieur Tolbac, were acquainted with my determination; both of them again offered me their purses. Supping one evening at the governor's, and talking of Constance wine, Monsieur de Tolbac asked me if I would not carry some of it with me to Europe; I very naturally answered, that the disorder in my finances, by the accident that had happened, prevented my making a little purchase of it, which I meant to have done, as a present for a lady to whom I had a particular attachment. He told me he would relieve me from this embarrassment by giving me, if I thought proper, an alverame of red, or of white, wine, or of both; I answered him that one would suffice, and that I would present it in his name to the person for whom I had intended it. " *No, said he,* " *'tis to you I give it, as a remembrance of me, and all the acknowledgement I ask, is, that you will write to me me when you get to France.*" He sent me the wine next morning. Monsieur Berg, to whom I had frequently mentioned the civilities I had received from Monsieur and Madamoiselle Cremon, told me, he would take upon himself the making my acknowledgements to them, and that he would send them, as from me, two dozen of Constance wine.

Where it was ordered that I should be in absolute want of every thing, I was not a little happy, and certainly very grateful, at meeting, among strangers, with men of so obliging and benevolent a disposition.

With the captain of the *Digue*, I agreed to pay 600 livres for my passage to France He was to sail in a few days. I was very cautious of using Monsieur du Berg's credit. I made up one single suit of clothes only, and a little linen. This was the whole equipage of an officer returning from the East-Indies. I had not only lost all my effects, but found myself 140 livres in debt.

My affairs here were but just settled, when the *African* came to an anchor at the Cape; she came to take in provisions; she left the Isle of France about the middle of January, and brought the following account of the *Indienne.*

Alas! this ill-fated vessel had lost all her masts in the storm, and after having kept the sea for more than a month, returned at length to the Isle of of France, in so bad a condition, that she had been since disarmed. The very rough seas, through which she struggled so long, had spoilt part of her cargo, and had filled the powder room with water, insomuch that the trunks of the passengers were afloat. Monsieur Moncherat, a good man I knew there, had looked over my luggage, and wrote me word, that but little damage had been done to any thing, except to the things in my cabbin.

We soon learned an odd accident that happened on board the *Indienne*. Among the transports who were sent to the isle of France, there was one of a good family, named *** He had assassinated his brother-in-law in France. On the voyage, he quarrelled with the supercargo, and when they landed, he stabbed him without ceremony, and broke the blade of his sword in his body. He fled to the woods, but was found, and committed to prison. He was tried and condemned, but while under sentence of death, there was a hole made in the wall of his prison, through which he escaped.

This very strange event happened two months before my departure.

During the tempest to which the *Indienne* was exposed, her mizen-mast carried away, fell into the sea. While they were hastily cutting away the rigging, they saw, in the middle of the waves, a sailor hanging by the round of the floating mast. He cried out, save me, save me, I am *** It was really this unhappy wretch. At

At the return of the *Indienne* to the isle of France, they suffered him once more to escape. When Monsieur de Tolbac heard this anecdote, he only said, *He that's born to be hanged, will never be drowned.*

Nothing had been heard, or could be learnt of the *Alliance*, which probably was lost.

For me, nothing could be more fortunate, than to receive my effects on the eve of my departure, and to be no longer on board the *Indienne*, which was likely to be detained some time at the isle of France.

We did not sail till March 2. I paid all my expences with bills of exchange upon the Treasurer for the Colonies, at six months, by which I lost twenty-two per cent. discount.

Of the Governor, and of Monsieur du Berg, who gave me several natural curiosities, I now took my leave. I had presented him with some of mine. Madamoiselle Berg gave me three perroquets from Madagascar; they had grey heads, and were of the size of sparrows. My landlady furnished me with fruits, and weeping; wished me, as did her family, a good voyage.

I now, with much sensibility and unaffected concern, left these good people, as well as their gardens of European fruit-trees, which, though in the month of March, were loaded with fruit. I re-

I rejoiced in the thoughts, however, of finding them in blossom in Europe, and of enjoying, in one year, two summers and no winter: but, what far exceeded the delights of a beautiful country and mild season, I was about to revisit my native country, and the friends I left in it.

LET

LETTER XXV.

DEPARTURE FROM THE CAPE.

ISLAND OF ASCENSION.

WE sailed, at two in the afternoon, March 2, in company with six of the fleet from Batavia. The other six went fifteen days before. We went out by the second opening of the bay, leaving Roben's Island on the left. We soon outsailed the Dutch ships. They kept company to the latitude of the Azores, where two ships of war waited to convoy them to Holland.

The Cape is reckoned by mariners a third part of the way from the Isle of France to Europe: another third they call to the Line: and the last, from thence home.

While sitting upon deck after dinner, in the most perfect security, eight days since our departure, we saw a great flame issue from the kitchen-

 chimney,

chimney, which rose several yards above deck. Every body ran forward. It was no more than a panic: an awkward cook had thrown some fat upon the hearth. It was mentioned by some of the officers upon this subject, that a few years ago, in a ship called the ———, the fire had catched the mast, and that all the rigging forward being on fire, the officers and crew were in distraction, and came in a tumult to tell the captain, who coming out of the cabbin, said very coolly, "My good friends, this is nothing, only bear away, and put before the wind."

For the flames, driven by the wind, in fact, ceased when all the sails were burnt. The man thus endowed with *sang-froid*, was Monsieur de Surville, an officer of great merit in the Company's service.

A S. W. wind, and a fine sea constantly, carried us before it very pleasantly, till we got to the Island of Ascension. We were near its latitude, March 20, 8 deg. S. but we had taken it too much eastward. We were obliged to run down the longitude, our intention being to anchor there, and catch some turtle.

The morning of the 22, we had sight of it.— This island is seen ten leagues off, though scarce a league and half over. One can distinguish a pointed hill, called the Green Mountain. The rest of the island is formed of small black and red hills, and the pieces of rocks near the sea were quite white with the dung of birds.

In

In proportion to the nearness of your approach, the more horrid the landscape appears. We coasted along shore, in order to anchor in the north-west. At the foot of these black hills, we perceived an appearance like the ruins of an immense city. They were sunken rocks, which have proceeded from an ancient volcano; they are scattered all over the plain, and as far as the sea, in strange shapes. The shore hereabouts is composed of them. Some are formed like pyramids, others like grottos, half finished arches: the waves break against them: one while they flow over them, and in running down again, cover them with a kind of table-cloth of foam! then finding flat pieces raised high, and full of holes, they beat against them underneath, and throw up long water spouts of various forms.

The shores here are all black and white, and were almost covered with sea-fowl. A number of frigate-birds hovered about our rigging, where they were taken by the seamen. We anchored in the evening at the entrance of the Great Bay, I went into the boat with the men who were to catch turtle. The landing-place is at the foot of a mass of rocks, which is seen from the anchorage, at the extremity of the bay on the right-side. We got out upon a large sand, which is white, mixed with grains of red, green, and other colours, like that kind of aniseed called *mignonette*. Some paces from hence we found a little grotto, and in it a bottle, in which the ships who touch there put letters. They break the bottle, and having read the letters, put them into another.

About

About fifty paces bearing forward, and taking to the left, behind the rock, to a little plain, where the ground broke to pieces under our feet, as if it had been a covering of snow. I tasted some of it, it was salt, which I thought very strange, there being no appearance of the sea's coming so far.

Having brought up wood, the kettle, and the sail of the boat, upon which our men lay down in expectation of night. It is about eight in the evening only that the turtles come on shore. The people were laying here at their ease, when one of them jumping up, called out in a great fright, *a dead man, here's a dead man.*—The matter was, by a little cross, placed on a small hill of sand, we perceived that some person had been buried there. The man had lain down upon this place without thinking; but not one of them would stay here a moment after this discovery; and we were obliged to comply with their whim, and remove about a hundred yards farther.

The moon rising now, began to diffuse a light over this dreary solitude, which, unlike agreeable views, so usually improved and rendered more soft and pleasing by her milder radiance, appeared only so much more horrible and dismal. We were at the foot of the Black-Hill, at the top of which we could see a large cross, put up, as we supposed, by some sailors who had been there. Before us, the plain was covered with rocks, from which rose an infinite number of points, about the height of a man.

A sparkling

A sparkling on the top of these points was occasioned by the moon; they were whitened by the dung of the birds that had rested there. These white heads upon black bodies, the one of which were upright, the other sloping, appeared like ghosts wandering over the tombs. The most profound silence reigned in this dismal region; a silence, now and then only interrupted and rendered more horrid, by the roaring of the sea on the beach, or the cry of a stray frigate-bird, frighted at the sight of man.

On the edge of the bay waiting for turtles, we lay upon our bellies as still as possible, this animal flying at the least noise. At last we saw three come out of the water; they appeared like black clouds, creeping along the sand. We ran to the first, but our impatience occasioned our losing it. She went down the cliff again, and swam away. The second was advanced farther, and could not escape, but was thrown upon its back. In the course of the night, and in the same valley, we turned above fifty, some of which weighed above five cwt.

Holes were dug all over the shore, where they had lain so many even as three hundred eggs, and had covered them with sand, in which they were to be hatched by the sun.

A turtle, killed by the sailors, was now made soup of, after which I laid me down in the grotto, where the letters are deposited, that I might enjoy the shelter of the rock, the distant noise of the sea, and the softness of the sand. I ordered a sailor to fetch me my wrapping-gown; but he dared not go by himself past the place where the man had been buried. No beings, certainly, can be at once so intrepid, and so dastardly superstitious as seamen.

On awaking after a very comfortable sleep, I found a ſcorpion and some crabs at the entrance of my cave. I saw no other herbs here, than a species of milk-thistle, or celandine. Its juice was milky, and very bitter. The herbage, and the animals were worthy of the country they were in.

I made shift to scramble up the side of one of the hills, the earth of which resounded under my feet. It was a perfect cinder, of a reddish colour, and salt. From hence, perhaps, proceeds the little covering of salt upon the shore, where we spent the night. A booby came and pitched on the ground a little way from me. I presented the end of my cane to him, and he took it in his bill, without attempting to fly away.

These birds easily suffer themselves to be caught, as will every other species unused to the society of mankind; a proof, this, that there is a sort of good-will and confidence, natural to all animals towards those creatures, which they do not think mischievous. Birds have no fear of oxen.

A number of frigate-birds were killed by our sailors for the sake of a piece of fat that is round their necks. They think it specific in the gout, because this bird is so swift: but nature, which has

has annexed this evil to our intemperance, has not placed the remedy for it in our cruelty.

The shallop, lay to, about ten in the morning to fetch the turtles on board. As the surf ran high, she anchored at a distance, and drew them on board with a rope.

We were employed in this tedious business all day. In the evening, the turtles that were not worth taking, were thrown into the sea again When they have been long on their backs, their eyes grow red as a cherry, and stand out of their head. There were many on the shore that had been left by other ships, to die in this situation,— a negligence altogether unpardonable.

LETTER XXVI.

HINTS ON THE ANTIQUITY OF THE ISLE OF ASCENSION THE ISLE OF FRANCE, THE CAPE OF GOOD-HOPE, AND EUROPE.

WHILE our sailors were getting the turtles on board, I sat me down in a chasm or cavern of the rocks, with which the country is covered. While our sailors were dragging their turtles aboard, a variety of reflections suggested themselves to my imagination at the sight of so horrible a disorder.

Were these prodigious piles, thought I, ruins of a great city, what memoirs should we have had of those, by whom it was built, and by whom it was destroyed! In Europe there is not a single column.

Alas! While so well informed in other matters, why do we thus remain in total ignorance of whence we came, and where we are? All the learned are agreed as to the origin and the duration of Babylon, now desolate and uninhabited; but by no means concur in opinion concerning the nature and antiquity

4

tiquity of the globe, the country of all mankind. Some maintain it to have been produced by fire, and others, by water; these, by the laws of motion; and others by those of chrystallization. The people of the western world believe it to be six thousand years old only,—while those of the East say that it is from all eternity.

Most probably one system only would be adopted, if all the world were like this island. Those pumice-stones, those hillocks of cinders, and those broken rocks, which still bubble and have bubbled up a kind of metallic dross, evidently prove it to have been the work of a volcano;—but how many years have elapsed since the eruption to which it owes its origin?

Had all this happened a very long time ago, surely these hills of ashes must have lost there pyramidical form, and have been rendered flat by the heavy rains, and the heat of the sun. The angles and out-lines of the rocks would not be so sharp and pointed,—it being one property of the atmosphere to destroy the projecting parts of every Body. Statues of marble carved by the artists of ancient Greece, exposed to the air for a series of years, no longer retain their original form; but are again reduced to mere shapeless blocks.

Why then cannot a judgment be formed of the antiquity of a body by the degree of decay it has suffered, in like manner as the antiquity of a medal is determined by its rust? Is not an old rock as much a medal of earth, engraved by time?

Let it likewise be observed that were this island very ancient indeed, these blocks of stone upon the surface of the ground, would have been before now buried in it, from their own excessive weight. This effect of a heavy body, though slow, is yet sure. The piles of shot, and the cannon, ranged upon the floor of an arsenal, in the course of a few years bury themselves. The greater part of the monuments of Greece and Italy, have sunk deeper than their surbases, and some have entirely disappeared.

Only tell me in how long a time a Body of a known form and weight, would be in burying itself in a soil of a certain known resistance, and you afford me an hypothesis or rather a data by which to solve all such phenomena. The calculation would be easy, were the data once known: in the mean time there is great reason to believe this island but of a modern date.

I have generally entertained a similar opinion, with respect to the antiquity of the Isle of France; but as its piqued mountains are already tabulated on the tops,—its rocks a third or forth part only sunk in the earth,—and their angles but a little blunted,—I am rather induced to believe it some ages more ancient than the other.

Of much greater antiquity than either, seems the Cape of Good-Hope. Here the rocks broken from the tops of the mountains are entirely buried in the earth, where they are found by digging. The foot of each mountain has a large and high Talus, formed of the broken pieces of the upper parts. These have been separated from their original situation by by the continued action of the atmosphere upon them In confirmation of this conjecture, there are by far the greatest quantity in those parts where the winds are used to blow, I particularly noticed this at the Table-Mountain, the part of which, opposite to the south-east wind, has a much more extensive Talus, than that part next the town.

On the top of the Table Mountain, I was particularly struck with some stones standing by themselves, the size of a tun or large cask, the angles of which are blunted. The pieces broken off from them have now no longer the sharp edges they seem formerly to have had; and are of no harder consistence than a white and smoothly polished gravel, like almonds. These stones are very hard, and in colour and grain, like plates of China, that have been much used.

These bodies in this obvious state of decomposition, are evidences to me of their great antiquity. In many places the rock is quite bare, nor is the bed of vegetable earth above two inches deep any where. It cannot then have been many ages since vegetables first grew there, though now common.

It were rash, however, to form any judgment from hence, because the summit of the mountain being neither of sand nor of porous stone, but of a sort of flint, white, polished, and very hard; the seeds of plants brought hither by the winds, may have remained a long time before they could be able to germinate.

The extreme deepness of the vegetative bed on

 the

the plains has also struck me, but from hence neither, can we decide as to the antiquity of the soil,—for where this bed is of a considerable depth, it may have been increased by the floods from the mountains after hard rains, or have been driven or washed farther off, in parts where it is thin.

Had we any where in Europe an high mountain standing by itself, with a flat summit like the Table, and not covered as that is, with a matter unfit for vegetation, a comparison might be made between the thickness of its vegetative bed, and that of any newly formed land alike insulated, for example, with the crust of earth which covers some of those islands formed in the course of the last century at the mouth of the Loire.

Till the contrary is proved by experiment, I will then presume that Europe is more ancient than the Cape of Good-Hope,—because the summits of the mountains are not so steep,—their sides incline more gradually, and the angular pieces of these rocks, yet uncovered with earth, are blunted and round.

No such rocks are here meant, as appear on the sides of mountains, which sea, torrents, or falling of rivers have rendered steep, nor the stones which the rain has left bare, by washing away the earth which covered them; and much less those flints in the fields, which the plough covers one year and uncovers the next: but those only, which by their weight and situation, are subject to the laws of gravity. I saw none of this last sort in the plains of Russia and Poland, Finland is paved with rocks.

rocks, but of a totally different shape. It is a series of small hills and vallies of solid rock, and may be called a petrified earth. Nevertheless as fir-trees grow on the tops of these hills, it should seem that they have been a long time in the air, which has decomposed them.——It appears even that in a climate less cold than the one I speak of, this dissolution would be very considerably accelerated; but that the snow covering the surface for six months in the year, and the ground being hardened by the frost, the effect of their weight is retarded.

No kind of rocks are so proper for these experiments, as such as have been found in the neighbourhood of Fontainbleau. It is a free-stone, in huge masses detached from each other, the edges of all which the hand of time has rounded off. Some of them are half, some two thirds buried in the earth, and others lay on the surface in heaps, as if brought thither for the purpose of building. These last, are probably the summits of mountains, which have not yet entirely disappeared. Each century has, perhaps, seen them farther and deeper immersed, and two thousand years ago, it is not unlikely, but that they were as lofty mountains as many at this day. The force with which the elements act, and the intrinsic gravity tends to preserve the globular form of the earth. In time, the mountains of Europe will be far less steep than they now are; in time, the sea will have dissolved the rocks by which its bounds are limited, and upon which it is continually breaking, in like manner as it has already destroyed those once famous ones of Scylla and Charibdis.

Long

Absorbed in these profound reflections,—I took from my pocket a book of ancient history, and opened a place wherein, speaking of some families of Europe, the author says, *so great is their antiquity, that their origin seems lost in the night of time*, as if their ancestors had been born before the sun. In another place, he speaks of the people of the North, as the fabricators of human nature, *Officina Gentium*; " as a torrent of bar-" barians, which the North could no longer con-" tain."

I am no stranger in the North of Europe, and have travelled through more than eight hundred leagues of it, but I do not recollect to have seen there one single monument of antiquity. Yet, we see durable traces of all populous nations every where else, and from the lowly steeple in a country village, to the pyramids of Egypt, every land where mankind have inhabited, bears testimony to their industry. The plains of Greece and of Italy are covered with antique ruins, why are they not likewise seen in Russia and in Poland?—because mankind can only increase according to the growth of the fruits of the earth where they inhabit; and because the North of Europe lay barren and uncultivated, while the South was covered with harvests of corn, vineyards, and olive trees. The people of the South, in their abundance, raised altars to every God. Ceres, Pomona, Bacchus, Flora, Pales, the Zephyrs, the Nymphs, were Pleasures, therefore they were Deities. The Virgins offered pigeons to the God of Love, and garlands to the Graces, praying to Lucina to bless them with good husbands, who should be faithful

and

and affectionate. Religion was congenial with nature, and, as acknowledgement was in every heart, the earth under this auspicious sky was covered with altars. They rose in every orchard to the Deity of the gardens; to Neptune on the sea-shore, and in every bower to Cupid: The Nayads had their grottos; the Muses porticos,—Minerva, perystiles. An obelisk to Diana, appeared in every copse, and the temple of Venus raised its cupola over the trees of every forest.

An inhabitant is no sooner driven from this delightful climate to seek a new establishment in the North; no sooner is he, with his unfortunate family, within the frigid zone, than he finds himself in a world, which, compared with his former abode, exhibits only the aspect of a waste howling desert. Heavens! what could equal the horror which seized him on the approach of winter! The sun scarcely presented his red and gloomy disk above the horizon,—the winds roaring through the woods, and splitting the trunks of the fir-tree and the oak,—the fountains congealed, and the course of rivers stayed by the freezing hand of Winter. Deep snows covering with a spotless robe the meadows, woods, and lakes alike. The plants, the flowers, the fountains,—every thing by which human life can receive comfort, or even support,—dead. He can scarcely breathe, nor dares he touch any object that presents itself to his eyes; for death is in the air, and every thing he sees, furnishes him with new cause of sorrow. When this unhappy creature hears the cries of his helpless infants, beholds their tears freezing on their livid cheeks, and their arms stretched

stretched out to him for the help he has not to afford them, discoloured and perhaps mortifying! How horrible must be his ideas of the land into which he is come? Can he hope for posterity from nature, or to reap harvests of grain from fields of adamant. His hand must tremble at opening a soil replete with death to its inhabitants. Nothing remains but to participate his misery with his flocks; with them to brouze on the moss and bark of trees, and continue to wander over a land, where a state of repose can be purchased only with life. How then can he think of building? A den or cavern dug in a rock, is his temporary protection from the cold; and if from the bosom of these snows, a monument of any kind should arise—what other can it be than a tomb?

The North of Europe was probably unpeopled till the Southern parts were nearly abandoned. The Greeks, harrassed by their successive tyrants, perferred the sweets of liberty to those of their native climate, which they therefore deserted; and carried with them into Hungary, Bohemia, Poland, and Russia, those arts, by means of which, man alone of all animals, can triumph over the elements, and bid defiance to the inclemencies of every climate. From the Morea to Archangel, an extent of five hundred leagues, no language is spoken but the Sclavonic, the words and even letters of which, are derived from the Greek.

We hence conclude Northern nations, for the most part, to be of Greek descent—They however, seem once more sunk into a state of barbarism; but are now emerging from it, under the influence of of a legislature more mild than that of former times. Peter the Great, has laid the foundation of their modern grandeur, and in our time, they live under the government of an Empress * who gives them laws worthy of Areopagus.

* The reader will please to recollect, that the text was written when this celebrated Empress was in the zenith of her power and popularity. *E.*

LETTER XXVII

ISLAND OF ASCENSION. DEPARTURE. ARRIVAL IN FRANCE.

REFLECTIONS upon this island for some time totally engrossed my contemplation. Pleasing objects are for our enjoyment, calamitous ones for our reflection. The happy man reasons but seldom—the afflicted mind meditates, and in meditation often finds relief from the evils which depress it. So true is it that nature hath made pleasure the universal pursuit of man, and when his heart is incapable of it, she places its seat in his head.

The Island of Ascension may indeed be said to be without earth and without water, but it does not occupy a place upon the globe to no purpose. The turtle has made choice of this coast to lay its eggs, which it does for three months in the year. It is a solitary animal that flies frequented shores. A vessel's anchoring here for twenty-four-hours will drive them from the bay for several days, and if a gun be fired, they will not return in many weeks. The frigate and booby are more familiar, being

being not so much experienced; but these, upon shores that are inhabited, keep upon the very summits of the rocks, and will not suffer themselves to be approached. This island is their commonwealth,—the primitive manners are retained, and the species multiply; for no tyrant can take up his abode amongst them. Doubtless the common mother of all beings has ordained that barren rocks and sands should be in the ocean, desolate indeed, but protected by the jarring elements, as a refuge and asylum, where the animal world may enjoy what even among mankind are deemed her chiefest blessings, tranquillity and liberty.

Almost all fertile and pleasant countries are deprived of their natural freedom, which this island still retains. Surrounded by the Atlantic it has escaped that slavery, which is the bane and disgrace of Africa and America. It is common to all nations, possessed by none, and is frequented by few but English and French ships, which stop in their way from India, to catch turtle. The Dutch being victualled at the Cape, seldom put in here.

No air can be purer than that of Ascension,—I lay two nights together on the ground without covering; I have seen rain fall from the clouds whose course was stayed by the summit of the green mountain, which however did not appear to be much higher than Montmartre—This stopping of the clouds is occasioned by attraction, which is always more forcible at sea than within land

Patients infected with the scurvy while they are

are here, are covered with sand, and quickly find their complaint relieved. Though I was very well, I held my legs for some time in this dry bath, and felt for several days after an extraordinary quick circulation of blood, which I could not account for. But I suppose that this sand being composed of calcareous particles, attracts to the skin the humours of the body it incloses; like those absorbent stones which are applied to a sting to extract the venom. It were to be wished that some able physician would make experiments in other disorders, of a remedy which instinct alone has taught to the scorbutic sailor.

We had one more night to pass on shore—At ten in the evening I bathed in a small bay, between the landing place and the main, surrounded with a semi-circular chain of rocks. At the end of this bay the sand is raised to a height of fifteen feet, and runs down to the sea in a slope. There are several rocks at the entrance, but they do not rise above the surface of the water. The sea, when much agitated, breaks over them with a prodigious noise,—I was obliged to gripe fast by the rocks, as the billows beat over my head almost every minute.

On the morning of the 24th the bar was very high, the ship hoisted a flag as a signal for us to come off. It was impossible for the boat to land at the usual place; she had been taking in a dozen of turtles that had been reserved, and was then swinging by a grappling iron at half a musquet shot from where we stood. Some of the strongest among the sailors pulled off their cloaths, and

and watching the moment of the surges leaving the shore, carried the luggage and passengers on board—running as fast as they could the whole way.

The officer who commanded was informed by me in plain terms, that I thought her very sufficiently loaden—twenty persons were on board, and as many remained on shore—but being desirous of saving the trouble of a second trip, they continued to go on board. In the mean time, a monstrous surge raising up the barge, broke the grappling, and threw her on the shore—eight or ten men up to the middle in the sea, expected to be dashed to pieces.—Had she brought up sideways, she had been lost, but luckily she was thrown in stern-foremost. Two or three waves succeeding, lifted her almost upright, by which means she shipped a good deal of water aft—The people on board in their fright jumped into the water, and were near drowning—but at length the united efforts of us all, set her once more afloat.

When she came back for us who remained, she narrowly escaped the like accident, and happy for us that she did so, for we were not hands enough to have got her off.—The ship must have sailed, and we had been left on an island whereon we could have found neither provisions, wood, nor water. And yet it is said there are some little ponds of fresh water at the foot of the Green Mountain—and a few goats, who finding no herbage but dog's tooth, are half starved. Cocoa-trees were planted here, but would not grow.

Ascension island on the South East, is composed of lava, and the North East of hillocks of cinders; whence I conclude that the wind was to the S. E. when the volcano rose from the sea—and that it blew gently, else the cinders would have been too much scattered to have formed the promontories of hills they now compose; further, that the internal heat, or combustible matter of volcanos is not kindled by the revolutions of the atmosphere, and that the commotions and tempests of the earth, are independent of those of the air.

Does it not rather seem that they depend upon the water;—of all the volcanos I have seen or know of, there are none but what are near the sea, or some great lake—I made this observation some time ago, when I was endeavouring to account for the cause of them—and being confirmed by nature, my opinion is the more likely to be a just one.

By five in the evening of March 24 we sailed. For near a month after we lived wholly upon turtle—They were kept alive all the time by laying them sometimes on the back, and sometimes on the belly; and by throwing sea-water over them several times a day.

One is soon tired of turtle, palatable and nutritive as it is—the flesh is very tough, and the eggs but of an indifferent taste.

Amidst great calms sometimes, and sometimes storms, we at last repassed the line. The currents

rents run northward very perceptibly; they more than once carried us ten leagues in four and twenty hours, when there was no wind. The 28th of April, in lat. 32 N. we saw an eclipse of the moon, at about eleven o'clock at night. We had several days of calms, which are said to be the intervals between the different winds which prevail in these latitudes. From 28 to 23 deg. N. the sea was covered with a marine plant, called *grappe de raisin*, or cluster of grapes. It was full of small crabs and the fry of fish. This, perhaps, is a means which nature makes use of to people the shores of islands with animals, which could not be transported thither by any other: the fish frequenting near the coast being never found in the main sea.

We now saw the pole star again appear above the horizon with much joy, and the pleasure was heightened every night that it rose. The sight of it made my evening walks very agreeable. One night at ten o'clock, as I was walking upon the quarter deck, somebody spoke in much haste and seeming fright to the officer who had the watch. He bid the man light a candle, and follow him along the forecastle. I took the same way they did, and presently we were not a little surprised to see a cloud of thick and black smoke issue from the hatchway.—The sailors of the watch were laid down very quietly upon one of the sails of the mizen mast, and when we called to them, were seized with terror. Two or three of the most daring, went down the hatchway with a lanthorn, crying out, that we should all perish. We looked about for buckets, but could not find even one. Some were for ringing the bell to call up the people, others for working the pump that was aft, to carry water below; every man proposed, but no man attended; the disorder cannot be described,

Being all ranged at length, with our heads stooping over the hatchway, we waited our destiny. The smoke increased, and we even saw gleams of flame issue from the crevices. Presently, however, a voice from below called out, that the fire had only catched some wood put into the oven to dry.—This moment of inquietude appeared like a century. Hard fate of seamen! In the midst of fine weather,—in the midst of the most perfect security,—and in the very hour of return to our native country, one unfortunate accident had well nigh brought upon us the most dreadful of all deaths.

While the crew exercised themselves by firing at a mark, which was a bottle hung at the end of the yard, the 16 guns were tried: we had five of them. This was done, that we might be prepared, in case we were attacked by the *Saltins*.*— Fortunately, we met with none. Our small arms were in such bad condition, that at the first firing one of them burst near me, and wounded the sailor that held it very dangerously.

* There is no English word for *Saltins*; but *Sallee* being about that latitude, I suppose the author means the Rovers of that place. *E.*

I per-

I perceived at noon-day, the 17, upon the sea, a long band of a greenish cast, in direction from North to South.—It was motionless, and extended near half a league. The vessel passed it at the South end. There was no swell upon it, nor near it. The captain, as well as the officers, agreed, that it must be a shoal, or flat,—it is not marked upon the chart. We were now as high as the Azores.

May 20,—we saw an English ship bound to America. They told us we were in 23 deg. longitude, which was 140 leagues farther to the westward than we imagined ourselves

In 45 deg. 45 min. N. May 22, we thought we saw a rock, over which the sea broke. The weather being calm, they hove out a boat: It was a shelf of surf formed by the bed of the sea. Two hours after, we found a mast, furnished with rigging, which appeared as if cut away from an English ship in stress of weather. We took it on board joyfully, for we began to want fire-wood, and, what was worse, provisions, having made but one meal a day for eight days past.

For some time the sky had been clouded over in the middle of the day, so that we did not know in what latitude we were. The 28, the wind blew so hard that the vessel could carry none but her lower sails. At eleven in the morning we perceived a small ship before us; we passed to leeward of her. There were seven men upon her deck, pumping with all their might, the water ran out of all the scuppers. We neither of us made much way, and, in tacking, sometimes passed so close, that I feared the next wave would have run us foul of each other. The Pilot, in his red night cap, called out to us through a speaking-trumpet, that he had not been four-and-twenty hours from Bourdeaux, and was bound to Ireland. We suspected him, by his haste and the bad condition of his vessel, to be a smuggler. It is customary at sea as well as on land, to form our opinions of strangers by their appearance.

About ten o'clock, this violent gale, however, subsided; the clouds separated into two long ranges, between which the sun shone out. All the sails were now set, and men placed upon the main-top to look out. Her head was kept to the North-East, that we might have the better chance for seeing land before evening.

We spied a small smack at four o'clock, which we hailed, but she did not answer; she was driving before the wind. At five o'clock a man aloft, called out, *land, land, to leeward*;—we immediately went upon deck, and many of the people ran up the shrouds; we presently distinguished rocks, that whitened as we approached; they were thought to be the mountains of Penmanmaur. We lay too during the night, and at break of day perceived the coast three leagues a-head, but nobody knew what land it was. The wind was scanty, and by no means suited to our impatience. At length we saw a boat, and hailing her, was answered, that she had a pilot on board.
Overjoyed

Overjoyed at hearing the voice of a Frenchman just come from his native shore, the crew ran with eagerness to the ship's side to see the piolt come aboard. " *What cheer, brother !*" said the Captain ; " *What land is that ?*" Belleisle, said the Pilot, ; " *D'ye think we shall have a breeze ?*"—*An'it please God, master, perhaps we may.*"

This man had brought with him a large barley loaf, which having been baked in France. we very soon eat up for him.

It was to all of us rather vexatious that the calm lasted all day: towards evening it freshened, and in the morning we were along side the Isle of Grois, and came to an anchor.

Here the scene soon thickened ; the custom-house officers came on board, and after them a crowd of fishermen. We bought some fresh fish, determining to eat our last meal together. During which, we got up. We sat down again, but we did not eat. We could think of nothing, we could look at nothing, but the coast of France.

All were instinctively agitated by the same sensibility. The crew were overwhelmed at the thoughts of their return home, with a joy that shewed itself in the most extravagant ways. I spoke to several, but could not get an answer from one of them: I therefore agreed with a fisherman to carry me and my baggage on shore and, having taken a hearty and friendly leave of the Captain, went into the boat, and was soon landed, thanking God, from the bottom of my heart, for having once more restored me in safety to my native country.

LET-

LETTER XXVIII.

VOYAGES AND VOYAGERS.

WRITERS have been long accustomed to try, in the beginning of their books, to gain the good-will of the reader: who very often does not read the preface at all. In my opinion, it is much better to wait till the end, or the very moment when he is going to form his opinion. Then it is impossible for him to escape without paying attention to the author's excuses:—The following are mine.

Whatever may be thought of my work, it has been composed with the best abilities in my possession; and nothing has been wanting to give it all the perfection I am capable of giving it. If it is ill-executed, it is not, therefore, my fault. For one should be blamed for doing ill, only when we can do better.

Should my style * be found imperfect, I shall be very glad to see its errors pointed out. It shall be my task to correct them. During the ten years

* This refers not to the present version, but the original. *E.*

I have

I have been absent from my country, I have almost forgotten my own language, and I have observed, that it is often of greater use to speak well, than to think, or even to act well. My conjectures, and my ideas of nature, are materials which I design for the construction of a considerable edifice; till I am able to elevate which, I submit them to criticism. Just censures are like thaws, which dissolve soft stones, but harden hewn ones. I shall trouble you with one more observation only, which I shall now make use of:—It was said, "*a saint began with a single stone, what, afterwards, became a magnificent abby.*" He achieved this miracle by time and patience: for my part, it is no wonder if I lost both the one and the other.

Being thus seduced to say so much about myself, of which it is so difficult to speak with decency, let us now go on to more important objects. It is rather singular, that there has not been one voyage published by those of our writers who have the greatest fame in literature and philosophy. We have no model of this so interesting species of writing, and we shall long want one, since *Voltaire*, *D'Alembert*, *Buffon*, and *Rousseau*, have given us none. *Montaign* * and *Montesque* have written their travels but have not published them. It cannot be said, that they thought those countries in Europe, where they had been, sufficiently known, since they have made so many new observations on even our own manners, which are so familiar to us. I believe

* Since the author wrote this letter, the manuscript of Monsieur Montaign's Travels through Italy, was found in an old chest, and published at Paris. *E.*

this

this species of writing, so little attempted, abounds with difficulties. It it necessary, that there should be an almost universal knowledge, a plan well arranged, warmth of style, and truth. One must speak of every thing.

Readers are of all tastes, and all must be pleased.— If any subject is omitted, the work is imperfect.— If all is said that can be said, it becomes diffuse and uninteresting.

The world of literature, notwithstanding, is blessed with many valuable writers of voyages, of whom *Addison* is, in my opinion, among the foremost.—He is, unfortunately, for the honour of our country, but not of his own—not a Frenchman. *Chardin* is philosophic, but prolix. The *Abbé de Choisi* saves the reader the irksomness of a sea-journal; he is agreeable, but that is all we can say of him. *Tournefort* describes learnedly the monuments and plants of Greece, but on such a subject as the ruins of Athens a man should write with more feeling. *La Hontan* speculates, and sometimes bewilders himself in the solitudes of Canada. *Lery* describes the manners of the Brasilians, as well as his own adventures, with a pleasing simplicity. From these different works might be composed one equally useful and excellent; but every man has a manner peculiar to himself. For instance, the sailor who wrote in his journal, that he "*passed by Teneriff at the distance of four leagues, the inhabitants of which place seemed very affable*, may be cited as an example."

It is usual for a great many travellers to speak on

on one subject only. This seeks after monuments, statues, inscriptions, medals, &c. If they meet with a man of extraordinary learning, they beg of him to write his name and some sentence in their *album*. Though this custom is a commendable one, I should prefer an enquiry after examples of probity, virtue, and greatness of soul, in the most eminent men of each place.—Had I written my voyages to the north, the world would have seen therein, the names of *Olgorouki*, the *Palatine Xatorinski*, *Duval*, &c. Remarkable buildings would not have been unnoticed,—such as the Arsenal of Berlin, and the Royal Academy of Cadets at Petersburg: As to subjects of antiquity, I confess that they inspire me with none but the most gloomy ideas. A triumphal arch is to me a proof of the weakness of human nature, and the uncertainty of its pursuits. The column, and the statue, remain, but the conqueror, to whose honour they were erected, is no more.

Such, in truth, is my unfashionable taste, that I prefer the tendril of a vine to a pyramid, and should, with far greater pleasure, import to France one nutrive plant, than the silver shield of Scipio.

Ah! It is nearly in the same proportion as the arts become naturalized among us, that nature herself is estranged. We are even so artificial, that we give to objects, merely natural, the appellation of *curiosities*, and seek for proofs of divinity among books, in which, *Revelution* apart, but vague reflections and general indications of universal order, are to be found. Yet, would we shew

shew the ingenuity of an artist, we should rather particularize the several parts of his work, than give a general difinition only of it. Nature presents to us relations so very ingenious, intentions so benificent, and scenes, which, though mute, and I might even say, imperceptible are so expressive, that they must influence the most inattentive mind, and excite an exclamation of, *surely there is a* GOD !

Genuine descriptions of natural objects are still so little known or used, that terms to express them are not even invented. Attempt but the description of a mountain in such a manner that it shall be recognized ; when you have spoken of the base, the flanks, and the summit, you have said every thing. But what a variety is discernable in these forms, round, long, flat, hollow. It is a mass of words without meaning or information. The difficulty is the same as to hills and vallies.—If a man were to describe a palace, he could do it without being the least embarrassed. It is of some of the five orders of architecture ; it is subdivided into sur-base, principal story, entablature ; and in each of these, from the plinth to the cornish there is not a single moulding without its proper name.

At the imperfect accounts travellers give of natural objects, we need not therefore be much surprised. In delineating a country, they tell you of towns, rivers, and mountains,—but the picture is as barren, and conveys as little idea to the imagination, as a mere geographical chart. Of Indostan, or of Europe, it is all one. The physiognomy,

nomy, if the expression may be allowed, is not there. Do they speak of a plant? they give a detail of the flowers, the leaves, the bark, the roots: but its port, its semblage, elegance, or inelegance are not to be defined—The similitude of an object depends upon the harmony, the unity, and connection of its several parts—for you may have the measure and proportion of all the muscles in a man's body, but you will not therefore have his portrait.

Such as have treated of nature by delineating their own excursions into foreign parts, though defective in point of expression, amply make up by the abundance of their conjectures. For a long time I was induced to believe, from the accounts I had read, that men might live in the woods in a state of nature. I did not find one single wild, and unknown fruit, that was fit to eat in all the Isle of France; and those I tasted, I did so at the hazard of being poisoned. Some few indeed were of a tolerable taste, but of these it would have been hardly possible to collect enough for the breakfast of a monkey—there are indeed several noxious roots, that are bulbous and of a sort called *Nymphea, or Water Lily*, but even these grow under water, where it is not likely our man in the state of nature would seek for them. At the Cape I expected to have found mankind better supplied. I saw artichokes of a fine fresh colour growing upon bushes; but they were so crabbed, they were not eatable. In the woods of France and Germany there is no other than the mast of the beach and the fruit of the chesnut—and these last but a short season. It is affirmed that in the golden age

age of the Gauls, our ancestors lived upon acorns, but the acorns of our oaks are too astringent; those of the green oak only being digestible. It is also rarely found in France, though very commonly in Italy.

In the forests of the north, firs yield a kind of apple, upon which the squirrels feed greedily, but I doubt they are not proper for the food of men. Nature would have dealt but hardly with the sovereign of the animal world, had she spread a plenteous table for every other race of beings, and left him destitute; but that he alone is endued with reason, and a disposition to society, without which the former would be but of little use to him. From this one observation we may draw the following consequences—that the most stupid peasant is superior to the most intelligent animal—which no art could teach to till, to sow, and reap,—that man is born for society, and incapable of living without it—and that the community owes to each individual that subsistence, which community alone can provide, and without which the individual must perish.

Travellers are still more faulty by often enough placing happiness any where, rather than in their native country. Their descriptions of foreign countries are so entirely agreeable, that they incline one ever after to be out of humour with ones own.

In my humble opinion, nature seems to have more equally distributed her good things, than we may at first apprehend. I know not whether to prefer a very hot, or a very cold climate. The latter is the more wholesome; moreover the cold is an inconvenience easily to be remedied, whereas the heat, is hardly to be endured, and can never be avoided. For one six months I have seen the landscape about Petersburg perfectly white; for another six months I have seen the Isle of France totally black. Add to this, the destruction occasioned by the vermin and the hurricanes, and which then shall we chuse? It is true that in India the trees are in leaf all the year round, and bear fruit without being grafted—and that the birds are numerous and beautiful,—but all things considered I give France the preference, especially if the constant spectacles of misery be considered in the estimate—for the sight of one man in a state of wretchedness is sufficient to effectually destroy my happiness. Can one think without horror that Africa, America, and a great part of Asia are in slavery? In Indostan all directions to servants are delivered with a stroke of a rattan; insomuch, that the cane has obtained the title of King of the Indies. Even in the boasted country of China, corporal punishments are inflicted for the most trifling offences. Among us,—culprits are even treated as men, and with some degree of consideration. How desolate, how rigid soever the northern climates may be deemed—nature in its rudest state will still in some respect, present me with a pleasing prospect. I have been witness of very affecting scenes even among the rugged rocks of Finland. I have seen there, summers finer and more serene than those of the tropics, days without night, lakes so covered with swans, ducks, woodcocks, plovers, &c. that one might say they had forsaken all other

waters

waters to come hither and build their nests. The sides of the rocks are frequently covered with moss of a shining purple, and the *Kloucva* * with its flowers of scarlet, and leaves of lively green, having spread abroad a carpet on the ground, meets with the stately fir, and round the dusky pyramid, twines its fragrant branches; forming retreats alike adapted to love or to philosophy. In a deep valley, and on the margin of a meadow, stood the mansion of a gentleman of family, where repose was undisturbed, save by the sound of a torrent of water, which the eye saw with pleasure, falling and foaming upon the black surface of a neighbouring rock. It is true, that in winter the verdure and the birds disappear together. Wind, snow, hoar frost, and hail envelope and beat upon the house, while chearfulness and hospitality reign within. They will go fifteen leagues to visit each other, and the arrival of a friend proclaims a festival for a week: † They drink the healths of their guests, their ladies, and their great men, to the sound of horns and drums. The old men sit smoking by the fire and relate the feats of their youth, while the young fellows in their boots, dance to the fife or tabor, round the Finland maid; who in her furred petticoats, appears like Minerva amidst the youth of Sparta.

Though most of their modes and habits are un-

* A beautiful kind of creeper with a red flower.

† The women are of their parties, and it is but just, that as they bear their husbands company in the war, they should preside in their entertainments. Instances of conjugal affection among these people are frequent and extraordinary. The wives of some general officers I have known, have followed their husbands in the field, from their first entering into the army.

couth, their hearts are not without sensibility— They talk of love, of pleasure, of Paris; for Paris is the metropolis of the female sex. It is thither that the women of Russia, Poland, and Italy come to learn the art of ruling the men, with ribbands and laces: and where the fair Parisian exerts her power with humour ever gay, and graces ever new, and tyrannizes over her English lover, who throws at her feet, his gold, and harder to part with, his melancholy! while she, from the very bosom of art, laughing, prepares a garland which binds by its pleasures every people of Europe.

Paris, I should certainly prefer to all other cities, not for its diversions, but because its inhabitants are a good sort of people, and live in liberty. What are to me its splendid coaches, its hotels, its crowded streets its public shews, its banquets, visitings, and friendships as soon dissolved as made. These numerous pleasures are productive of only superficial happiness, and enjoyment. Life ought not to be a mere spectacle. It is in the country only that a man enjoys the genuine feelings of his heart, and the pleasures of society with his wife, his children and his friends. A country life is preferable in every respect to living in towns. The air is pure, the prospects enlivening, the walks fine, provisions at hand, and the manners of men, better, because more simple. The lover of liberty depends upon heaven alone. Here the miser receives new presents hourly, the warrior gives himself up to the chace, the voluptuary places here his garden, and the philosopher may indulge his meditations without fear of interruption. Of animals, shew

me

me one more useful than the ox, more noble than the horse, or more faithful than the dog.

My own country present me with rural scenes most to my liking, not on account of their superior beauty, but because I have been brought up there. In a man's native place there is a secret attraction, a something affecting, which is not the gift of fortune, nor can any other power than nature communicate it. Where are the games of our infant days? —days when pleasure abounded without forethought and without alloy? Ah! what joy have I experienced at finding a bird's nest!—With what delight have I cherished and caressed a partridge—received the strokes of its bill—and felt under my hand the palpitation of its heart and the fluttering of its wings! Happy the man who revisits the scenes where every thing was beloved, every thing was amiable—the meadow he had ran races in! Or the orchard he had ravaged! More happy he, who has never quitted you, paternal roof, sacred asylum! The wanderer returns indeed, but does not find his home :—of his friends, some are dead, —some gone away; his family is dispersed, his protectors extinct——but life is no more than a short voyage; and the age of man like a winter's day*

* Such is the language of true sensibility, of which genius alone is the natural organ of communication. No writer has more of this happy talent than *J. H. B. De Saint Pierre.* It seems the distinguishing feature of his mind, and characterises all his compositions. It is this, that has rendered him so popular with all his countrymen, even in the vortex and paroxysm of political mania! It is this which makes his *Studies of Nature* equally interesting to all readers. It is this which preserves him amidst all his eccentricities from ever hazarding the least offence against morals or religion. *E.*

 I will

I will not however think upon its troubles, but call to mind the virtues, the good offices, and the constancy of my friends. Perhaps their names and my grateful acknowledgment may continue to live even in these letters—Perhaps they may sometime reach even to you, amiable inhabitants of the Cape! Unhappy African, who, on the rocks of Mauritius bewailest thy truly wretched lot; it is not for my feeble hand to alleviate thy griefs, or dry thy tears—but if happily I may have induced thy tyrant-masters to look upon thy ill-fated race with regret, and upon their own implacable cruelty with remorse as the cause of such incalculable sufferings—I have nothing more to ask of India—I shall have made my fortune.

Paris, Jan, 1, 1773.

LETTER XXIX.

TREES.

SOME madrepores are among the curiositie I have brought home, and these are very common in the seas of India; the islands in general being encompassed with them. They grow under water, and form forests of several leagues extent, in which fishes swim about, as birds fly in the woods. The madrepores do not bear fruit, nor can they be included in the vegetable system. They are the work of an infinite number of small animals, who unite their efforts for the formation of these plants of the sea. The shrubs which I have sent with the madrepores, are called litophites, and are, as well as the corals, equally the work of small animals. This, which you may look upon as a mere conjecture, is confirmed by microscopical observation. The chymical experiments on this matter are rather uncertain, because the reasonings of chymistry are founded upon the dissolution of the subject. At length, however, a conclusion is drawn from the regularity of these works, in favour of the opinion, that they are produced and effected, by beings actuated by a spirit of order and intelligence. After all, a shrub is not more difficult to make than an hexagonal cell of wax, as formed by bees. The dispute subsisted for some time; but all the world is now agreed

That every flower is inhabited is my opinion, and in this island wholly alone. † Do not think I mean to adopt the Grecian fancy of the Hamadryads, that every laurel had its Daphne, and that every one unfortunately killed by a quoit, is the inhabitant of one sort of tree; or that all who die of self-love should be lodged in the Narcissus. Could I absolutely confirm the truth of this system, I should not thereby prove the purpose of universal happiness to be advanced. The legs and arms may be lopped off from the sisters of Phaeton, for a clown to make faggots of. My inhabitants have no such fears—but they are wise, and they are ingenious.

The support of this opinion, I am well aware, will be more difficult, than of that with respect to the madrepores. Men interest themselves little about what passes at the bottom of the sea, but it is

* All the sponges have the figure of plants, and are branched in so many different ways, that we could hardly believe them to be the work of marine insects—their texture is so compact, and their fibres so delicate, that it is inconceivable how these animals can lodge in them. Bougainville on Nat. Hist of Isle de Malouines. *E.*

† See an Essay on the subjects of chymistry, which was published in 1771, by Dr. Watson, then Professor of Chymistry, since Reg. Prof. of Divinity of Cambridge, and now Bishop of Landaff. *E.*

widely

widely different with flowers, which are objects generally known and used, and have a received opinion affixed to every thing relating to them. And yet I cannot see why our plants, which resemble the madrepores in every other respect, should not, in being inhabited also.

Let it here be well considered, that every machine of a natural construction has an internal organization, which tends to a certain effect, by certain means. For example; in the ear there is a thin elastic concave membrane, called the tympanum, adapted to the reception of sounds; and in the eye, a sort of transparent and convex membrane, which collects the rays of light upon the retina. The ear is evidently contrived for the purpose of hearing, as the eye for seeing: never will a blind man see by means of his ears, nor a deaf man hear with his eyes. If then a tree is a machine, one part of it must be appropriated for the bearing of flowers, another for the spreading of the roots, both of which would, in that case, make their appearance, at the extremity of the plant assigned to them by Nature:—but should we plant a willow at the water's edge, with the head downwards, the roots would in due time bear leaves. But we are not for this reason to expect an hydraulic machine to sprout from our planting a common pump in the ground, or that laying in a supine posture, any animal incapable of turning himself, his claws or his legs would, in process of time, grow out of his back.

No alteration of position whatever, can affect the parts so as to cause either to perform the office of the other; in every machine which has been investigated, each part produces its proper effect, nor can it be instrumental to any other. The laws of nature are simple, universal, and constant.

A tree, in my conception, is a republic, and not a machine. As soon as a branch of a willow is planted on the margin of a river, the little animals which were inclosed in it, betake themselves to those parts where their labours are most immediately necessary—All secondary considerations are laid aside. The leaves are deserted and fall off. Some employ themselves in closing the breach that has been made in their habitation, by surrounding and covering it with a bourrelet, or pad. Others have pushed forth in the earth, long subterraneous galleries, in search of provisions and materials for the use of the community. If they meet with a rock, they turn their course another way, perhaps surround it with their labours, to form a support for the fabric they are constructing. In some species, as in the oak, they drive down a long pivot, or tap-root, which supports the whole habitation; each nation has its different manners: Some build upon piles like the Venetians, others upon the surface of the earth, as the savages raise their cabins or huts.

In order to remedy evils, or correct errors, they employ themselves in making magazines for provisions. Population among the little republicans is very rapid, because of the ease of subsisting. They live upon oils and volatile salts, with which the air and the earth abound. To obtain those of

 the

the air, they have recourse to the method practised by sailors when in want of fresh water, and as they spread out their sails in rainy weather, these display leaves, as so many surfaces, which, that they may not be carried away by the wind, are most ingeniously fastened by one point of support, at the extremity of a pliant and elastic tail or stem.

A great many habitually ascend through the trunk with drops of liquor, others again descend by the bark with the superfluous aliment.

Were the leaves formed by the sap, as may be imagined by some, the fruit and flowers might be so likewise: but, graft a wild stock; the fruits of the graft shall be good, while those of the stock shall not be changed in the least. If the sap which has ascended by the trunk of the graft, and has descended again by its bark, had partook of any quality, it would have shewn itself in the fruits of the stock. But this does not appear, and why it does not is evident: the animals of the stock bring materials to close the orifice made for inserting the graft, which on their arrival, the inhabitants of the graft receive and fabricate of them excellent fruits: whilst those of the stock continue to form their usual indifferent ones. The materials are the same, the ducts are in common, but the artificers are different. It may be asked, how these beings are protected from an inclement winter. They, as other animals, have instinctive precautions for their safety; they invelop their houses with coverings, proportioned in number and texture to the climate they are designed by Nature to to inhabit. The trees of the north, as the fir, the birch, &c. have three several barks—those of hotter countries have a sort of cuticles only, by which the sap descends.

These little wise creatures shew their sagacity in another respect—they proportion the height of their edifice to the size and extent of its base. In laying their foundations, they meet with a variety of obstructions—another tree—rocks—or an improper soil, when they have reached a certain depth. In the air, they are not restrained, except by considerations of safety. We have a strong proof of this in plants which twine and cling; for they spread themselves to a very great extent without stopping. Some of the *liannes* have shoots so long, that it would be difficult to find the ends of them. The beans which climb, rise to an extreme height, while the marsh bean scarcely attains to three feet—these are, notwithstanding, equally long lived. We see also, that trees growing on mountains, are low in stature: those of the same species in deep and sheltered vallies, that have no fear of the winds, rise with more boldness to a far greater height; and I am persuaded, that if an elm, in the course of its growth, were to pass through a number of terrasses, its inhabitants would with courage lay a separate foundation in each, and raise the head to a height that would be prodigious.

A curious experiment is made by the Chinese, which will confirm what I have just advanced. They choose upon an orange-tree, a branch with its fruit, which they bind hard with a brass wire, and

and cover this ligature with wet earth, upon which is presently formed a bourrelet, or pad, with roots; they then cut off this little tree, and with its large fruit set it upon a table. Had it been left in its original situation, it would have formed a second stage of orange-tree. Here then we have another proof that trees are not machines, because they can always grow, and have no determined size.

* Monsieur Bougainville says, that in Otaheite weeping willows are allowed to be planted before the houses of great men only—and that it is known, that by bending the branches of this tree, and planting them in the ground, the shadow may extend as far, and in what direction you please.—Of this tree the dining-hall of the kings of Otaheite is formed. *E.*

LETTER XXX.

OF FLOWERS.

THE productions of Nature, of which our eyes will not enable us to form a judgment, are infinite, and are we therefore to doubt of their existence? Shall we say the animals, of which I speak, are void of the several senses of taste, sight, or feeling? As well may we doubt that the Romans, who built the amphitheatre of Nimes, eat, drank, or slept, because the historians, who tells us of this building, do not make particular mention of their doing so. Your garden is watered daily, and you ask whether its inhabitants drink? You know that when plants deprived of air, decay almost immediately; and you again ask, whether they breathe? Some flowers are known to close, and shut up their leaves in the night; and others not only do so, but even change their colours.—Among trees also, there are some that close their leaves entirely in the evening, as the tamarind-tree. Can we then deny the influence of the light upon them, when its effects are so evident.

The

The trepidation and contraction of the sensitive plant, upon the approach of the hand towards it, has been attributed to the animal heat; but this cannot be the case, because I have seen it equally to move and contract upon being touched with a stick, a stone being thrown towards it, and even by the wind *. Its powers of motion and contraction can proceed, therefore, from no other than an intrinsic cause.

Do any object that these animals depart from the universal system of self-preservation; that all others employ themselves in labours useful to themselves, and these, in making flowers, which answer no purpose but the pleasure and gratification of mankind; and which, after all the pains and trouble bestowed in their formation, can scarcely be said to exist for a day. A reply is ready from the continuation of the account of their proceedings: the mother-country, and speaking of inhabitants, the expression I think may be allowed, being now too populous, the next care is to send forth colonies. The fine weather in the spring, is the time chosen for this purpose, and

* A new species of Sensitive Plant has been lately discovered in the marshy parts of North America, which has been transplanted to England, and grows there. It is called the *Dionœa Muscipuia*, or *Venus Attrapemouche*. Its leaf is no sooner touched by a fly, or other insect, than it folds itself over its prey, and remains in that compressed state till the captive is entirely consumed. It will close up equally if touched by a straw, hair, or pin. Experiment has not yet ascertained, whether this plant derives its nourishment from the flies it takes; but it seems very likely that it does so, and if this be the case, the *Attrapemouche* tends more than all hitherto known, of the different species of the Polypus, to confirm the analogy between animals and vegetables. *E.*

for

for providing sustenance for the emigrants. Sugar, milk, and honey are collected, and deposited in buildings constructed with admirable ingenuity. The heat and action of the sun is now of the greatest consequence, as well to bring to perfection the provisions, as to promote and accelerate the sponsalia.

This wonderful and profoundly politic people, when they colonize, unite their colonists by ties the most forcible that nature knows, or is capable of. They adopt the measures of government when establishing our settlements on the Mississippi, who sent out very few persons but such as were newly married.

Little hollow tubes are erected by the males, on the tops of which they form lodgments of golden dust, from whence they descend to the bottom of the flowers, where the females expect them with impatience.

It would seem that the flower is the work of the female; it is hung with the most beautiful sattins; purple, sky-blue, black. One may fancy it a bridal-chamber, whence are exhaled the most fragrant perfumes; or it may be called a vast temple, in which at once are celebrated an infinity of nuptual ceremonies: Each leaf is a bed; each stamina a bride; and many families inhabit under the same roof.

The females, often enough, make their appearance by themselves upon one tree, and the males upon

upon another. Perhaps in these republics, the stronger sex keeps the weaker one in subjection, and will not admit them to associate upon public occasions, though there doubtless may be a necessity for making use of them upon particular ones. Like the Amazons of old, who were served by slaves of the male sex, but allied themselves with none but free people.

In the palm-tree, the female alone is employed in preparing the conjugal bed; which, when perceived by the male, he submits himself to the disposal of the winds, and is by them transported upon these beds, called by the botanists, Prolific dust.

On this occasion, I probably seem to our artificial naturalists, transported by my imagination, beyond the bounds of probable reason; let me, therefore, return to my subject, and speak of the form and shape of flowers; which is always circular, whatever be the form of the fruit. Their leaves, or coronets, are disposed around as mirrors,—plain, spherical, or eliptic; so as properly to receive and reflect the heat to the focus of their curves, for the due formation of the embrio which contains the seed. The flowers that yield seed are single ones, because, the placing of one mirror behind another, would have answered no end.

Of vegetables, whose juices are viscous and less liable to ferment, such as bulbous and aquatic

tic plants, my little geometricians construct reverberating machines, in the form of furnaces, which are portions of cylinders, funnels, or bells; observable in lilies, tulips, hyacinths, jonquils, lilies of the valley, narcissuses, &c.

Such as commence their labours early in the spring, adopt also this prudent mode of formation, witness the primrose, crocus, snow-drop, &c.

Some build exposed to the air, and grow but near to the ground, as the daisy and pissabed, form mirrors nearly plain. Those, on the other hand, that are something more in the shade, as violets and strawberries, form mirrors that are more concave.

Such as attempt to transplant themselves in hot weather, contract the circumference of the flower, in order to diminish the effect; such are the blue-bell and pink, &c. Others, as the pomegranate and wild poppy, rumble up their leaves to shelter the disk from the sun, the two great heat of its rays rendering such a protection necessary. It is the same in papillonaceous flowers, whose form is rather calculated to re-unite the direct rays of the sun, than to collect a-new their reflected heat.

Their attention is also exemplified in the flowers of summer which have large cups, are fastened to ligaments, by which they are rather suspended than supported; they quickly lose their flowers;

flowers; of this kind, are the wild poppy, the poppy, the flower of the pomegranate, &c

Another species also merits notice, of which the sun-flower is one, whose leaves are disposed as radii round the circumference. The flower is here placed upon a flexible knee, by means of which, the inhabitants are constantly turning it towards the sun. One might fancy them so many academicians, directing a telescope, or reflecting mirror, towards that luminary.

Similar description is likewise remarkable with respect to the colours of flowers; white and yellow being the most adapted for collecting the reflected rays. The generality of spring and autumnal flowers, are of those, or such like, bright and clear teints; the degree of heat being so small, makes the use of active mirrors necessary.

Many flowers peculiar to these periods, which are of a deep red, as the anemony, piony, and some sort of tulips, have their centers black, as most proper to absorb the rays immediately. The summer flowers are of deeper colours, and less adapted for reverberation. In this season, we frequently see blue and red, but black very rarely, because it never reflects at all. Poppies, which are of a deep brown, are, if exposed to the sun burnt up before the flower is developed.

Of plants, their height, their size, their colour, and the form in which they are cut, or scolloped, seem all combined in wonderful harmony. Considered

sidered in this light, flowers, instead of being mere objects of pleasure, are fit subjects of study for the ablest geometricians.

In all her dispositions, nature is equally bountiful and just. Things for our use are furnished to us with simplicity; for superfluity and enjoyment, with magnificence. Corn, olive-trees and vines, are instances of the former; flowers, and many other beautiful natural productions, of the latter.

India animals, as they differ from ours in their wants, are equally different in their operations.—In our climates, heat is necessary; our animals therefore, form the flowers before the leaves; and farther north, they build a solid flower, and cover it with scales. These are ranged in a conoid form upon a sort of espalier. The fir tree and the birch, would be parched up in hot countries, and therefore they never grow there.

In the Eastern hemisphere, the trees are full of spreading leaves, under the shade of which grow the flowers. Their circumference is never very compact, as may be seen in the orange, or citron trees.

On such as have but few leaves, as the agathis, the various sorts of palms, the date, cocoa, and latanier, the flowers grow in pendant clusters. In this inverted state, they are not liable to be scorched by the sun, having no other heat than a reflected one. Trees of Europe, bearing flowers in clusters, bear them upright, as the vine, lilac, &c.

Thus in our temperate climates, the flowers seem to seek for the sun; in India, to avoid and shun it; the greater number either growing close to the trunk of the tree, or hanging down in bunches as those above-described.

LET

LETTER XXXI.

FRUITS

IN opposition to the system for which I contend, it may be alledged, that my animalcules, reasoning too much from consequences, seem therein even to be wiser than men. Wherefore is this, but because the animal is endewed with an instinct, equal, in effect, to that experience which man is ever arriving at, and never attains. The spider, weaves as soon as it issues from the egg. The portion of intelligence afforded to each species, is perfect from the beginning, and suffices for all the wants of the animal. It is a general observation, that, the smaller the animal, the greater its industry. Among birds, the swallow is more alert than the ostrich :—of insects, none is so small, nor is any so laborious, as the ant. Activity and adroitness, seem given to the weaker animals as a compensation for the want of strength; and mine, being so much smaller than all these, I am justified in believing, that they are also more intelligent.

A spe-

A specific quantum of heat being amassed, sufficient to unite the families at the bottom of the calice, or cup of the flower, the whole nation is employed in carrying thither honey and milk. This last is a sustenance apparently designed for all animals when in their infant state; even the yolk of an egg, dissolved in water, is converted to a consistence like cream. The colony then takes up its residence in the part called the Bourgeon, or bud. The provisions are ranged around, under the appearance of milk, which is soon after changed to an oily and more solid substance.

That this colony may be protected from accidents to which it might be liable, it is, together with its provisions, enveloped in a shell. This covering is sometimes as hard as a stone; great care, however, is taken to leave an opening, as in nuts, or small holes at the end, covered with a valve.—by this outlet the young family find egress. Not one single grain is known, but what is, in its organization, suited to this purpose.

In advancing this, however, I do not attribute to them a greater degree of intelligence than is seen in other insects. The spider lays its eggs in a bag, which also has its orifice. The silk-worm shuts itself up in a pod, of a texture wonderfully compact, except in that part towards the head, which is so contrived as to allow it to escape from its confinement at the proper time,—this precaution is common to all vermicular insects. But all animals that unite their labours, have infinitely more ingenuity in their proceedings, than those which work individually;—these, exceed in ingenuity all others; for, while they construct the building, and collect provisions for the support of the infant colony, lest the work should be destroyed by birds, or other animals, it is environed with a substance of a nauseous taste, as the external coat of walnuts, which is bitter, or fortified with prickly points, as the shell of chesnuts. These operations of my animalcules originate from the same cause, which directs the rabbit to dig itself a burrough in the earth; the lapwing to suspend its nest by a few threads; and the duckling to take to the water, before it has seen the drake swim upon the surface. Let us not wonder then, that the rose-bush is armed with prickles, and protected all over by the same means, which the chesnut has provided for its fruit alone.

Such a covering is commonly seen among shrubs that grow on the borders of the woods, and are exposed to the ravages of beasts that feed there.—The sea-rush, the bramble, the black and red thorn, the gooseberry tree, and even the nettle and thistle, which grow by the way-side, are furnished with prickly points for their defence. They are in fact to the woods, as frontier towns are to a province.

Observe particularly that the colony once supplied with the necessary provisions, have various modes of transplanting, or transporting themselves—those suspended aloft in the air, have nothing to do but to suffer themselves to fall down. The fruit drops, and after having rebounded a few times, rests perhaps thirty paces from the parent

parent tree. And here I must remark that those fruits which fall from a great height, are rounder and harder in proportion to their fall. The acorn, the mast of the fir tree, the chesnut, the common nut, the pine apple, are in their several ways protected from the violence of the stroke they receive in coming to the ground. Nature having precontrived, when she raised them so far above the earth, that their return to it, should not be attended with ill consequences. On the other hand, the artificers of the linden tree, which grows in moist and swampy grounds, know very well, that should they construct unwieldy coverings, their weight would bury them in the same place they fell. Wherefore, their seed is fixed to a long fibre or feather, with which it is let down by degrees, and carried away. by the winds. The willow, which grows in the same kind of soil, has its tufts of feathers as well as the reed. The seeds of the elm, are placed in the midst of a large follicle or purse; by means of these, which serve them as wings, they are transported to any distance. By the construction of its seed, I should be induced to think the elm designed for the inhabitant of the valley. We need no longer wonder that the cherry and peach tree rise but to a middling stature. A full grown peach which should fall from the height of an elm, would not go far. How then, you will say, do those that are mere shrubs, such as the blue bell, artichoke, thistle, &c. for they cannot roll away from where they lit. I answer, that these also affix their colonies to a kind of wings, and they are then transported by the wind. In autumn you may see the air full of them. They are suspended with equal industry as ingenuity, and however far they travel, the seed always falls perpendicular; and there are some sort of peas with elastic shells, which when ripe, shoot forth their seed to the distance of ten or twelve feet. Do you now think that a plant is no more than an hydraulic machine?

As the inhabitant of the chesnut, and other fruits which I have mentioned, protect themselves from the attacks of the birds—so the strawberry, and the rasberry, make their enemies subservient to their purposes. The former, are warriors, the latter politicians. They environ themselves with a substance, alluring to the eye and grateful to the taste. The birds feed upon this substance, and are nourished by it; and by a natural operation, sow the seeds again in the earth. They devour the fruit, but this does not damage the seed, which is too hard to be affected by their digestive powers. Many other fruits that have stones in them, are sown by the same means. This finesse is not peculiar to the animals of our hemisphere. The nutmeg is a kind of peach, growing in Molucca. The nuts of it bring in a large revenue to the States of Holland; who, that they may reserve to themselves the benefits arising from it, have endeavoured to destroy and eradicate this tree in the islands that do not belong to them; but their attempts are in vain: a particular species of sea fowl, sowing soon after they have eaten it. Thus weak is man, when he militates against nature: a whole nation could not extirpate one single vegetable.

For

For the encouragement of population, the king of Prussia once gave orders to cut down some forests, to provide lands for new married people. It was represented to him, that this measure would occasion a scarcity of timber; to which he made answer—"I had much rather have men in my dominions, than trees." Can it be supposed that the sovereign ruler of all things, would not rather chuse for his subjects, animate beings, than mere uninformed machines?

Animalculæ, we have perceived, moving in the juice of plants—and though too minute for us, their various operations being imperceptible to our organs, even when assisted by the best microscopes: yet they as certainly labour, act in concert, and perform every thing related of them, as the animal inhabitants of the madrepores and litophites—for as these are the plants of the sea, the others are, in like manner, the madrepores of the air.

Perhaps you think they differ in their construction, because the madrepores do not bear fruit—but this is an opinion rather started, than to be received. For it is to be considered, that they live in a fluid, where their fruits can neither fall nor roll; to what end then should they environ the colony with a cumbersome body; or with a lighter substance, like the wad which surrounds the seeds, which are to fall in the water.

A milky juice, however, has certainly been seen in their flowers, like that in the seeds of our fruits,

fruits, which milk is dispersed in the sea like the spawn of fish.

We all know arts and manners differ, in different elements; a sailor and a citizen are both men, but a ship and a house are by no means constructed alike.

Our Lilliputian architects, of the plants in the air, live in an element which appears to be in perpetual motion,—the most gentle zephyr is to them a hurricane. They have taken the most prudent precautions to secure the foundations of their edifices, and to transport their families without risk of their being damaged or scattered abroad.

Such of them again as build in the sea, live in a fluid, which is not altogether so easily put in motion, and when once agitated, moves in waves and large masses. The drops are not so active and penetrating as the globules, of which the air is formed, and which are incessantly dilated and contracted, by different degrees of heat or cold. They do not, therefore, require to be so carefully inclosed, as those seeds, which are liable to be so easily dissipated. Their milk is besides of a more viscous nature, not easily dissolved.

Had animals of the water inhabited a still more solid element, for example, the earth, they would not have been exposed to any sort of agitation. And it is probable that they would then have had no occasion to put down roots, to raise a stem, spread

spread out leaves, fashion flowers, or fabricate fruits, as do those that inhabit the air.

My assertion is incontestable. The truffle has none of the parts above-mentioned, nor has it any use for them. To what end should there be flowers on a plant that never sees the sun, or roots to a vegetable not exposed to any shock? I have heard many people say, they cannot divine by what means the truffle is re-produced. Its reviviscency is, in my opinion, effected by the communication of its animalculæ with each other, through the interior parts of the soil it grows in, where reigns a calm eternal and undisturbed. The fluid being tranquil, the communication cannot but be easy—no vessels are necessary, for the little inhabitants may swim along in safety. One would be almost sorry that the animals of so charming a fruit should be so indolent, and of such apparent incapacity: but the endowments of every being, are proportioned to its necessities—and man, of all beings the most indigent, is at the same the most intelligent. It is to be wished, indeed, that he were the happiest; and yet the inhabitants of the truffle, though less sensible than others, may perhaps be more contented.

This, let me hope, will account for the ordinary causes of vegetation. If you are not yet satisfied, I will now speak of its extraordinary productions: and my best mode of doing this, will be by anticipating such objections as I think you may probably make to what has been already advanced; and the first is one, which you will say, perhaps, all the laws of hydraulics cannot obviate.—That a young

young tree, full of sap, frequently puts forth branches and leaves, without bearing the flowers natural to its species; but a portion of the roots being cut off by an experienced gardener, it becomes fruitful. Whence is it, that it does not bear, unless deprived of a part of its nurture?

I reply, that those animals which have a sufficiency, or superfluity of provisions, are not solicitous to expatriate themselves. They seek to enlarge the tenements in their present occupation; they fabricate wood alone; but no sooner are their provisions cut off, than they find it absolutely necessary to send from home, such part of the inhabitants as can no longer subsist in the environs.

Do you next ask, Why a tree, damaged, by the stripping of its bark, or otherways, in the spring subsequent to the accident, shall bear an unusual number of flowers; afterwards of fruit, and then die?

Strange, it may doubtless seem, that on the eve of its death, it should be more prolific than formerly; but the reason is plain: the inhabitants being assembled together to debate on the pub lic calamity, reason thus:—

"A breach is made which we cannot repair! Our ramparts and covered ways are broken up: and if we remain here, we must perish by cold or hunger: Let us then depart." They immediately go to work, construct flowers, and take refuge in the fruits: The mother-country thus abandoned, the following year the tree dies.

In

In every seed, it has been said, there is an entire plant, with its seeds also, which contain still future plants; and they again their seeds, and so on, *ad infinitum*. But this exceeds my powers of comprehension: for there must be a certain degree of gradation, wherein the matter is no longer susceptible of form; form being no more than the bounds, or limits of matter. If it were otherwise, there would be as much matter in an acorn as in an oak; and if it has the principal forms only of the oak, the question is, where are those that it has not, and that are equally essential to, and equally constituent parts of, the oak in its mature state, as those which are retained?

The forms can never be left out but for want of room; the space of the second being much less, the number of forms must be again diminished. And as every decreasing magnitude must necessarily come at last to nothing; and these imaginary glands are continually diminishing, there must of consequence a period arrive, when the race of oaks would be extinct and at an end. Yet this is the hypothesis upon which the generality of people reason, when they would account for the causes of vegetation.

After much talking upon this subject, some of my friends have professed themselves, from motives of compassion, unwilling to believe the existence of these animalculæ. Can it be possible, say they, that myriads of beings should be created, to be destroyed, merely for the sustenance or pleasure of mankind? And that, were my opinion a just one, they would rather continue in error, than give their assent to so cruel a truth. But I can see no

reason

reason why we should reject any system for compassion's sake. Anatomists have no such scruples when they form a system, every thing that comes in their way falls a victim to the knife. An English gentleman once caused a great number of bitches, big with young, to be opened, for the discovery of the laws of generation—but he did not gain the information he sought. Others have been mentioned, and very justly condemned, by Voltaire, for having taken out the bowels of a living dog, to shew the spectators the lacteal veins. I would by no means encourage the practice of such barbarous experiments; but my system does not affect the life of the animals, whose existence it is meant to prove. For as they are too minute to become the objects of vision, so neither can they be affected by our powers of digestion.

FINIS.

J. CUNDEE, PRINTER,
Ivy - Lane, Paternoster - Row